CHILTON'S
AUTO
RESTORATION
GUIDE

CHILTON'S AUTO RESTORATION GUIDE

Burt Mills

CHILTON BOOK COMPANY
Radnor, Pennsylvania

Copyright © 1975 by Burt Mills

First Edition   All rights reserved

Published in Radnor, Pa., by Chilton Book Company
and simultaneously in Don Mills, Ontario, Canada,
by Thomas Nelson & Sons, Ltd.

Designed by Anne Churchman

Manufactured in the United States of America

Library of Congress Cataloging in Publication Data

Mills, Burt.
    Chilton's auto restoration guide.

    1. Automobiles—Restoration. I. Chilton Book
Company. II. Title. III. Title: Auto restora-
tion guide.
TL152.2.M54 1975   629.28'7'22   75-28436
ISBN 0-8019-6250-1

2 3 4 5 6 7 8 9 0   4 3 2 1 0 9 8 7 6

This book is fondly dedicated to my wife

PAT

*who has good naturedly put up with my
interest in old cars, and who took most of
the photographs used in this book.*

*It is also dedicated to my neighbors who
have been good sports about this hobby.*

Acknowledgments

Acknowledgment is gratefully made to the following, who either furnished photographs used in this book, or allowed photographs to be taken on their premises:

Antique Auto House, Loveland, Colorado.
Bart's Vintage Cars, Colorado Springs, Colorado.
Genuine Automotive Parts, Englewood, Colorado.
Rippey's Veteran Car Museum, Denver, Colorado.

Contents

SECTION I

From Junker
to Jewel

Introduction

So you think you'd like to restore an old car? Maybe you've seen some sleek beauties at old car shows. Perhaps you've drooled as you've watched a parade of antique cars roll by. Some particular model may have struck a nostalgic chord that took you back to earlier years when a similar car played a part in your life. Or are you simply looking for a good hobby?

Discouraged by the price tag on a perfectly restored classic car, you may have decided one is out of your reach. The average person attaches a highly inflated value to old cars. It's a common belief that any well-preserved or restored Essex, Peerless or Velie is now equal in value to a new Cadillac. The thought of performing a complete body and mechanical restoration job may seem mindboggling.

Before: Decrepit looking but basically solid cars like this '29 Packard Phaeton give the impression of a real junker to many, but offer a challenge for restoration.

After: A complete professional restoration has turned the same '29 Packard into a real "jewel" to be admired and enjoyed. (*Restored by Rippey's Veteran Car Museum, Denver.*)

The delusion that restoration is both extremely difficult and expensive helps keep the price of restored cars high. This mistaken belief has undoubtedly scared away a lot of would-be old car restorers.

Another widely accepted, but mistaken, belief is that old car restoration is strictly a man's hobby. It doesn't have to be. There is absolutely no reason why the hobby can't be enjoyed by women too. Any woman can do any of the restoration tasks, from rebuilding a motor to making a new roof for a convertible. Some particularly heavy jobs may require the efforts of two people: it doesn't matter whether these are two men or women. Mutual interests and hobby sharing are good ways to find a compatible mate, as well as make a marriage successful. Car restoration can be a fine husband and wife enterprise.

Of course, Duesenbergs, Rolls Royces, Bugattis and the like are high priced. They always have been. But there are still plenty of other makes around from the Twenties, Thirties, Forties and Fifties that are restorable. Many can be had for a low price: a restorable car can be purchased for as little as $150, possibly less. Restoration is not overly difficult, nor is it pro-

There'll be no trouble finding parts for this '42 Ford, making it an easy restoration for the beginner and a roadworthy car when finished.

hibitively expensive. The average man or woman can turn a derelict into a well-restored machine. It's interesting work. All it takes is common sense, patience and good judgment. In fact, it's really fun! It's a good way to relax from everyday tensions. It's also a good investment, as well-restored cars only increase in value.

This book is written for the beginner–restorer. It explains in necessary detail all the average man or woman needs to know to make an acceptable restoration. This book tells you how to do the many different jobs involved in car restoration. The basic functions of the various mechanical components are described. This book explains what you should look for in choosing a car and discusses the problems you should expect as you work along. It answers questions you may pose during the restoration. The tools you'll need for an average restoration are listed. You'll learn how to diagnose needed repairs. Repair as well as replacement procedures are described. Included is information on the chassis, motor, drive train, brakes, body, etc. In fact, all you need to know to make a completely acceptable restoration is included in this book.

So don't put off the fun, thrill and satisfaction of restoring the old car of your choice. Good luck, happy hours and happy motoring!

CHAPTER 1

Basic
Requirements

Car restoration can be anyone's hobby. You don't need an M.I.T. degree, nor do you need a machine shop. You can restore an old car if you have average intelligence and don't mind getting your hands temporarily dirty. Don't be scared of car restoration, it's nothing to get uptight about. Don't let some of the lingo used by car repairmen intimidate you. After all, they have to impress someone with their great knowledge. It's easier than you think, if you'll plan your work and follow some simple rules. You don't need to be a mechanical genius or strong as an ox. Machine shop services are easily purchased when needed. All you really need is the car, garage space, some tools, determination, and some spare time. Your self-confidence will grow as you get into the hobby.

Space   Of course, the more space available the easier, but you can get by very nicely with a lockable garage space; half of a normal two-car garage will do. I've restored many a car in our garage. Attempt restoration in a carport only if you live in a warm, dry climate, and can screen it off for privacy. There should be electricity for an extension light, so you can see what you're doing. An electric outlet is handy for any power tools you may want to use. A cement floor is preferable, so you can level the car, as well as for ease in moving around under the car. So you see, space is no problem.

You'll find a workbench with a small hand vise very useful. You can easily build a workbench if you don't have one. Some restorers make a simple removable wooden top to place over electric appliances (washer, home freezer) already in the garage, using this as a workbench. If you do this, tack some old pieces of carpet or a rag rug on the bottom to keep from scratching the appliance. A few shelves and hooks for parts and tool storage will help too. A sheet or two of plywood nailed to the garage rafters makes a fine place to store parts during the restoration. You can work on small parts at a card table as you watch TV, if you like. Not everything has to be done in the garage.

If you're going to work on the car during cold weather, you'll need a source of heat so you don't freeze. But don't risk a fire by getting a space

6

Small homemade workbench with peg board on wall provides ample space for restoration tools and working. Keep fire extinguisher on hand for safety.

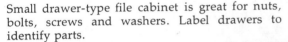

Small drawer-type file cabinet is great for nuts, bolts, screws and washers. Label drawers to identify parts.

Electric space heater serves double duty, providing heat and helping to dry wooden window moldings. Note hand striping on '25 Franklin hood panels and the replated nickel hardware.

heater too close to papers or cleaning rags. *Store gasoline or solvents in sealed containers, well away from the heater.* A home fire extinguisher is highly recommended.

You may wonder if it'll take forever and a day to restore a clunker: it's certainly not an overnight job, but probably won't take nearly as long as you think! Obviously, the amount of time depends upon the car you've selected, the condition it's in, and your own plans for it. How you plan

Time Schedule

your work makes a lot of difference. If you give enough thought beforehand to scheduling your restoration, then work along methodically, you'll be surprised how quickly a good restoration job can be done.

Another variable is the amount of work you'll do yourself. Plating, welding and machine shop work must be done for you. However, if you'll spend an hour or two some evenings a week, plus four or five hours on a weekend, you should be able to complete the job in a reasonable time. Plan on spending four months to a year.

Before you begin the restoration, you should subscribe to one or both of the hobby's big magazines. Both are predominantly filled with classified ads listing old cars, parts and literature for sale. These ads might be the only source for an elusive headlight lens or an original equipment carburetor which would otherwise take months to locate. The two magazines are: *Hemmings Motor News,* Box 380, Bennington, Vt. 05201 and *Cars & Parts,* Box 299, Sesser, Ill. 62884.

You can save many hours by finding out as much as possible about your particular car before starting the work. Write the parent company if it's still in business. Antique, classic and old car clubs can usually provide helpful information. Specific make car clubs can furnish loads of technical information. It'll be worthwhile to look into national and local car club membership. Many car magazines carry listings of car clubs and there are yearly club directories published. You'll find club members are helpful and a good source of information and parts. Many clubs have active social programs you'll enjoy.

Cleanup   The initial phases of car restoration can be mighty dirty jobs. Some of the mechanical repair jobs create a mess, too. However, the overall restoration process isn't that bad. There are several hand lotions available that make cleanup easy. Rub these into your hands before starting a job and you can wash off grime and grease with soap and water afterward. These contain lanolin, so you're lubricating your skin at the same time you're working on your car. Many new, powerful detergents make it possible for you to clean up your car's parts without getting dirty yourself. You should sweep and tidy up after each work session, so you'll have a clean place to work next time.

Car restoration is an excellent way to wear out your oldest clothes. Old blouses and shirts, slacks and denim jeans are great—just toss them in the washer after each job. Work gloves can be worn for added protection with some jobs. Don't worry about the dirt: you can work on your old car over the weekend and still have presentable hands in the office on Monday.

Tool Chest   You won't need as many tools as you might think and they aren't excessively expensive. You no doubt already have some available. Most old cars come equipped with a pretty fair set of tools; some may still be with the car. It's impossible to list every tool you might need for a wide variety of jobs, but the standard ones are listed here. Normally, around $150 will be more than adequate if you're starting from scratch. Remember you can borrow or rent some tools; also, you can easily sell any you don't want to keep once the job is done. You can frequently locate used tools through the classified ads in your newspaper and at garage sales.

Just which tools you'll need depends upon the extent of the restoration job and the tools you already have on hand. You may find some in the car you buy. Generally, the following lists will suffice:

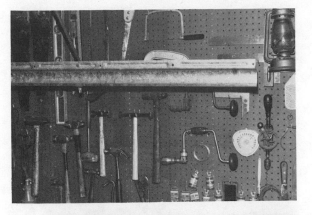

Simple, easy-to-assemble hand tools are all that are necessary for average wooden body structural repairs.

This small group of tools will allow the restorer to make most engine repairs. Many of these tools were found in old cars, some were purchased for specific jobs. Good strong tools are a wise investment.

A wide selection of tools isn't necessary for the average body-framing restoration job.

Straightening fenders and other body metal requires only a few tools. This simple group will handle most of the jobs you'll come across.

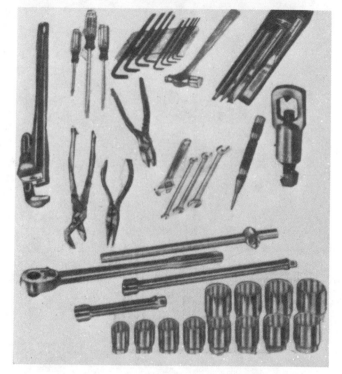

Tools used for mechanical restoration work.

MECHANICAL RESTORATION WORK

1 set open end wrenches: 3/8" × 7/16" to 15/16" × 1"
1 set box end wrenches: 3/8" × 7/16" to 15/16" × 1"
1 set socket wrenches, with drives and ratchet, same sizes
1 adjustable 8" wrench
1 set allen head wrenches (also known as hex key sets)
1 set open-end midget ignition wrenches
4 regular screwdrivers, assorted sizes
2 Phillips-head screwdrivers, different sizes
1 punch and chisel set, 3-piece
1 hacksaw with extra blades
1 set pliers: slip-joint, adjustable, electric or cutting
1 ball-piened hammer, 8 or 12-oz. size
1 variable size nut driver

1 nut splitter
1 set metal files
1 thickness gauge set, .0015 to .035 inch blade sizes

BODY WORK

Many of the tools listed for mechanical work can also be used for body work. You'll need some additional ones, however. If your car has a wooden frame body, as most did in the Twenties and early Thirties, you'll want the following items: (steel bodied cars of the late Thirties and Forties will require fewer woodworking tools).

Average assortment of tools necessary for body work.

1 fine-toothed crosscut saw
1 claw hammer
1 set wood chisels
1 metal tape or folding ruler
1 wedge bar, about 16″ size
1 electric hand drill (use a hand brace if you want)
1 set assorted wood bits
1 set assorted metal bits
1 level
1 inside–outside trisquare, ruler and depth gauge
1 set of C clamps, 8″ opening

FENDER WORK

You can do most of the body and fender work with a few simple tools, leaving only extensive repairs that require welding for the body shops. These should do it:

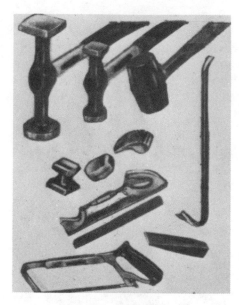

Assortment of tools usually required for fender work.

2 bumping hammers: 3½" head, 5" head
1 heel dolly (used for shrinking metal)
1 all-purpose dolly (for roughing work and beating panels)
1 combination dolly and spoon (for fender edging)
1 set assorted body files
1 file holder

It may sound like a lot of tools, but it really isn't. Chances are that you won't need all of them. Some you may already have. You won't necessarily need all of them at one time if you plan to do all the mechanical work before starting on the body and fenders. Also bear in mind that you can probably locate good sets of used tools: some can be borrowed, others rented.

When buying, remember to choose good quality tools. Don't try to save a buck or two on cheap ones. Cheap tools break and the damage to your hands and elbows can be very painful. All the tools listed can be purchased from mail-order houses or your local hardware or automotive supply store. Some car clubs make arrangements for members to get discounts on purchases of individual tools or complete sets. No brand names are recommended, just be sure to buy good tools.

The wrench sets listed for mechanical work should be Standard Society of Automotive Engineers (SAE) measure, unless you're restoring a foreign car, in which case you'll need metric measures.

CHAPTER 2

How to Choose
Your Car

This is when the fun begins! Choosing the car you want to restore can be an exciting experience for any man or woman. Because of myths that have become accepted truths about certain cars, you'll need to be on guard constantly. Everyone has heard about the car that belonged to the little old lady who loved it, talked to it and drove it only on sunny Sundays. There are other claims that are about as ridiculous. So approach old car buying warily. Take your time and don't hurry into your first purchase.

Selection depends upon what car you want and how much you want to pay. It also depends upon how far you're willing to travel for the car, as traveling expenses should be added to the cost of the car. The degree of restoration you want to tackle is also a factor. Only you can answer these particular questions.

There are many sources of old cars: you'll find them everywhere. Drives through the country and small towns may help you locate some. You'll see

Plenty of work—and fun—ahead, making a jewel out of this hopeless looking '19 Cadillac touring car, but it can be done.

them in vacant lots or behind garages in the cities. Talking with service station managers and garage owners in outlying areas will often turn up leads. I located a 1923 Franklin through a service station attendant who was repairing a loose trailer hitch on my car. A friend of mine located a Stanley Steamer through a gas station attendant who asked what the fellow was doing in that neck of the woods.

Auto wrecking yards and junk yards are often good sources. Many restorable cars are scrapped just to get them out of the way. Another excellent source is the classified pages of your newspaper: many papers carry special listings for antique cars; farm auctions and auctions to settle estates often contain a car or two. Be careful not to get carried away at auctions and bid more than the car is actually worth to you. Many auto buff magazines carry listings—I've bought many a car this way. In answering ads, ask for specific information, request a picture of the car (offer to return the picture;) and enclose a stamped, self-addressed envelope. When you receive this information, you'll know if you want to follow up.

Members of car clubs often know what's available and can give you some good leads. Keep asking around. You should have no difficulty finding a variety of cars from which to choose. You may have trouble locating a specific make, say a 1923 Marmon Boat-Tailed Speedster or a 1933 Chrysler LeBaron Phaeton. But if you're not too particular in your choice of make, model or year, a restorable car is easily located.

Determining Price

You don't have to know a lot about cars to make a sensible choice. Bear in mind that there were great differences in the original cost and quality of cars. These differences still will be present to some extent. The true classic with a coach-built body was rare and expensive when new. It will command a top price today. The more expensive a car was originally, the more complicated it is mechanically and the more expensive it'll be to buy and restore. Sometimes the extra quality built into an expensive car makes restoration less extensive. You'll have to equate these factors. Orphan makes or special interest cars are generally priced higher because of their rarity. Sporty models and convertibles will bring more than standard coaches or sedans. The present condition of the car, the difficulty of making repairs (parts and time) and any problems involved in getting it home, all affect the price you should finally settle on.

The handy checklist included in this chapter will help you decide if you want a given car and approximately what it'll take to restore it. Since you'll probably be looking at several cars before you decide on one, get some copies made on one of those copying machines and take a preliminary checklist with you when you look at a car. The fact that you're reviewing the car's condition this carefully may help you negotiate a lower price. Be realistic when checking out the condition. If you need the help of a friend, get it. A garage can usually give you estimated repair or replacement costs. It's better to estimate problems as slightly worse than they look or sound, and more difficult and expensive to repair. This way you'll have more bargaining power. You'll also have some pleasant surprises instead of ending up with a bad investment.

Sellers of old cars may tell you all sorts of things—some of which they may even believe themselves! Watch out for the seller's friend who's on hand when you're looking at the car. He probably doesn't know a damn thing about the car, but may try to pass himself off as an expert. He may be

PRELIMINARY CHECKLIST

Date _____

Owner's name _____   Address _____

Make _____

Body style _____   Year _____   Model _____

Price _____   Accessories _____

Radio   Heater   Spotlites   Other

Can owner furnish title _____   Car now licensed? _____   Car was last run _____

General appearance _____   Inside or outside storage? _____

Check Before Starting Motor

Oil in base? _____   Coolant in radiator? _____

Water drops in oil? _____   Oil in coolant? _____

Visible oil leaks? _____   Visible coolant leaks? _____

Visible cracks in motor block? _____   Cracks in cylinder head? _____

Fan belt tight? _____

Check Before Driving Car

Does brake pedal hold when pressed down? _____

Any signs of leaking brake fluid? _____

Any grease leaks around rear wheels? _____

Air in tires _____   Horn work _____   Lights work _____   Wiper work _____

Checklist on Body and Fenders

	Excellent	Good	Fair	Poor	Repairable
Grille					
Front apron					
Left hood					
Left cowl					
L. F. fender					
L. runningboard					
L. F. door					
L. R. door					
L. quarter					
Rear panel					
Rear apron					
R. R. fender					
R. quarter					
R. R. door					
R. F. door					
R. runningboard					
R. F. fender					
R. cowl					
R. hood					
Front bumper					
Rear bumper					
Headlights					

	Excellent	*Good*	*Fair*	*Poor*	*Repairable*
Park/side lights					
Taillights					
Windshield frame					
Door handles					

Report on Test Drive

MOTOR

	Yes	*No*			*Yes*	*No*
Start easily				Pull evenly		
Run evenly				Any knocks		
Idle evenly				Emit smoke		
Noise in motor when cold				When warmed up		

INSTRUMENTS
Oil pressure _____   Generator charge _____   Overheat _____

CLUTCH
Will motor stall with brake on? _____   Clutch slip? _____
Does clutch grab when pedal is slowly released? _____

TRANSMISSION
Clunking or grinding sound as you go through the gears? _____

	Acceleration	*Deceleration*
Low		
Second		
High		

Universal Joints

Any thumping or banging noise coming from near middle of car on acceleration and deceleration? _____

DIFFERENTIAL
Any whining noise at moderate speeds? _____
Any chucking noise at slow speeds or decelerating? _____

STEERING

	⅛	¼	½	None
Amount of play in steering wheel				

Front wheels shimmy? _____   Steer easily? _____
Pull to one side? _____   Wheel return after corner? _____

BRAKES
Stop car quickly? _____   Evenly? _____
Brakes grab? _____   Any grinding noise? _____
If hydraulic, does pedal hold position when pressed? _____
Does handbrake hold? _____

WHEELS AND TIRES
Do wheels match? _____   Complete hubcaps? _____
Tires? L.F. _____   L.R. _____   R.R. _____   R.F. _____   Spare _____

INTERIOR OF CAR

	Excellent	*Good*	*Fair*	*Bad*
Front cushion				
Front seat back				
Rear cushion				
Rear seat back				

	Excellent	*Good*	*Fair*	*Poor*
R.F. door				
R.R. door				
L.F. door				
L.R. door				
Kick panels				

	Excellent	*Good*	*Fair*	*Poor*
Headliner				
Side panels				
Inside visors				
Window shades				
Door handles				
Window cranks				
Ashtrays, vanities				
Pedal pads				
Other				

trying to help his friend or impress you with his great knowledge. You can't tell the guy to get lost, but there's nothing wrong with telling the seller you'd prefer to talk with him alone and may come back at another time. If you take a friend along with you, don't make it look as if you're ganging up on the seller.

Like many other purchases, buying an old car is often a battle of wits. It's part of the fun of ownership. You'll hear all sorts of claims about the various makes and models. You'll probably be quoted phony original prices on some cars. You may be given a story about some famous person or well-known local personality who once owned the car. In most cases this shouldn't change the car's value, though occasionally it can. You may be looking at an old heap standing in a shed with four flat tires, covered with chicken droppings that hide most of the rust, while the owner tells you that the car drove fine when Uncle Jess parked it there three years ago. Chances are it was pushed into its present location ten years ago because Uncle Jess couldn't find anyone to take it off his hands.

There are some partially restored cars that turn up for sale. The owner may have been transferred to another city, and unable to take the car to the new location, or one is available because of a divorce or death in the family. These may be good bargains. However, beware of the seller who says he's lost interest in the car. Find out why he lost interest, especially if you see other old cars on hand. He may have encountered a very expensive repair or replacement problem that contributed to his losing interest. You should also be wary of the person who tells you he turned down a much larger offer a week ago. I've had this pulled on me at least ten times. I usually reply that he should have taken it, as it's far more than I will offer. Beware of the seller who says he's promised the car to another person, or that he's holding a deposit on the car, but if you'll up your offer a certain amount, he'll let you have it. Once a price is given you, repeat it to the seller and let him see you jot it down. It's an old trick to give one price to get you interested, then when you've decided to buy the car, claim you misunderstood the price or what's included in it.

I certainly do not mean to imply that all old car sellers are crooks—nothing of the kind. The tactics mentioned shouldn't deter you from bargaining on a car. It's as natural for the seller to try to get the highest possible price as it is for the buyer to try to get the lowest possible price. If you've got an accurate appraisal of the car's worth and restoration costs, you can usually strike a fair bargain.

Don't be scared away from a make or model you'd like just because of the car's appearance. It may look hopeless: flat or missing tires, sagging doors, fenders dented and rusted, broken glass, seat cushions and top shredded. The whole thing may be covered with odds and ends of junk and bird droppings; wasps and field mice love to nest in secluded old cars. But remember that most old cars were pretty well built, made of solid materials, If they're largely complete, they can usually be rebuilt and restored.

Legal Requirements

Be sure to check your state's requirements for licensing an old car. These regulations vary from state to state. Generally a properly endorsed and notarized title will do. A notarized bill of sale will usually suffice if a title isn't available: many states didn't issue titles twenty or more years ago. In any case, be sure the person selling the car has the legal right to sell it. Make sure you get a receipt. Check to be sure that the motor and serial numbers are correct and correspond to the numbers on the paper. Information regarding body style, body number, etc., should correspond to the actual car. Be sure that your legal instrument of sale is properly signed and notarized. Imagine the anger and frustration of restoring a car, only to find you can't title or license it!

Preliminary Checklist

When you see a car you believe you'd like, there are some checks you'll want to make. First of all, get directly to the owner for negotiations. Ask questions about the ownership and title; if there are no plates on the car, ask when it was last driven. A registration slip will tell you when the car was last licensed. Stickers on the doors or firewall should show dates the car was serviced. Compare the price with prices of other cars you may be considering. Ask about delivery to your garage. Get all the information you can by asking questions and making comparisons. If you know someone who has a similar make, get that person's opinion. It's a good idea to wear old clothes when climbing in and around old cars. They won't guarantee a lower price, but it won't matter if they get soiled or torn.

TEST DRIVE

If the car is running, you'll want to take a test drive, remembering that most old cars won't perform to today's standards. Before starting the motor, it's wise to make a few checks. See if there's oil in the base. Check the dipstick for water drops in the oil that could indicate a cracked block, head, or blown gasket. See if there's coolant in the radiator and that there are no signs of oil in the coolant. Check the fan belt to make sure it's reasonably tight. On many cars the water pump and generator were driven by the fan belt.

When starting the motor, see how quickly the oil gauge shows pressure. The amount isn't as important as the fact that there is pressure. Listen for knocks in the cold motor before the oil circulates. Bad knocks that sound from deep down in the motor could indicate badly worn or burned-out bearings. Upper motor knocks aren't as important, but they can indicate worn camshaft and valve mechanisms or wrist pin wear. A glance at the ammeter gauge will tell you if the generator is charging. Sometimes tapping an apparently inoperative gauge will make it spring into action. The heat gauge will take longer to respond than the other gauges, but you should soon find out if the car is overheating. Overheating can be caused by a clogged or sluggish radiator core, a faulty or leaking water pump, a cracked motor or cylinder head. It could also be due to a leaky hose or a blown cylinder head gasket.

Once the motor is running, before any heat or pressure builds up, remove the radiator cap and see if any bubbles are coming up through the coolant. The coolant should be moving, but should not contain any bubbles. These can indicate a blown head gasket or a cracked cylinder head.

If the engine hasn't run in some time, starting may be difficult. You may need jumper cables from the battery in another car. Warmup may be slow and the engine may run unevenly. These things can be caused by worn points in the distributor; sparkplugs that need cleaning, regapping or replacement; sticky valves; a dirty or clogged gas line or filter. An unevenly running engine usually isn't a serious problem. You'll enjoy the tuneup you can give it.

If you can take a test drive, by all means do so. Once you've got the motor running, checked the gauges and listened to it as it warms up, you're ready.

With the hand brake set, let the clutch out slowly without giving the motor much power. If the motor starts to stall, that's good: it indicates the hand brake works. As the car starts to move, notice at what point the clutch takes hold. The farther out the pedal is before the car starts to move, the more wear there is in the clutch. A weakness in the clutch operation isn't anything to scare you away: clutch plates can be easily resurfaced or repaired; clutch throw-out bearings can be replaced; pedal linkage can be adjusted.

As you drive, go through the gears slowly. Listen for unusual clunks in the transmission and differential, but remember that many older cars didn't have the quiet synchromesh transmissions: low and second gears will normally make some noise. What you're listening for is an irregular grinding sound that indicates excessive wear or missing teeth on the gears. Transmissions can be repaired, of course. New or rebuilt gears can replace worn ones. You may want to replace the transmission rather than repair it—there's no real problem here, unless your car is extremely rare.

Before you attain any speed, possibly before you shift into high gear, check the brakes. Early cars usually had mechanically operated brakes and they're simple to repair. Later cars had hydraulic brakes, a little more complicated, but easily repaired. For testing purposes, see how quickly and evenly you can stop the car. Notice if it pulls to one side when the brakes are applied, indicating a grabbing brake. The check on the brake system at this point is simply for an overall evaluation and for your safety during the test drive.

Check the steering for excessive play. More than a half-turn without the car responding may indicate worn bushings. Bushing replacement isn't difficult and will correct most steering faults. In some cases new king pins may be needed. Front wheel shimmy indicates worn king pins. Often an antishimmy device installed between the front axle and tie rod will postpone rebuilding the steering system for many miles. If the car pulls to one side when you release the wheel, it could be due to different sized or underinflated tires, or it could be out of line. To check basic alignment, park the car parallel to a curb: check the distance from the curb to the front and rear wheels; the distance should be the same. I once bought a 1932 Chrysler without doing this and later found it to be nearly two inches out of line.

During your test drive you'll be able to estimate overall condition of the motor, clutch, transmission, brakes and steering. Don't be overly alarmed by rattles or squeaks. The test drive should give you a good idea of what repairs will be necessary. Record these findings on the checklist for future reference.

STATIONARY TEST

If the car isn't in running condition, arrange to hear the motor run before you buy it. If this can't be done and you're still interested, there are some tests you can make to assure yourself that it can be made to run. The owner shouldn't object to these. With the car out of gear and the ignition off, use a crank to spin the engine. It shouldn't turn too easily, as that would indicate poor compression, meaning the pistons have worn the cylinder walls excessively. A ring job will correct this, and you can do it yourself without much difficulty. If, on the other hand, you can't budge the motor with a hand crank, the motor may be set up or seized. This usually indicates a broken connecting rod, burned out main bearings, or worse. A seized engine is no reason for the beginner–restorer to decide against a car if the rest of it seems restorable. Usually replacement engines can be located. They can be rebuilt, often using many parts of the original engine, and installed to replace the seized engine.

If no crank is available, your problem is more difficult, but you can still check to see if the engine is free and will turn. Put the car in high gear, with the hand brake released, and get someone to help push the car. This won't be easy, but it'll show you if the motor will turn over. Don't use another car to push or pull the car you're testing. If you're unable to push the car because of lack of room or flat tires, jack up one rear wheel of the car. Put the car in high gear with the hand brake released. Turn the wheel by hand. As you rotate the wheel, it will operate through the drive train and cause the motor to turn. There will be some play here, but nothing to worry about.

If the motor is free and will turn over, you can eventually make it run. However, you should get a sizable price reduction if the motor is seized. As previously mentioned, this requires either engine replacement or extensive repairs. You may want to investigate the possibility of locating a replacement engine before negotiating a final price on the car.

In checking the motor before purchase, look over the outside for cracks or splits in the cylinder head or block. This is easier on an "in line" engine than on a V-type. Cracks aren't always apparent because of oil, grease and accumulated grime. They're pretty risky business. The simple cracks on the outside of the water jacket can be repaired by an additive to the cooling system. More serious ones will need welding. Worst of all are the cracks you can't see, inside the head or block. Symptoms are oil in the cooling system or water in the oil. If you're not convinced that the motor is without cracks, ask the owner outright if the block or head is cracked. Also, you're not out of line in asking him for a written guarantee that he'll give you your money back if you find such a crack in a reasonable time. Guarantees are not the best answer, of course, and the beginner–restorer should plan on finding a replacement motor if the block is cracked. In some instances only a block or head needs to be replaced and most of the other engine parts can be used in reassembling the motor. If a complete replacement motor is located, choose the best parts from each for the rebuilding job.

JUDGING THE BODY

Once you've made your decision on the mechanical condition of the car, you're ready to check the other parts.

Dented or rusted fenders and running boards don't create any real problems. The time and expense of repairs or replacements should be taken into consideration in arriving at a price for the car.

The radiator shell, headlights, bumpers and other plated parts aren't crucial, as they can usually be replated. If they're badly pitted, this means replacement or replating. Remember that these are cosmetic, rather than functional, repairs: they should be considered in that light, but included in your estimate of restoration cost.

Rust, rot and corrosion are the biggest enemies of the car's body. They can be serious if they've gone unchecked over the years. In many cases, however, they look far more expensive and difficult to repair than they really are. This is good from the buyer's position, as many sellers don't realize how easily these repairs can be made.

Remove old finish and hammer out dents before priming and painting dented and rusted fenders, as required on these from a '27 Hupmobile.

On most older cars, the body is framed in wood. A steel or aluminum skin is formed over it and attached to the wood. If the wood has rotted, the body panels will have no support. If they're steel, they probably will have rusted through in some spots. Usually the firewall is sheet steel, with the first structural wood being in the cowl section, windshield and dash supports. If this is rotten, the whole section will sag. This makes the doors sag too, as they either hinge on it or close to it. Door and body panels that cover the rotten wood usually look pretty bad: doors won't close properly, and sections of the body have no strength.

These conditions should be taken into consideration when evaluating the car. Remember, you can replace the wood yourself and rusted-out metal can be replaced or repaired easily. Neither of these tasks is beyond the capabilities of the beginner–restorer, whether a man or woman.

On cars with all-steel bodies (usually around the mid-Thirties), wood was used only for attaching trim pieces or as roof bows. As age caught up with these cars, the metal supports rusted through. If the rustout is in door frames, door posts or other structural places, replacement is a little more difficult, but you can do it. You may want some of these replacements welded in place, so consider this expense when evaluating the body on your checklist.

EXAMINING THE INTERIOR

The interior of an old car that has sat in a shed or outdoors for a number of years can easily scare the uninformed buyer away. If a door has stood ajar, a window is down or broken, or the roof has leaked or is missing, the interior of the car will be a mess. It can be enough to scare you away from the hobby. Often children will have played in the car, breaking or twisting knobs and levers and tearing the upholstery. Mice and rats may have nested in the car; bees and mud-daubers may have called it their home. All this can be pretty discouraging. As the cloth webbing on the seats rots out, springs may push through, exposing the padding. The seats may appear impossible to repair, causing you to think the car will need all new seats and cushions. Leather splits and cracks, upholstery on doors and side panels may be rotten or motheaten. You may find fungi growing in the car. These conditions can be easily repaired by the beginner–restorer. They should be noted on the checklist in evaluating the car to determine a fair price.

Remove rotten upholstery panels, seats and floorboards to start restoration. Use what you can as patterns to make new components.

Carpets, floormats, pedal pads and other trim items aren't difficult or expensive to repair or replace. Tires, tubes and batteries are readily available. Your only problem will be the cost involved. You'll want to include all these on your checklist to consider when you figure the cost of restoration.

Occasionally one will come across an old car that doesn't have any nameplate or other identifying insignia. This may be an orphaned make or a car that has been changed over the years as new parts were added to replace worn or damaged ones. Occasionally this "found" car will be only part of the original vehicle, abandoned for one reason or another. A discovery of this kind can be a really fascinating one, especially if inspection shows that the machine can be put into working order. I once "discovered" the rusting corpse of a small truck in the logging area of Ontario. So many parts were missing that it was hard to identify. After scraping away years of rust on the block, I found the name "White." Since I was on a fishing trip, I had to leave the old truck for someone else to restore it.

Unidentified Corpse

You won't have too much trouble identifying most old cars, unless you've encountered a rare, long-orphaned make. If the radiator shell, hubcaps and other parts that normally carry a trademark are gone, you'll have to do some searching.

Look on the firewall, inside and out, to see if there's a plate of some description. If so, this should be handled carefully so as not to obliterate any printing or stampings on it. If there's no identification plate of this nature, look along the frame for any stampings. Check the cylinder head and the engine block, looking for a name and number. If you locate a name, number, initials or other trademark, it'll give you something to go on.

Of course, if you locate a name that is familiar, you should have no trouble in running down the correct information. Should the car turn out to be a make still manufactured or one that belonged to a family of cars still being manufactured, you're in luck. Write the parent company, enclosing all the information you can find on the vehicle. Send along photos too, as they may help in identification.

Should you find information indicating the car is one that is now an orphaned make, contact the national club representing that make. Again, send as much detailed information as possible along with photos.

Several directories are published annually, listing the names and addresses of the hundreds of car clubs. These are published by companies that publish automotive periodicals. You can buy one for under $2, or may find one in the reference room in your public library, usually a great source of information. Even if they don't carry what you're looking for, they have book lists that help. You can also write the Head of the Automotive History Collection, Detroit Public Library, a great source of helpful information on all makes of cars.

Once you determine the make, year and model you shouldn't have any trouble making a satisfactory restoration. There is next to no chance that you'll find a car that can't be identified. It may take some time, but eventually you'll run it down. The efforts you made in identification will add interest to the car.

Tallying up the results on your checklist, you should estimate the cost of restoration. You undoubtedly have a price in mind that you're willing to pay for an unrestored car. You can get comparison prices from many sources: newspaper ads, magazine ads, prices quoted by other sellers and buyers, prices indicated by car club publications all help in setting a price range in your mind. With a general idea of what you want to spend on the initial car, plus the estimate on repairs from your checklist, you should arrive at a reasonable price. Your own judgment of the seller's personality

The Big Moment

must be taken into consideration to determine your opening bid. Naturally, you'll bid low, explaining how much it'll cost you to restore it. The seller will counter with a higher price, stressing the good points of the car and discounting your estimate on restoration costs. This is where your detailed checklist can be extremely helpful to you: through give and take, you'll arrive at a price.

When you've settled the deal, be sure you get everything that goes with the car. Sometimes there'll be an extra rim hanging on a wall or a box or two of odds and ends. This is especially true if someone has started repairs on the car or it's partially dismantled. Get everything that belongs with the car and take it along even if it looks worthless. If you want to, you can always discard unneeded parts or possibly trade them off to someone else.

Since half the joy of restoration will be showing your friends how much you accomplished, be sure to take some snapshots of the car. Try to get one as you first saw it or before you moved it. Both inside and outside shots will be fun to look at after you've completed the restoration. Many people take pictures regularly during the restoration process—an interesting group of pictures to show to skeptical friends.

CHAPTER 3

Starting
General Restoration

Usually, the first thing you'll have to do when you bring home your new acquisition is to convince some of your friends and neighbors that you haven't taken leave of your senses. Tell them the noble old crate is in far better condition than it appears—it'll be restored in no time. There'll be plenty of snide remarks about how much you were paid to haul it away. There'll also be some bawdy remarks, all of which have to be answered with good humor. Some viewers may be genuinely interested; you can appreciate their questions. Invariably you'll be asked outright what you paid for the car. A husband and wife should level with each other on the price: as

When hauling a car on a trailer, be sure car is securely chained so it can't move in any direction. Have proper lights for night towing.

for the others, if there's no way they can find out, shock them by quoting a real zinger. It'll start your investment appreciating.

You shouldn't have any trouble getting it home. Drive it if you can. Rent or borrow a tow bar and safety chain if you plan to tow it: be sure you have it properly lighted after dark. You can haul it on a trailer made for this purpose. There are also people who make a business of transporting cars, if you want it brought that way.

Assuming that you'll be working on it for some time, you want to get it into the best possible position in your garage. Place the car so you can open all doors without hitting anything. You should be able to get around it completely. If the restoration will require dismantling the car, buy four good strong jack stands. Don't use blocks or pieces of wood; *never leave a car on*

When loading car on trailer, be certain ramps allow clearance for all underparts to avoid damage. Put chocks under trailer wheels to prevent movement.

If the car is a real basket case, rent a small trailer or borrow a pickup truck. Bring everything home at one time. Load parts carefully to prevent damage.

You have a choice of jack stands. Center one is homemade from rear axle case. Choose stand with wide base for solid support.

hydraulic or mechanical jacks while working on it. Make it safe and solid before you remove the wheels. Also remember that an old car is attractive to children who may want to play on it. It's a good idea to take the ignition key out of the car and hang it someplace until you need it.

Jack stands are adjustable, so jack the car up to sufficient height to allow you to get underneath it easily. Be sure the car is level from front to back, as well as from side to side. This is extremely important. Each jack stand should be under a flat spot on the frame of the car or where the spring crosses the axle on semielliptic springs. If you place the jack stands directly under the axle on transverse spring cars, put the stands far enough toward the outside so you can't tip the car. On cars with independent suspension, place each jack stand under the coil spring socket or on a flat spot on the frame. Don't place the stands under the brake drums for any reason.

Actually, on all cars, it's better to put the stands under the frame near enough to the frame ends so you won't get a teeter-totter effect. Jack stands under the frame also take the weight off the car's suspension system and

When placing the car on jack stands, set stands toward end of axle to give wide base of support and prevent any tipping of car.

will make working on these components easier. Also, once it's on the jack stands be sure that it's extremely safe and solid. Remember, it'll be your gut or head if anything gives way and the car comes down once the wheels are removed.

It helps to have an electric outlet nearby. You'll never get enough light from a ceiling bulb, as there'll be shadows and dark spots. A good, well-insulated electric extension cord with a metal protector for the bulb is best. A reel type that can be fastened to the wall and will retract when not in use is just great. Have a heavy duty extension cord for use with an electric drill; all sorts of attachments can be used with a small drill. One of the handiest is a small wire brush attachment.

Identifying Parts

You'll want plenty of containers for storage. Avoid pickle and peanut butter jars, as they may break if you drop them and can also break if you drop a heavy bolt or nut into one. Beer or soft drink cans with tops removed are good, as are coffee or shortening cans. Boxes are handy for larger items. Use a felt-tipped marker and freezer tape to identify parts: mark cans and jars plainly.

Freezer or masking tape labels on coffee or beer cans identifies nuts, bolts, washers, to help in reassembly.

Properly marked boxes for storing small parts during restoration will save many headaches when the time comes to put things back together. String tags help on parts too large to put in storage boxes.

Some of the nuts, bolts, springs and washers will look alike and you may not see the need for any additional identification. You may think you'll remember where the various parts came from, but the importance of identifying all small items you remove can't be overemphasized. You may not be working on the car every day and you'll sure as hell forget where some of them came from. Mark your storage cans "dash," "left front door," "carburetor parts," "windshield trim," and so on to save you many hours later and get parts back where they actually belong.

For some reason, cars seem to be referred to as "she." Call yours "he," "she," "it," or give it a name—you'll be spending a lot of time together. First thing to do is to make a thorough search or cleaning. This must be of the entire car, inside and out. It is absolutely necessary in your restoration job, and it makes more sense to start inside.

Clean out every nook and cranny—you're apt to find a lot of them! A good place to start is the dashboard, if there are glove or map compartments. Some cars had compartments for tools and maps in the kickpads in the cowl panels. Take everything out. Keep the money, keys, screws, bolts, nuts, washers and other small parts that may have ended up there. You may find some interesting memorabilia, letters, grocery lists or gas ration coupons. (I'd like to know the real story behind a large screen glass earring I found in the kickpad compartment in a Reo.) Some owners stored owners' manuals, parts catalogs and service orders in these compartments. Discard old condoms and other odds and ends of junk that used to find their way to these spots.

Decide if these panels have to be replaced: obviously, in this clean and search process, don't remove any panels that look OK to you. If a panel is good enough to keep as a pattern, do so. Otherwise, you'll have to make up new patterns when the time comes. Once you've searched this area, removing any interesting materials or salvageable parts, put the rest in the discard can.

Get a large galvanized garbage can with a cover for weekly trash pickups. Galvanized is best, as it is strong, won't burn and gas won't dissolve it, as it will some plastics. The weekly discard can get pretty heavy, too. Put the can out with the regular trash collection or arrange to haul it to the dump yourself. A weekly discard is best, otherwise you'll find yourself knee-deep in junk you'll have to plow through for weeks. It's also better for reducing fire hazards, as well as much easier to work around. Try to keep your work area clean, as this will help keep you from tracking dirt into the house.

Door panels often offer up some real goodies. Many old cars had compartments in the doors or door pockets. Again remove any small parts, interesting papers, even little screws and washers, then get rid of the rest. Remember to store these discoveries in a can marked to show where they came from. If the door panels have to be replaced, try to keep the best one to use as a pattern.

Inside Esmerelda

Use blowing cycle first to clean out crevices, then follow up with suction to pick up dirt. Sift through dust as you empty the bag to retrieve any tiny parts.

Next is a dirty job, but it's interesting and important. You may want to take a decongestant tablet beforehand. Use a good whiskbroom and the vacuum cleaner, if you can. When using the vacuum cleaner, start with a clean bag. Use the machine on the "blowing," or exhaust, cycle first, especially under the dashboard. Then, by hand, pick up any small parts that suddenly appear. Keep dust and small trash picked up and emptied regularly in the trash can. After the blowing operation with the cleaner, put it in normal operation to pick up the dust and dirt that you've loosened. The use of a vacuum cleaner and attachments makes the cleanup job easier.

SEATS AND RUGS

Remove all seat cushions and seat backs. All sorts of things will turn up—bits of costume jewelry, wrenches, screwdrivers and other odds and ends. Look for any factory information, handbook or parts manual. Receipts for work performed will give you information on the car's condition. Lift out the rugs, floor mats and padding, saving all screws, washers and other small parts.

Some cars had battery boxes and tool storage compartments under the front seats, as well as places for storing jacks and tire tools. Some models had storage compartments for side curtains and top boots. Search through these carefully, saving anything that looks interesting. While you're working with the battery box, be sure to see which terminal on the battery is grounded (attached to the car frame) as this can make a difference should you need to get a replacement battery.

As you search through these parts, try to sort the findings into the cans and boxes I mentioned. Although some of the bolts and screws may be rusted and you won't want to use them again, they're handy for determining thread size and diameter of replacements.

Seat cushions, rugs, upholstery panels and headliners should all be cleaned as well as possible before storage. You may not have had to remove all these parts, but any you did remove should be cleaned. Anything you can hang in direct sunlight for awhile will help dry up mildew and prevent rot. Brush and vacuum all parts as best you can before storing them on those pieces of plywood nailed to the garage rafters.

HANDLES, CRANKS AND REVEALS

Inside door handles and window cranks are commonly held in place by a tapered pin that runs through the handle and the shaft. These are hidden from view by a spring-backed escutcheon. Gentle prying with a thin-bladed screwdriver or table knife will push the escutcheon back, exposing the pin. A drop of light oil on the pin will free it so you can drive it out with a nail or small punch. Naturally, you drive from the tapered end—either all the way out or far enough so you can grip it with pliers and pull it out. Save it along with the spring and the escutcheon.

Some cars used handles that slipped over square shafts, held in place by a screw on the end. These, of course, come out easily, though a drop of oil may be necessary to avoid stripping the head. Others used a little hexagon key and these must be removed by using the appropriate size allen head wrench to unscrew the threaded key. No matter which system, there are no real problems in removing door and window hardware: just don't force anything. Let any bolt or screw that doesn't want to budge soak for awhile in oil. There are several special rust-removing oils that will help, too. Always use a lubricant before applying pressure.

In removing the window and windshield reveals (those frames around the glass) your job is a simple one. The more expensive cars used wood trim held in place by a few plated screws. Clips were often attached to the back where they wouldn't show. Remove the screws and washers; *pry gently so you won't split the wood*. Occasionally there'll be little metal prongs attached to the inside of the wood. These slip into slots in the metal part of the door. Notice that the upright pieces usually come out first. You can determine which piece to remove first by seeing which piece of wood overlaps the other.

On lower-priced cars these reveals or frames were metal. Some were finished to resemble wood or painted to match the dashboard. These, too, are held in place by screws and the method of removal is the same. You don't want to apply much pressure, as these can be easily bent out of shape.

Once the frames are out, mark pieces on the inside to indicate where they belong. All markings on car parts that would indicate whether right or left hand are made from inside the car facing forward. These simple marks where they won't show will help identify them should you have to refinish them before re-installation.

DASHBOARD AND FRAMES

It's better not to remove the dash panel if you can avoid it, but don't be afraid to tackle if it has to come out. The biggest problem in removing the dashboard is in rewiring and reconnecting the gauges. If you feel you have to do it, get some little string tags to label each wire or tube you may have to cut or disconnect. Removal of the dashboard is covered in detail in the section on body restoration.

Don't hesitate to take out seat frames. A good soaking with oil will loosen the bolts or screws holding the frames in place. In some cars you may want to remove the floorboards first to make seat frame removal easier, as it often takes two wrenches or a wrench and a screwdriver to turn these out. Save any seat-moving mechanism and label it to help in later reassembly. If you don't take a snapshot, a simple sketch will usually do as well, so long as you remember to keep things in approximate proportion, marking left or right, front or back, on the sketch.

Occasionally you'll find a bolt or screw that will break rather than twist out. Don't get uptight about this, as you can always drill it out later and use a replacement.

After cleaning the inside of the car, removing all those parts you feel need repair or replacement, you should do somewhat the same job on the rest of the car.

Many old cars had tool storage compartments attached to the front fenders or built into the splash aprons along the running boards. Others had clips on engine pans or on the engine side of the firewall that held tools. Some

Outside Clean and Search

had compartments underneath the running boards. Rear decks on coupes and victorias, as well as rumble seat compartments on roadsters, coupes and convertibles, all provided storage space. Trunks on coaches, broughams and sedans were another place for storing tools. Look through all of these places and don't throw anything out that may be used again as is, or as a pattern in making a replacement.

By now, you've gone over the car far more thoroughly than you could have before you bought it. You've got a good idea of what you're going to need to do. The car is pretty well stripped down for repairs; you've removed the inside parts that must be repaired or replaced. It may look pretty rough at this point, but don't let it shake you up. This first all-important search and clean operation will show you the condition of the important body parts and help you decide what you need to do. Also, this operation may have turned up some tools and parts that will prove very handy as you work along on the car.

Diagnosis and Treatment

You're not ready to start "fixing" yet, no matter how anxious you may be. It's best to plan your work: you should diagnose that which needs to be done and make a list of these jobs. Decide what parts can be repaired and what parts must be replaced. For repairable parts, decide which you can repair yourself and which will need machine shop or welding that you can't do. Don't underestimate what you can do by way of repairing parts. Also, don't plan on replacing anything that can be repaired. A good portion of the fun in restoration is the work you can do yourself.

The more thought you give to the jobs that must be done, the easier it will be for you to do them. Your work so far has been only cleaning and diagnostic work on the body itself. Usually it's wiser to get all the mechanical restoration done before starting body restoration.

While making up a list of the jobs to be done, based on what you've come across so far, be honest with yourself. If you've bitten off more than you think you can chew, this might be a good time to seek help. Remember,

Car ready for restoration, with wheels and some sheet metal removed. Mark parts as you remove them; take photos or make sketches of assembly methods to help when you put things back together.

this is just a list of things you find need repairs: detailed directions on how to make these repairs are found in the following chapters. Refer to your original evaluation sheet as you make up this list. Extra time spent here will save you many hours and dollars later on.

To help you make an accurate appraisal of mechanical conditions so you may plan your work, the following checklist should suffice. Then I'll discuss in detail the directions on how to make these checks.

1. Check the cooling system for effectiveness and leaks. Include the water pump, upper and lower hoses, heater hoses, fan belt and radiator.
2. Electrical system: generator, voltage regulator for output and shorts, starter, distributor, sparkplugs, coil, condenser and points, as well as lights and horn.
3. Check for excess carbon on piston tops and sparkplugs.
4. Investigate for any oil-fouled sparkplugs.
5. Examine seating of valves and valve clearance.
6. Check compression of each cylinder.
7. Operate clutch to detect play or slippage.
8. Check transmission for ease in shifting.
9. Examine brake system, both foot and hand brakes.
10. Operate steering gear to detect wear and play.
11. Check differential for excessive play.
12. Examine springs and shock absorbers.

Your initial evaluation of the car may render some of these unnecessary. How to make each of these checks and the necessary adjustments and repairs are explained in subsequent chapters. Basic chassis restoration will be covered first.

MECHANICAL PARTS

Once you know what replacement mechanical parts you'll need, you have several options. First check automotive supply stores: these are a good source of engine parts, gears, clutch parts, brake linings and fittings, elec-

Obtaining Replacements

Without too much difficulty, you may locate repair shops with parts on hand for old cars. Replacement parts are sometimes less expensive than extensive rebuilding of badly worn parts.

trical components, mufflers, exhaust pipes, etc. Many cars used parts that were furnished by the same supplier originally, so are interchangeable; many parts were made to the same specifications by different companies. The knowledge the sales help can offer concerning specifications and interchangeability of parts can be most helpful to you. You may want to take a part down and ask them to match it for you.

If your car is a make that's still being manufactured, a dealer can sometimes give you advice on parts, though very few will still have parts on hand for cars over ten years old. An inquiry to the manufacturer may bring helpful information on parts availability and suggestions.

National and regional car clubs are a great source of parts. Most issue periodic publications containing lists of parts for sale and parts wanted. Over the years I've bought parts from individuals all over the country, and have never been cheated. However, in fairness to you as well as the seller, ask for specific information concerning condition, price, crating, mailing or shipping costs.

The many commercial car magazines usually contain a section on parts wanted and parts for sale: these are a good source. Also, if you spot an ad offering a car like yours for sale, the owner may have some extra parts.

One of the best immediate sources is a local auto club. Club members usually know of parts available and gladly help other members locate them. They usually expect reciprocity when the time comes that they are in need.

Don't overlook the classified ads in newspapers. Many papers carry listings of antique or classic cars; some carry listings of car parts for sale. These ads often turn up useful leads.

Occasionally you'll come across an obscure part on an orphaned or really old car that you just can't seem to find. In these rare instances, you can usually find a machine shop that will either repair your old part or fabricate a new one for you. These shops are listed in the yellow pages of your phone directory. A friend may be able to refer you to one that's been helpful.

Another possibility for obscure parts repairing or fabrication is the hobby–machinist who has his own small shop in a basement or garage. These hobbyists are most accommodating. A surgeon once made a carburetor part for a Phantom III Rolls for me. A manager of a large clothing factory made door latches for a '41 Lincoln Continental for me. A school teacher who repaired antique guns as a hobby made me a set of bronze spiral windshield-wiper gears to replace worn fiber gears. These hobbyists love a challenge, do excellent work, and are glad to help. The cost is often so low it's embarrassing.

As a last resort you may have to substitute a part, using whatever you can get to do the job. This type of substitution lowers the value of your car somewhat and should be considered only if you can't find the necessary part or manage to have one made for you. Of course you can always be on the lookout for the genuine part, and if you locate it, replace the substitute.

LOCATING BODY PARTS

Body parts are usually easier to locate than mechanical parts. You have the same sources as you do for mechanical parts: national and regional car club publications; local car club members can help; ads in the nationally

Replacement fenders and other body parts for many old cars are readily available. However, you may have some trouble finding parts for low production or rare models.

known car magazines—either ads you run for parts wanted or someone else's car parts for sale.

It's seldom that you'll find body parts, fenders, grilles and the like at a car dealer's, though this occasionally happens when a dealer has been in business for many years. It's worth a try.

Car wrecking yards are a possibility for some makes. Yards that still have old cars on hand are becoming fewer as time passes and new regulations concerning wrecking yards take effect.

Be sure to check into the possibility that other cars made by the same manufacturer had interchangeable parts. You can frequently spot fenders, aprons, doors and other body panels that were the same on certain families of cars.

Headlights, taillights, door handles, bumpers and many trim parts were manufactured by independent suppliers, thus identical parts can be found on several different makes of cars. This was more common in the Twenties and Thirties before the depression wiped out the independents.

Local body and fender shops can rebuild almost any sheet metal part for you. However, this may take some investigation, as so many shops are simply geared to replacing panels, fenders and bumpers and don't have the time or inclination to do repair work. Usually members of a local car club can tell you of shops that will repair body parts and do the job right.

Replacement of fenders, aprons or grilles with better ones from the same make car is often easier and less expensive than repairing the originals. Since the replacement will be identical, this won't lessen the value of your car nor change its' authenticity. Doors and other body panels can be switched from one car to another, using the best parts of each to make one good one.

If you have room and are able to locate one, it's wise to buy a "parts car." These are usually wrecked ones or cars that aren't worth restoring. They offer a great source of replacement parts. Often these cars can't be titled and are available at very low prices. Remember to protect any parts car you buy from further deterioration by storing it properly, covering exposed parts, and using oil and grease to prevent rust. Sometimes several restorers buy a parts car together, though some arguments can arise over who gets which part.

With diligence, you can usually locate the body and fender replacement parts you need in all but extreme cases, though it may take some time to do so.

Obviously, the directions throughout this book cannot possibly cover each make of car. Manufacturing techniques and methods varied from maker to maker, sometimes from model to model. This is especially true of earlier cars and smaller manufacturers. Later, as mass production took over, less could be done by hand and things became more standardized.

Car manufacturers who initially developed a specific part or mechanism held patent rights. Often they were sold or traded to other companies in exchange for rights they might have held. Also, as companies tried to copy parts and features successful on certain makes, their offerings would be much the same, but enough different in design or assembly to get around the original patents.

Supply companies made many component parts for cars, often similar, but sometmes with slight variations ordered by the manufacturer. Frequently a part would be supplied to a car manufacturer by two or more suppliers. Though these serve the same purpose when on the car, they might be quite different in the way they were assembled. This is especially true of electrical and carburetor components.

The restorer will find differences in specific systems and parts discussed in every chapter. The overall descriptions of the workings will apply, only details will differ. Manuals on specific makes are often available; also, owner's manuals can give detailed information on certain models, if more specific directions or information are required. So don't get discouraged when you find variances on the typical systems and parts described, as these can't be avoided.

SECTION II

Mechanical Restoration

CHAPTER 4

Basic Chassis Restoration

The hardest part of the restoration will be disassembling the car. This is when you get out, get under, and get it apart. Years of dirt, grease and road tar will have formed a scale, making nuts and bolts hard to remove. Plenty of scraping with a putty knife and scrubbing with a wire-bristled brush will expose the threads. You can lubricate them before working with wrenches.

Take heart: the car will go back together a hundred times more easily. So, if you can get it apart, don't worry about putting it back together again.

There are several products that allow you to get your hands filthy, yet clean them with soap and water. Buy these at hardware stores or supermarkets. These usually contain lanolin, so they're good for your hands, too. If you're working in a shortsleeved shirt or blouse, rub the lotion on your forearms up to the elbows.

Depending upon the condition of your car and your restoration plans, choose only what you feel is necessary from the following directions. No need to remove any part that doesn't need repair.

Disassembly

WHEELS AND TIRES

First, remove the wheels and store them out of your way. You'll probably want to paint them. Any badly worn tires may as well be removed and discarded. This gives you more room to work. Put the wheel studs or nuts back on the hub now to prevent loss. A drop or two of oil on each will help prevent rust.

BUMPERS AND SUPPORTS

The second step is to remove the bumpers from the car. Don't bother to dismantle the arms or brackets from the face bars at this time. You can do that later more conveniently. In removing the bumper assemblies from the

When removing a bumper face bar, you can easily support it with your knees or a box as you loosen nuts.

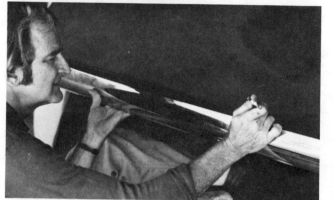

Rear bumper is easily removed by loosening nuts holding bumper brace to brackets.

Bumper braces offer a spring action to face bar and are usually attached to face bar at ends. When replating face bar, be sure to refinish braces.

To replate bumper face bars and refinish supports, remove them from the car as a unit, then disassemble.

chassis, you'll discover two different types of mounting. Each requires a different removal pattern. On some cars there were curved bumper arms that ran at right angles to the face bar. These arms ran parallel to the chassis or were attached to the end of the chassis. If your car was assembled this way, just remove the holding bolts on each side. Once you've done this, you can lift off the whole bumper assembly. On other cars, a bumper support ran parallel to the face bar and was attached to it at the ends. In these cases, simply remove the bolts where the support was attached to the frame ends and lift off the assembly.

Don't let it throw you if the nuts holding the bumper supports don't want to budge. After accumulating years of rust, dirt and grime, they may be hard to turn. Scraping with a wire-bristled brush should remove a lot of the rust and scale, exposing the threads. Follow this up with a good soaking in oil and rust remover. After a little wait for the lubricant to do its job, you should have no trouble. Save these nuts and bolts in a properly identified can.

On rare occasions you may have to use a nut splitter or hack saw on a stubborn nut. Aside from a little extra work, it isn't a serious problem. You'll have others to match for replacements.

Once you have the bumpers off the car, you can decide if you want to send them out for plating. If this is the case, then disassemble the braces and arms. Mark them to identify right and left, front and rear. Store these for later refinishing; you can send bumpers to a plating shop at any time. Usually, if the plater knows he's going to get the plating for your entire car, he'll naturally give you a better job and lower prices. Get an estimate first, and ask to see some of his work. If your bumpers are badly pitted and rusted, you may want to hunt up replacements. If you don't feel you want to spend the money for replacements, bumpers can be sanded, primed and painted. They'll give just as good service as the shiny plated ones.

LIGHT ASSEMBLIES

Next to come off should be the headlight and taillight assemblies. Usually the headlights were mounted on a crossbar that went from fender to fender; occasionally they were mounted on individual stanchions that bolted to the chassis, or fenders. On some cars the mounting bars reached only from the fender to the radiator shell.

Plan to take the headlights and bar off as an assembly. Occasionally horns were mounted on brackets attached to this cross member. Disconnect the wiring, tagging the wires, if necessary, so you'll know how to put them back together. Usually they'll fit together only one way.

When reworking headlights, remove crossbar support for refinishing at the same time.

A socket wrench and either an open-end or box-end wrench will be needed for headlight removal. The plunger-type oil can that will squirt up to these nuts will help. Normally the bolts that hold the headlight assembly go through the fender brace (the curved brace from the frame to the edge of the fender). Road grime, rust and scale will make a good scraping a necessity here. With patience they'll come loose. Later you can remove the headlights from the bracket or crossbar more easily on a workbench.

FENDERS AND BRACES

The fender braces should be removed from the chassis and come off as a part of the fender. This is especially true if the fender has been dented or the metal torn, as the brace will help maintain the natural arc of the fender as you repair it. Usually, it's not necessary to remove the fenders from a car to repair them.

Remove the bolts holding fender to frame and running board. Remove fender brace with fender to help maintain arc of fender during repair.

Small cars usually had one brace per front fender, at the highest point in the fender curve. Larger cars with longer front fenders sometimes had a second brace roughly halfway back. Cars with side mounted spares usually had a brace from the bottom of the fender well to the frame.

The fenders themselves were bolted to the chassis frame, fender braces and ends of the running board. They were also bolted to the curved portion of the splash apron. You'll be lucky if your car was made with the bolts threaded into nuts secured to the frame. Most did not. There's considerable scraping and oiling to be done before these nuts will come off. This is a two wrench, or wrench and screwdriver, job. Don't let it throw you if you have to saw a couple of bolts or use a nut splitter. Only tear metal around the bolt as a last resort.

Don't try to save the old fender welting, the fabric-covered cord that fits

Remove rust and grime before attempting to remove bolts holding fenders to body, apron and running board. Use plenty of solvent to remove rust.

between the fenders and the chassis or body to prevent squeaks and keep moisture out. New and better fender welting is readily available at a very low price.

There was usually an apron, a vaguely U-shaped piece of sheet metal that fitted at the bottom of the radiator shell between the chassis ends. It was there to hide the front axle and springs. This should come off if you remove the fenders.

Remove bolts holding front apron to frame and fenders. In some cases, bumper supports must also be removed.

From time to time you'll come across a nut you can't loosen. Perhaps it's corroded to the point where it won't hold a wrench. If a pipe wrench won't grip either, you'll have to saw the bolt, use a nut splitter or try to drill it out. Only tear the metal around it as a last resort and then just enough to free the bolt. You can pound the metal back in place, have it welded and use a larger washer for strength when you reassemble the parts.

SPECIFIC TOOL USAGE

There are correct ways to use tools that will help you get the job done easier and save banging or scraping knuckles. You must take care to fit the

Some luggage racks only require removal of a couple of nuts. Others are more complicated, but will come off easily.

right wrench to each nut and bolt. Scrape off all rust and scale before fitting the wrenches. Don't use an adjustable wrench if you have another wrench that fits. On some screws or slotheaded bolts, you may want to run a hack saw blade through the slot a few times to ensure that you've got enough metal to twist against. As with wrenches, fit the proper size screwdriver in the slot to prevent unnecessary play and slippage.

Be sure the handles of your tools are free of oil and grease and your hands aren't slippery. Once you start applying the leverage you need to break loose some of these threaded devils, you don't want your hands to slip. *Point sharp tools away from yourself;* if they slip, you won't get gouged. Use common sense in working with tools and you'll avoid injury.

Rear fenders are removed essentially the same way as the front ones, but more easily. Usually the nuts into which the bolts were threaded were secured to the wheel arches. This makes it a one-wrench or one-screwdriver job. You'll find a drop of oil or rust remover on the secured nut and exposed threads will help, along with the suggested scraping. Many times the head will twist off. Don't get uptight if this happens, as you can drill out the remaining bolt. You can always place the nuts and bolts in a different position when reassembling, if you don't want to drill out broken bolts.

Some cars had an apron over the gas tank; others had small panels between the fenders and the gas tank. These will come out like the front apron. Sometimes the apron covering the gas tank was bolted through the back of the body. In closed cars this poses a problem, since it's difficult to reach both ends of the nut and bolt. Usually a wrench fitted so it will turn

Bolts hold gas tank to bracket on the frame. Some cars have straps that circle tank and attach to brackets. Be sure to rinse tank with water to remove all traces of gasoline.

against the body metal will hold itself in place while you turn the other end. Be sure to keep steady pressure on it to prevent its slipping out of place. Sometimes you'll need a helper to hold one wrench while you turn the other end.

SPLASH APRONS AND RUNNING BOARDS

If you feel you need to take off the side splash aprons and the running boards, don't hesitate. The procedure is about the same as for the fenders. To prevent scraping your shins after you remove the running boards, remove the supports, too. You'll find some of the nuts and bolts hard to twist, as they've been exposed to everything on the road for the life of the car. Scrape them off as best as you can and soak them with oil or rust remover. Start with the bolts attaching the running board to the fenders. Usually there was a steel piece between the fender and running board to stiffen the assembly. You will also find the running board bolted to the splash apron. Remove the bolts and the running board will be free to lift off. In the Twenties, most cars used wooden running boards; later on these were replaced with steel stampings. Wooden ones may be rotted to the point that you'll need to split the wood to remove them and saw out the bolts. You can easily make replacement boards out of plywood. Both wooden and steel boards can be recovered with new matting easily.

You may find the splash aprons attached either to the chassis frame or the bottom body sill. You'll need to get under the car to remove these. In some cases it will take a second person to hold a wrench, as you may not be able to reach both nut and bolt.

Taillights. On most old cars the taillights were secured to the rear fenders or chassis by a simple bracket. Some cars, usually the deluxe jobs, had a taillight on each side of the car. Some had a center mounted taillight in conjunction with the spare tire carrier. No matter how many lights, the removal process is the same.

First disconnect the wiring, tagging the wires if necessary. Remove the light and bracket as a unit at its mounting location on the fender or chassis. Usually two or three bolts and a backing plate were used. Since these bolts will have been exposed to the same road conditions as the headlight brackets, they'll require a good scraping and lubricating before you can remove them.

Once off, you can determine if there's any plating you want done. In some cases the inside reflector may be rusted because of a broken lens. Usually a good cleaning will remove most of the rust. If not, it's easy to spray a coat of aluminum paint on the reflector. You can't do this to repair a headlight reflector, as you need all the candlepower reflection the lamps will give. But for rear lights, it's OK.

SPARE TIRE CARRIERS

Only remove the spare tire carriers if you feel they can't be repainted in place. With side-mounted spares, this was usually a curved tubular bracket attached to the frame by three bolts. With rear mounted spares, it was either a one-piece brace attached to the frame or two separate brackets. If you want to remove them, clean the bolts and nuts thoroughly and lubricate them before applying any pressure. This will usually be a two-wrench job and may require the help of a second person. Once off, identify the holding bolts. The brackets can be sanded and painted whenever you get around to it.

What you have now is probably a sorry looking mess. Hopefully, you don't have any skinned knuckles or bruises. You shouldn't have if you worked carefully. Depending upon your restoration plans requirements, you have a car that's stripped down to the point where you can proceed with repairs. Anything that needs repair or replacement should be off the car now.

It will be easier for you to work on the motor later on if you remove the radiator grill or shell. You won't have to remove the radiator unless you have to repair it or make front motor repairs. Six to eight bolts or screws are all that need to be removed to lift off the grill or shell. There may be a fastening at the top of the shell, but it's usually on the radiator itself. The long center pin in the hood usually fits into a slot on the grille and the cowl. With these slots removed, the hood will lift off. Don't try to save rotted or torn hood lacings, as replacements are readily available.

HOOD

If you need to do any repair work on the hood, it's much easier to do if you take the hood apart. The hood is usually made of four pieces of stamped steel. Three long pins hold these pieces together and act as hinges when the hood is raised. These pins usually slide through alternating loops in the hood panels. A good dose of oil at each joint should loosen the pins so they may be driven out. The easiest way is to stand the hood upright on the cowl (widest) end. Put a couple of layers of newspaper under it to soak up spilled oil. Try to get oil to run down the pins by dripping it on the exposed ends, as well as along the slots. Let the hood stand for a while, flexing the hood panels occasionally to work in the oil. You can get a long rod from your hardware store, the same diameter as the hinge pin. These are inexpensive; you should have no difficulty determining the size by matching it to a small bolt that fits the hole. Usually the center one will be the same diameter as the side pins, but make sure: if they're both the same diameter, one rod will do. Measure it for length too, since you don't need it more than a couple of inches longer than the pin you're going to remove.

Remove holding slot on radiator shell and firewall; hood will lift off. Drive out center and side pins to separate into component parts.

On some cars these long pins are tapered slightly. Try to determine this beforehand. When you start to drive out the pin, drive it from the narrow end toward the wide end. Start with the center pin first. Lay the hood flat on the floor, with one end against some lumber to avoid damaging the end of the hood. Place a small punch or bolt at the end of the pin and give it a couple of sharp taps. As the pin starts to move, use the long pin. Use a wooden block against the end of the pin so you won't be hitting the long driveout pin directly: this will keep you from flattening the end. A drop or two of oil along the slots from time to time will help the pin slide out. With the center pin removed, the hood will be in two pieces.

Use the same process to remove the pin that hinges the two side panels. This will divide the hood into four individual panels, each easy to handle. You may want to remove the hood attachment clips and lifting handles at this point, especially if they're to be plated.

With as many of the aforementioned parts or panels removed as you feel necessary, you've done the dirtiest and most difficult part of the disassembly.

At this point, you're ready for the chassis–frame restoration. Put plenty of newspapers down under the areas you'll be working on. These will make daily cleanup easier. Using a putty knife about one inch long, start scraping. You've got to remove years of accumulated road grime, grease, rust and scale. What the putty knife won't remove will probably come loose with the wire brush.

Restoration

Use putty knife and wire brush to clean the chassis after it has been stripped down. Chassis and underparts should be repainted before assembly.

Start at the front of the chassis and work toward the rear, doing one side at a time. If you've got one of those wheeled creepers, it'll speed up the work, but one isn't necessary.

You'll find it easier if you work on the inside of the chassis–frame first. Most are of channel construction, so start at the inside top and work back. You'll need your electric extension cord so you can see what you're doing. The accumulation of dirt and grease will come off. It's a good idea to position yourself for this job so the stuff doesn't fall on you as you work along.

After you've scraped one section as clean as you can get it with your putty knife, use a wire-bristled brush to get at the hard to reach places.

Occasionally there'll be such an accumulation of dirt and grime that it won't come off with scraping and brushing. In these few cases, you may want to daub on a small amount of kerosene. A narrow paint brush is fine for this. The kerosene will loosen the worst spots. Remember not to smoke while you're doing this; keep the kerosene from splashing on the hot bulb in the extension cord; don't let the lamp bulb touch newspapers which will flare up easily, especially if they're kerosene soaked. *Never use a wire brush on any metal that is still wet from the kerosene.* You can easily cause sparks as the metal bristles rub against the soaked metal parts, and cause a fire.

From a practical point of view, it's best to do a relatively small section at a time. Perhaps about two or three feet at a time would be the easiest area to handle. This way you can reach everything easily. Clean out dirty and oily papers regularly: you'll give yourself a better place in which to work, and reduce any fire hazard.

Sometimes you'll find it easier to use a good strong solution of detergent and water instead of kerosene for hard to reach places. This is especially true if you're going to wire brush them anyway. *Never use gasoline,* as it's too risky. Also, when using kerosene be careful about inhaling the fumes.

Although you'll be spending most of the time cleaning and scraping, remove any part you think needs replacement or repair. For instance, you may find the frame or box that holds the battery is corroded or rusted out. If so, remove it now. Do the same with exhaust pipe or muffler brackets, if necessary. There's no need to clean a part that you'll be discarding later on.

When cleaning any section of the chassis–frame, go halfway across any cross members you may come to. You can clean the other half when you work on the other side of the car.

When you've completed one side or plan to stop work for the night, it's a good idea to spray on a rust-inhibiting primer. These come in aerosol cans, are inexpensive and easy to use. They'll protect the chassis from further deterioration. Later on, if you want, it's an easy matter to use a spray coat of black enamel. Aerosol sprays are suggested, as they'll reach places a brush can't. The time you take to spray a coat of enamel on the frame will be worthwhile.

Once you've worked your way around the chassis–frame of the car and removed parts to be replaced, it's a good idea to evaluate the job you've done. It's easier to redo a small portion now than later on. You'll be happier with the overall restoration if each portion is completed to your satisfaction.

This is a sensible time to reevaluate your checklist. You can see how accurately it reflects the work to be done: you may find additional chores you hadn't anticipated; you may find that some of the parts you thought would have to be replaced can be repaired satisfactorily. With this part of your restoration behind you, you can look forward to the remainder as easier, a lot cleaner and much more fun.

This makes a good show-off point: let those skeptics who had a lot to say when you started the job eat their words; it's a time to enjoy what you've accomplished.

REFURBISHING PARTS

You have some latitude in refurbishing parts, depending on the condition of these parts, your ability, willingness, time and money. Repairs of individual parts are covered in the appropriate chapter. Generally parts that can be refurbished can be considered in five main categories.

Mechanical Parts. After a thorough cleaning of the part, you should be able to gauge the amount of wear, and the amount of refurbishing necessary. Badly worn parts will usually have to be replaced. Other less worn parts can be rebuilt to give satisfactory service. Worn or chipped teeth on gears can be rebuilt by welding in new metal and grinding it down to the proper fit. Worn shafts can be built up the same way. New bearing metal can be poured if replacement bearings aren't available. Broken parts can usually be joined by welding.

Rusted or corroded parts can often be cleaned with a wire-bristled brush or grinding wheel. Detergents, solvents or kerosene will in most cases remove corrosion, and the exposed metal can be smoothed with emery cloth or compound.

Bent parts can be straightened in some cases. However, it may be necessary to heat the metal before attempting to straighten it. Once it's straightened, be sure you know what caused the metal to bend in the first place so you can prevent it from happening again.

A common mistake is assuming that worn parts must all be replaced. In many cases a worn part can be reworked to make it satisfactory. When rebuilding parts that mesh or work with other parts, you should consider the adjoining pieces: make sure that they fit together properly after rebuilding one part. Try to diagnose what caused a particular part to wear; if it was because of a faulty adjustment of another part, or lack of good lubrication, correct the cause to prevent future problems.

Body Parts. A thorough cleaning will turn up areas in bodies or fenders where refurbishment is necessary. Disassemble parts only to the point where you can work on damaged components easily. Determine and eliminate the cause of the damage or excessive wear.

If a body panel or door has a badly rusted spot, it's best to cut out the rusted metal, leaving strong metal around the spot. New metal should be cut to fit and welded in. With the weld properly ground down, the seam won't show when primed and finished. Though you probably can't do any of the welding yourself, you can usually cut out the old metal.

Many times, tiny holes will show up once the rust is removed from a panel. You'll want to work on both sides of the panel to make a good repair and prevent future rusting. New metal can be flowed in—either lead or metal from a welding rod. Once this new metal is in, properly ground and refinished, the repair won't show.

Most rust-through can be repaired and the condition that caused the problem corrected. This is most frequently evident at the bottom of panels and in seams. Be sure there is proper drainage to prevent a recurrence.

Hammering out dents in fenders and panels can restore the part to its original contour. Careful filing and sanding will give the smooth surface necessary for refinishing. Care must be taken not to stretch the metal out of shape when pounding it out. Bent body parts, especially small ones, can often be straightened in a vise. Most of the body and fender repairs can be done by the beginner–restorer, with only the welding jobs requiring professional help.

Plated Parts. These include the body hardware as well as accessories and radiator shell, headlights, bumpers, etc. Many times these will clean up surprisingly well when a strong detergent–water solution is used with a fine scouring pad. Be careful not to scratch a plated surface with a coarse scouring pad or sandpaper. Parts that won't clean to a satisfactory degree can

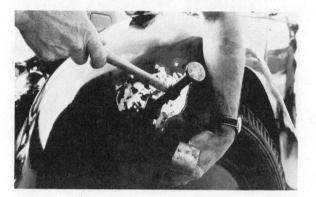

Use dolly and fender hammer to pound out dents. Always hold dolly behind metal you're pounding to avoid stretching metal. Filing and sanding will provide smooth base for primer coat.

always be plated. Early cars usually had brass plating; later on, nickel was used; still later, chrome replaced the nickel. Some cars used stainless steel or a polished aluminum: these can be rebuffed to the desired degree. The plating will usually cover the threaded areas too, though some platers will take care to see that this doesn't happen. You may have to rethread some parts before you can reassemble them.

Occasionally, on headlight rims and other thinly plated metal parts, you may find cracked and brittle metal. That won't render the part impossible to repair in most cases. A machine shop or plating works can solder these parts and flow in silver solder in cracks; when ground and buffed, they can be replated to your satisfaction.

Small plated washers, spacers, bolts and nuts can be easily cleaned by scouring and buffing, sometimes even filing lightly with a fine file. If necessary, these can be replated.

Radiator shells may be rusted on the top; in some cases the metal may be cracked. New pieces of metal can be welded on the inside under these spots and silver solder flowed into cracks and deeply pitted spots. When this is ground down and buffed, it can be satisfactorily replated.

On cars with cast grille inserts in the radiator shell, care must be taken in straightening any bent metal, as it is apt to break. Sometimes heat must be applied so the metal can be bent back into shape. Broken parts can be welded in place and replated if necessary. Radiators having a stamped grille insert are easier to repair, as the bent metal can be straightened. Often it's necessary to disassemble many of the grille parts to straighten them properly. They can then be replated or repainted as necessary.

Door handles and interior hardware were sometimes cast in pot metal,

Restorer has choice of finding replacement bumper or installing brace behind broken face bar and attaching center grille guard to retain bumper on this '35 Plymouth.

Bolts hold grille panels on this '39 Buick. Missing bar can be welded in, others straightened. Grille can then be replated to good as new condition.

which won't stand much bending or pressure. Handle these carefully and avoid too much force. Cars with the plating applied over bronze or brass have hardware that's easier to work on. In either case, the first procedure is a thorough cleaning to remove as much corrosion and dirt as possible; then take it from there.

Upholstery. Cloth upholstery can be refurbished with a careful and thorough cleaning. Whisk broom and vacuum cleaner first; any cleaning fluid or washing is used afterward. This won't remove worn spots and won't mend torn spots, but it will make the upholstery more presentable, and easier to work on. Any small tears can be repaired by sewing or patching, whichever will look better. Any panels with bulges or tears should be removed and repaired. Sometimes a few additional plated screws will hold a panel in the proper position. Any loose material should be stretched and secured back in place. Many times headliners only need to be pulled back into position over doors or windows. Quarter panels often need to be stretched over the backing form and reglued. The covering on seat cushions should be securely attached to the frame: tacked if the frame is wooden, clipped if the frame is metal.

Leather upholstery should be softened and cleaned: either saddle soap or a leather softener should be applied to make the leather supple and easy to work with. Once in this condition, tears can be stitched or patches sewn in underneath the tear. Any leather that has pulled loose should be firmly secured, either by tacking or with clips. Unprotected leather on the bottom part of doors can be covered with a scuff pad you make yourself. Often new panels cut to fit certain areas can be covered with leather or matching vinyl and installed, if reupholstery isn't practical.

Many cars with leather seat cushions had a substitute material used on other parts of the seats and door panels. If this material is cracked or torn it can be easily replaced. Sewing leather isn't too difficult. Small areas can be stitched by hand, using a curved shoemaker's needle. Longer seams can be run on a home sewing machine with a heavy needle. Vinyls can be easily cut and sewn, making repairs and refurbishment of this type upholstery possible.

Faded and worn leather can be redyed once the leather is properly cleaned and the surface repaired. There are leather "paints" on the market that will work satisfactorily. You can find spray finishes for headliners, cloth and coated fabric, allowing you to freshen up these components without replacement.

Carpets and rugs were usually made of quality material; unless worn through, they can be made to look good and give satisfactory service. The biggest contributor to wornout carpets was dirt that was left in the carpet and held in moisture, causing rot. The underpad should be replaced if it can't be patched or reversed. The carpet edging may have to be replaced and in many instances can be sewn on by hand. There is an iron-on binding that I've seen used satisfactorily.

Sometimes a single piece of carpet was used for the entire rear compartment. If only a few spots are worn badly, the carpet may be cut and bound, with new pieces cut to fit the areas worn through. In this instance, the original carpet might cover the driveshaft tunnel, with new pieces on each side. Also, new pieces of carpet or vinyl can be cut and placed over the worn spots. This will work for front carpets, where there usually was a leather or rubber inset for the driver's feet. Carpet on door bottoms and dash kickpads can be cleaned and made as presentable as possible. If these aren't satisfactory, new carpet pieces can be cut, bound and installed in their place.

Paint. You'll be surprised what a thorough cleaning can do for an old paint job. Of course, this won't put back nonexistent paint, nor will it fill scratches and chips. But many times it will show a finish that can be restored. It's worthwhile to keep the car's original finish as long as possible, provided it looks acceptable to you and protects the metal underneath.

After a thorough washing with a detergent solution to remove old grime, dirt and wax film, rinse the car thoroughly with clear water. Be sure joints and crevices are all cleaned out. If the finish looks just dull at this point, you can probably avoid repainting. Use a fine cleaning or rubbing compound: don't use a power polisher, as you're apt to rub right through the finish. Take one panel at a time, use the compound sparingly, and rub the finish to remove the film. When the panel is dry, use a clean soft cloth to remove the rubbing compound. The finish should appear bright and have a good luster. If there are rub marks or spots you missed, use the rubbing compound again. After it dries, remove the residue; you will find the old finish as good as it will come back. If this is satisfactory to you, go on to another panel. When you've completed the car panel by panel, decide if the appearance pleases you. If it does, then give the car a good wax job. If only certain panels aren't quite what you want, consider refinishing only these panels, leaving the others in their original condition. Remember, the paint may have faded over the years, so refinishing panels will take some paint matching first.

This has been a quick summary of refurbishing mechanical and body parts to help you determine what has to be done. The operations are covered in detail in chapters pertaining to individual parts. The important thing to remember is that a great majority of parts can be repaired and refurbished for satisfactory use. Only badly worn or damaged parts have to be replaced, often with a part from another car, not necessarily a new one.

CHAPTER 5

Suspension System

The requirements of suspension systems have changed greatly over the years. The development of the lower pressure balloon tire was probably the most instrumental factor in these changes. These tires came into widespread use in the mid-Twenties. They allowed cars to be driven at higher speeds and corner faster. The flexing action of the balloon tire took on part of the job that had previously been supplied only by the suspension system. As car speeds increased, new highways allowing higher speeds came into being. Suspension systems on old cars had to be rugged and simple. Only later did they become a complex assortment of springs, shock absorbers, levelers and antisway bars.

Suspension system is a term applied to include the springs and shock absorbers. On some makes there may be tie, or radius, rods to hold the axle in place. The purpose of the suspension system is to protect the car and passengers from bumps.

Springs

Spring restoration is a relatively simple job. You look for any broken leaves, worn or missing parts and worn bushings. A good cleaning will make all the parts clearly visible for inspection. There were five kinds of springs in common use, as well as combinations of these various kinds. The springs you'll be dealing with are either full elliptic, semielliptic, quarter elliptic, transverse or coil.

Broken main leaf on full elliptic spring can be replaced by removing holding spring clips before removing center bolt. Spring leaves can be reassembled, replacing only the broken leaf.

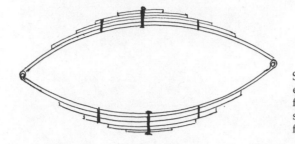

Sketch of full elliptic spring. Joined at each end of main leaves and attached to frame and axle at the middle. Shorter springs could be used when these are fitted.

Full Elliptic. These springs were a unit of two semielliptic springs attached to each other at the shackle end. With this type spring, the center of the upper spring was attached to the chassis. The center of the bottom spring was attached to the axle. Because there were two springs doing the work of one, each spring could be shorter. This gave more room between spring centers. It also gave a soft ride. The two springs were attached to each other by a pivot pin through the shackle end, as there was no need for a movable shackle.

Sketch of semielliptic spring. Center bolt is often off-center, depending upon car design. Eyes in each end of main leaf hold shackle bolts.

Semielliptic. These were the most popular springs, mounted parallel to the chassis–frame of the car, one at each corner. Each end of the main leaf was attached to the chassis. One attachment was stationary, while the other (the shackle end) was movable to allow the spring to compress. Varying numbers of shorter leaves were added, all being secured by a main bolt at the center. The leaves were held in alignment by spring clips. The center of the semielliptic spring was attached to the axle, either on top of it or underneath. The rear springs were longer than the front and usually had more leaves, because when the car was loaded with passengers, it had more weight to support. The rear spring of large sedans often had more leaves than coupes or roadsters of the same make. This was because of the heavier body weight and passenger capacity.

Quarter Elliptic. These were literally half of a semielliptic spring. The main leaf was attached to the chassis–frame at one end and the other to the axle by means of a spring shackle. Normally quarter elliptic springs were used on light cars. They were mounted parallel to the chassis in most instances; however, on some makes they were mounted at an angle to both the chassis and axle.

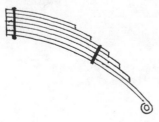

Sketch of quarter elliptic spring. Thick end attached to frame and to axle shackle by eye at end of main leaf. These were used in pairs on light cars or in conjunction with semielliptic springs on rear of heavier cars.

Rear transverse springs were attached to shackle, which was mounted on brake backing plates or to axle mounted hangers.

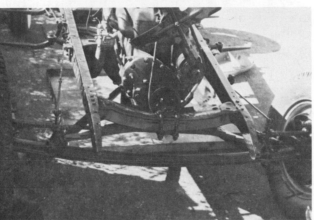

Front transverse springs were attached to shackles, in turn attached to spring hanger mounted on axle.

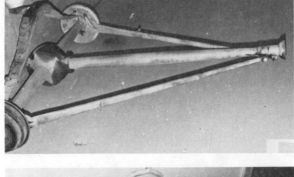

Rear radius rods attached to the tubular driveshaft just behind universal joint on Fords, Mercuries, Lincoln Zephyr and Lincoln Continental with transverse springs.

Front radius rods held axle in place, allowing transverse spring to handle only up–down axle movement.

Transverse Springs. These were semielliptic springs, but were mounted parallel to the axle. They were attached to a crossbar on the chassis front and rear, at the center point of the spring. The shackle ends of the spring were attached to the axle. On a few cars, the shackle ends of the spring were attached to the front wheel housing. Cars with transverse springs had to have braces to hold the axle at right angles to the chassis. These were tie rods or radius rods. Some ran parallel to the frame, others were set at an angle to the axle and frame, forming a triangle with the axle. These braces allowed the springs to absorb only the up-down motion of the axle and prevented front-to-back axle movement.

Coil Springs. Though occasionally used on older cars, coil springs became popular with independent suspension developed in the Thirties. The coiled steel spring was attached to the chassis at the top and to the axle at the bottom. Spring sockets kept the diameter of the spring constant, making the spring contract and expand on demand. Like transverse springs, these required a radius rod or brace to maintain the position of the axle.

Plenty of grime and dirt to scrape off all fittings before getting at the coil spring. Bottom of spring is attached to wishbone at top of frame-mounted holder.

Dual coil springs, on independently sprung rear axle of '33 Mercedes, are easily removed by loosening bottom brace. Web strap controls downward movement of axle. Shock absorber controls upward movement. New bendable pipe is used here to replace exhaust pipe.

If you placed the supporting stands under the chassis when positioning the car in your garage, the whole suspension will be easier to work on. It won't be supporting the car in any way and all joints will be hanging loose.

To detect worn spring shackles on cars with semielliptic or quarter elliptic springs, grasp the hub end of the axle. You should not be able to move it forward or backward. If the axle will move toward the front or back, something's wrong. It can be a rubber bushing or it can be worn bolts in either end of the spring. It might be in the bolt(s) attaching the spring to the axle. Once you're sure the attachment to the axle is secure, search out the source of play. By removing the bolts that go through the eye or loop at each end of the spring, you can see if they're worn. If they are, you should replace them.

Testing the System

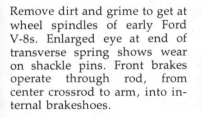

Rear spring hanger attaches to backing plate on rear wheel of '32 Ford. Knob above spring hanger holds the connecting rod of shock absorber.

Remove dirt and grime to get at wheel spindles of early Ford V-8s. Enlarged eye at end of transverse spring shows wear on shackle pins. Front brakes operate through rod, from center crossrod to arm, into internal brakeshoes.

Use the same test on cars with transverse or coil springs: if you get a front-to-back motion of the axle, check the rubber bushings on the radius rods or braces. Check the point where the radius rods or braces are attached to the frame of the car. With coil springs, see if the brackets or spring sockets holding the coils to the chassis and axle are tight. With transverse springs, check the shackle bolts for wear, as well as the center bolt in the spring and the attachment to the chassis.

On cars with full elliptic springs, you can expect an inch or two of front-to-back movement. The cars were designed for one side of the axle to compensate for movement of the other side. However, this movement should occur only after you've applied considerable pressure. Check the pivot pin connecting the two main leaves of the spring unit. You can easily spot wear on this pin. Also check the bolts attaching the spring to the axle, as well as the bolts attaching the spring to the frame. There shouldn't be any play in any of these bolts.

Unless you've discovered a broken spring leaf, center bolt, shackle bolt or pivot pin, worn or missing spring clips or rubber bushings, your job will be one of cleaning and lubricating.

REPLACING WORN PARTS

When replacing broken or worn suspension system parts remember that there will still be some compression to the spring, even though the car's weight is off it. Use a jack to lift the axle to the point where you remove this compression. Usually you'll find a castellated nut and cotter pin on shackle bolts. Remove the cotter pin and back off the nut. If you have to use force to remove a bolt or pivot pin, you need to raise or lower the jack to relieve the pressure. These parts should fit snugly, but shouldn't have to be forced. If you have to tap a part to start it moving, use a wooden block to protect the threads. A little graphite powder or light oil will help in removal and reassembly. When replacing a broken leaf, you don't have to remove the spring from the car. Remove any spring clips that hold the leaf. (These are the U-shaped brackets with a bolt across the open end; they hold the leaves parallel.) Remove the bolts holding the spring to the axle. Remove the center bolt in the spring assembly. This will allow you to pull or push out the broken leaf. You now insert the replacement leaf. With the spring in this position, it's a good idea to lubricate thoroughly between the leaves. Position the replacement leaf so the center hole lines up. A punch or screwdriver will help you do this. Do not *force* the center bolt into place: it will fit easily once the leaves are properly lined up. Tighten the nut to compress the spring and replace a cotter pin if one was used. While doing this, ensure that the leaves

Rear spring shackle of '28 LaSalle attaches to spring at top and frame at bottom. Leather boot covers leaves to hold in lubricant. Grease nipples on shackle allow for easy lubrication.

Forging for front spring-shackle combine to hold front bumper support on '32 Chrysler. Solid drop-forged axle lowers car's center of gravity. Front hydraulic shock absorber attached to spring platform on axle.

remain parallel by slipping the spring clips over the leaves, but don't try to insert the bolt in the clip until the spring has been compressed. Tighten the bolts holding the spring to the axle and replace cotter pins.

Replacing a leaf in a transverse spring is more difficult, since the center portion of the spring is attached to the cross member. To do this you must lift the chassis with a jack unless the car is already on jack stands and the axle is hanging free. Unless it's the main leaf that's broken, you don't have to remove the shackle ends of the springs from the spring hangers. You must carefully remove the center bolt and long U bolts holding the leaves in compression. It's better to remove the center bolt from the spring before you start on the long U bolts. Because of the compression in the spring, you'll find the leaves will spring apart when you remove the U bolts that have held it under compression. With the spring shackles still secured and the center bolt removed, the spring can only move upward when compression is released. The cross member to which it's attached is usually channeled, so the leaves aren't going to fly around. Do look for some pressure on the nuts as you back them toward the end of the threads.

With the leaves now freed, you can remove the broken leaf and replace it with a new one. Reassemble the leaves in proper order. Some restorers have used a much longer bolt to run through the hole in the center of the spring leaves. This is then tightened to the point where they can install the U bolts holding the leaves in compression. With these bolts tightened, remove the overlong bolt and replace it with the regular length bolt. Spring clips along the spring should be tightened when the leaves are properly compressed.

LUBRICATION

A good way to lubricate springs is to force them open. In some cases, you should remove the bolt through the bottom of the spring clips. You may want to loosen the center bolt, as well as the bolts holding the spring to the axle. Use a jack between the axle and the car frame. By extending the jack, you'll force the spring leaves open. This will allow you to either spray in light oil, or you can apply it with a paintbrush. The spring should be cleaned of road grime and dirt before opening the leaves. Once the spring is properly soaked, you can tighten the center bolt and the bolts holding the spring to the axle. Tighten the spring clips last. There may be grease fittings on the shackles: if so, be sure to force enough grease into the fitting so that the old grease appears at the edges.

Bushing on pivot pins (steering knuckles) must be driven out for replacement. Steering arm has adjustment on end to take up for some wear.

WORN BUSHINGS

There are two types of bushings in the suspension system. Rubber bushings are easier to replace. These are normally in joints and act to take up play and keep out dirt. There may be metal bushings in the spring eyes, shackles and spring hangers. After removing the bolt or pin that goes through these openings, you can tell by looking or feeling if a bushing is worn. Locate a replacement bushing, if possible, before removing the present one. If you can't locate a replacement, then remove the old bushing and take it to an automotive repair or machine shop. They may be able to match it with a similar sized bushing from another make of car or a machine. Bushings are normally pressed into place. Occasionally the outer measurements will be greater on one end than the other, indicating the direction from which they were pressed in place. They can be removed by pressing from the smaller end. Usually you can force the old one out and the new one into place by tapping or using a large, fine-threaded clamp. Use a piece of wood between the bushing and the hammer or clamp. Be sure to lubricate the bushing before inserting the bolt or pin that fits in it.

You can normally buy replacement rubber bushings. If not, buy a piece of solid rubber the thickness of the bushing, trace a pattern and use a razor blade to cut it out.

A new silicone compound, contained in a tube with a needlelike nozzle, makes rebuilding rubber bushings easy. You simply insert the nozzle into the worn rubber bushing and squeeze the silicone compound into the bushing. This compound fills the area and quickly solidifies. It makes a new bushing on the spot. It's tough, resilient and wholly satisfactory. It can only be used to replace worn rubber bushings, however, not metal bushings. The product was designed for replacing worn rubber bushings in steering systems, but works fine wherever rubber bushings are used.

SHOCK ABSORBERS

There are three types of shock absorbers and several varieties of each type. One was designed to control only the rebound motion of the spring—

it did nothing on the compression or upward push. It only helped control the speed at which the spring returned to its normal load position.

A second, compression type actually aided the spring as it took road shocks. In effect, it acted as an auxiliary spring on the upward motion only.

Sometimes called a "stabalator," friction-type shock absorber was connected to axle by strap. These controlled only the downward, or rebound, motion of axle. Replacement webbing is easily obtained and installed.

Different kind of friction-type shock absorber, as on '29 La Gonda helps control axle motion both up and down. Tighten nut to increase pressure on spring arms to give stiffer ride.

Hydraulic shock absorbers on '32 Buick controlled upward motion only. Fill these by opening plug at top. Disconnect rod from axle, then work it up and down to free shock of air.

It was attached by an arm or plunger to the axle, with the shock absorber housing on the frame of the car.

A third was the double-acting type. This helped the spring absorb the compression and it acted to control the spring's return motion too.

Double acting hydraulic shock absorber on '36 Buick controls both up and down motion of axle. Two bolts hold the case to chassis.

Remove holding bolts to take shock absorber off frame. Hydraulic shocks are easily rebuilt. Remove arm from shaft.

The shock absorber that only controlled the return action of the spring was usually contained in a round case attached to the car's frame. Like all shock absorbers, there was one per wheel and placement was on the outside of the frame. Later, as frames became wider, the rear shock absorber was often placed inside the frame. To allow front wheel turning space, frames remained narrower at the front than at the rear. With the rebound-type shock absorber, a center bolt held the cover on the case. Inside the case a heavy web strap was wound around a spring loaded axle. One end of this webbing was attached to the axle. The spring mechanism in the case, working through the webbing, kept the axle from dropping back into position too quickly, causing a rebound action. This type shock absorber is easily inspected and repaired. An excellent replacement for the webbing which often rotted or broke is the woven belting used in Army and Navy uniforms. It can be bought at surplus stores and costs very little. Be sure to clean the spring mechanism and coat the moving parts lightly with oil or graphite. Clean the outer housing with a wire brush and spray with a rust-inhibiting primer. Later paint it the color of the running gear on your car.

The shock absorber that acted only on the upward motion of the axle was either a hydraulic type, or a coil spring inside a round housing. The rod or plunger was attached directly to the axle, or to an arm connected to a rod to the axle. On the hydraulic type, the rod or plunger pushed hydraulic fluid through a small hole into a chamber. This action tended to slow the upward movement of the axle. In the spring loaded type, the rod pushed against a coil spring and this action slowed the movement of the axle. You may need to replace the rubber or felt packing on the hydraulic plunger. You can easily make replacement packing if you can't buy ready-cut ones. The hole through which the fluid is forced, as well as the return hole, must be cleaned. New hydraulic fluid can be put in through a threaded plug near the top. Be sure the hole admitting air is cleaned, too. While checking shock absorbers, be sure that brackets attaching them to the frame are tight. Also check the connection to the axle.

The double-acting type, usually hydraulic, used the plunger to force fluid one way on compression, then the other way when the axle moved back to its normal position. These double-acting types were sometimes supplied with fluid from a central reservoir. The movement of the rear shock absorbers could be controlled by the driver for a soft or hard ride.

First check the fluid level at the shock absorber and at the central reservoir if there is one. A threaded plug can be removed for fluid level inspection. Before unscrewing any inspection plugs, be sure all dirt around the plug is removed. Any dirt that might fall into the opening can cause trouble. Check the packing or washer on the plunger: these should not let fluid bypass them. New washers or packings are easy to obtain and install. While you have the mechanism apart, check the small orifice through which the fluid is forced to make sure it's not clogged. Check the air outlet and bypass orifice, too. When filling a hydraulic shock absorber, work the plunger a few times to be sure all air is removed. Replace the filler plug tightly.

Double-acting types are complicated, as there are two compartments for hydraulic fluid. As the plunger moves one way, it forces fluid from one compartment to the other. As it returns, it forces the previously moved fluid back into the original container. Washers or packings on the plungers, as well as both orifices, must be checked before refilling. Air must be worked out of each compartment before replacing filler plugs.

Shock absorbers that are controlled by the driver are the double-acting type: a lever controls the length of the stroke the plunger can take. The longer the stroke, the softer the ride. The control works on the back wheels only. Aside from being sure the control operates freely and is firmly attached, it requires no attention.

On cars with a centralized reservoir for the fluid, small-diameter tubes connected each shock absorber to the central tank. You fill this type by filling the reservoir and "bleeding" (letting out any trapped air) each individual absorber. To force air out of the tubes, fill the reservoir and open the threaded plug on one shock absorber. Disconnect the plunger on that absorber. Work the plunger up and down until fluid runs out the plug hole. After this operation, reconnect the plunger, tighten the filler plug and do the same for each shock absorber. You may need to refill the reservoir during this operation if the lines were previously dry. Buy shock absorber fluid at any auto supply store. This "bleeding" job is tedious, but easy. When completed, you'll like the better ride you'll get with properly operating shock absorbers.

Wheels

You must have made a preliminary check when you were considering the purchase. Obviously you want all wheels alike. It wasn't uncommon as cars became old and changed hands many times for someone to switch wheels. Any wheel that is badly rusted, or on which the wood is rotted or broken, should be replaced. Wheels that are bent will probably have to be replaced, too.

There are four basic types of wheels: artillery (wood), wire, disc and pressed steel. Some makes offered a choice of wheel styles, making more than one kind correct for some autos.

If your car has wooden spoke wheels, make sure the spokes are sound. Check that portion of the spoke that extends through the metal rim: it should be solid and without splits or chips. The spoke should extend through the metal rim about a half inch. Be sure that the wood is sound where it's bolted to the metal hub and that rust on the hub isn't more than superficial. Most damage to wooden spoke wheels was caused by the weight of the car settling for some time on the rims or tires that rotted out, allowing the rims to touch the ground. You may find wood rot, a badly rusted-out rim or spokes that split or rotted. If you have a good wheel, a cabinet maker can make replacement spokes. If necessary, you can frequently locate replacements.

Wooden wheels had separate rims on which the tires were mounted. These rims were held to the wheel by a series of bolts, usually carriage type: one with a round head but squared shank that fit into a square opening in the back of the rim. A bolt on the threaded end held a specially shaped lug that fit the contours of the rim. When this was tightened, it held the rim securely on the wheel. Cars that had artillery wheels usually carried only a tire mounted on a rim as a spare.

Artillery wooden wheels used spokes that extend through the steel rim. Bolts through hub plate held wheel solid. A separate split rim bolts to the wheel.

Rims for artillery wheels were "split" and had to be made smaller or unlocked before a tire could be put on or removed. There was a three-pronged tool made for this job: each prong was threaded and these were attached to the rim after it had been removed from the wheel. A handle on the device expanded or contracted the prongs, opening or closing the rim. These handy tools are still available through some mail order houses; they beat the factory's suggested method of prying the rim with a chisel and pounding it back with a hammer. There may be a rim spreader with your car, as many owners acquired one. If not, save your knuckles and temper by getting one. They don't cost much.

There are two varieties of wire wheels and two ways in which wire

Welded steel spokes on Willys Knight wire wheel made strong, lightweight wheel. Wire spokes were fitted individually on some older, as well as some foreign, cars.

wheels are mounted. One type is a center lock, still used on some European sports cars. The axle hub is tapered and splined; the wheel hub is similarly tapered and splined. A threaded hub cap forces the wheel onto the axle hub and holds it in place. These wheels often have individually threaded spokes and require careful alignment, produced by tightening or loosening spokes to make the wheel turn evenly.

Threaded knock-off hub holds wheel on splined shaft, as on this Mark IV Jaguar and other foreign cars.

The more common type of wire wheel had welded spokes and the wheel was bolted onto the hub. In some cases the bolts holding the wheel to the hub were concealed by the hub cap; in other cars these bolts were visible and the hub cap smaller. Since the spokes are welded in place instead of threaded, individual spokes cannot be tightened. A bent spoke can usually be straightened by pounding from the opposite side. Broken spokes can be straightened and welded. Missing spokes can be made by securing a steel rod, the same diameter as the spoke, cutting to proper length and welding in place.

Each type of wire wheel had a snap-on rim like the artillery wheel or was the drop center type in which the rim and wheel were made as a single unit. The drop center wheel became most popular because it was lighter, cheaper to build and easier to mount tires on. The bead of the tire was held against the rim by air pressure.

Disc wheels were popular for a time and were used by many manufacturers as standard equipment or as an option. They were round pieces of steel with a hub in the center and a rim at the outer circumference. Disc wheels were not as flexible as the artillery or wire wheel and sometimes warped. At first, these wheels had a separate rim—the snap-on type—similar to one type of wire wheel. This ring fitted around the outside part of the wheel, locking the rim and tire in place. A few disc wheels in later years were made with drop center rims. Disc wheels were heavy and some drivers complained that they reacted to crosswinds. Cars with disc wheels usually carried only a tire mounted on a rim as a spare.

Disc wheels were popular in the Twenties. Detachable split rim held tire and was bolted to wheel, as on this '25 Essex.

Pressed steel wheel gave look of spoked wheel and provided strength, was lightweight and inexpensive, as on this '35 Plymouth.

Pressed steel wheels were developed in an effort to give the appearance of a spoke wheel, yet have the durability and strength of steel. There were different designs: some looked much like a chrome plated artillery wheel; others had a wavy or fluted design. They were of the drop rim type and were bolted onto the hub. These were less expensive to manufacture and were the forerunners of the wheels used on contemporary cars.

Hub Caps. Originally the hub cap was designed to protect the axle end. These were threaded and screwed on to protect and hide the nut holding the wheel bearing to the axle. They were often packed with axle grease to provide lubrication for the wheel bearing. They were usually marked with the insignia of the car or some identifying design. Later, as cars adopted the bolt-on type wheel, hub caps became larger to hide the wheel lugs. These became highly decorative. Later on, hub caps were largely replaced with wheel discs. Wheel discs allow a lower cost wheel and the choice of wheel discs became an optional extra.

On an old car where the hub cap literally protected the nut and bearing, you can have a split one welded and rethreaded at a machine shop if you can't locate a replacement. Hub caps that won't clean and polish to suit you can be replated. Damage to hub caps came mostly from scraping against curbs, etc. A dent can frequently be hammered out and will clean up satisfactorily. Replacement caps aren't difficult to locate and usually won't cost you much.

In reworking the wheels, you must make sure they're solid and safe. You may be driving your car at higher speeds than those for which it was originally designed. This can put extra strain on wheels when cornering and braking. You want them to be dependable and safe. Rusty spots should be confined to the surface; if rust has eaten into the metal, the wheels must have new metal welded in or the wheels must be replaced. The spokes on wooden wheels must be solid and free of splits or rot. Wheels must be "true," meaning they shouldn't be crooked as they turn. The rims shouldn't have any dents that can cause damage to a tire or allow it to come off.

To restore wooden spoke wheel, scrape and fill spokes. Sand rim and hub plate. Avoid using liquid paint remover.

Refinishing wheels is an easy job, but takes a little time. If you plan to refinish wooden spoke wheels, you have the most time consuming job. They were often black or car color. Varnished natural wood wheels cost extra and are an asset to your car's value. If the present wood wheels are not natural wood varnished finish, you can make them so. Finishing a wood wheel is like any other wood refinishing. You scrape and sand the old finish off. A liquid paint remover isn't recommended for this type job, as you're apt not to get the remover out of the crevices. When the old finish is completely removed, sand the spokes, hub and rim smooth. Since the hub and rim will be painted, you can either mask off the spokes and paint them now, or do that job later. The spokes may take a coat or two of shellac, with a light sanding between coats. Apply stain only if you want other than a natural wood finish. Finally, apply enough coats of varnish to build the hard finish you want. You should sand lightly between coats of varnish.

You don't have to remove all the old finish if you're going to paint wood wheels. However, you do need a smooth surface to cover, so a thorough sanding is necessary. Use a filler on any small checks or cracks in the spokes. Either use a coat of shellac or primer to build up the surface for your final coatings. Sand lightly between coats. It's not a bad idea to give wood wheels a final coat of clear varnish after painting them, as this added protection is worthwhile.

Refinished wooden spoke wheel required plenty of scraping, filling and base coats before final enamel color coat. It's good to give coat of clear finish to preserve wheel.

Many wooden spoke wheels had a stripe on each spoke, as well as on the center hub and wheel rim. If you want to apply a stripe it's easy, and does dress up the appearance. Use thick paint and a brush that's made for striping. Apply the stripe on the spoke first. Stripes on the wheel hub and rim are best made by mounting the wheel on the car and turning the wheel while holding the brush steady against it. When doing this, have a cloth saturated with turpentine or thinner handy in case you flub. A coat of clear varnish to protect the striping is recommended.

Disc or wire wheels were often painted contrasting colors to give a sporty appearance to the car. Discs usually had some striping near the hub or rim, or both. The quality of the paint job you'll get depends largely on the care you take in preparing the wheels for painting.

The old paint doesn't have to be removed unless you think that's necessary to get a smooth surface. You can either sand the old finish or use a liquid paint remover. If you use a liquid remover, be sure all traces of it are completely rinsed off before applying a primer or base coat. Some restorers take wire wheels to a place that does sand blasting; for a couple of bucks per wheel, you can get it cleaned down to the bare metal. Companies that letter gravestones often will do this sand blasting for you. Once the wheels are sand blasted, be sure to clean out any particles of sand remaining in crevices and give them a prime coat before the surface has a chance to start rusting.

It's wise to build up at least two coats of primer paint on a wire or disc wheel before applying your finishing coats. Be sure to sand lightly between coats, as you want a smooth finish.

If your wheels are the drop-center type, be sure the inside of the rim is free of rust and scale. Since these wheels held tires that used an inner tube, you must have a smooth inner surface to prevent chafing. Usually a rubber or fabric inner flap was used to protect the tube. Some wheels had a rubber ring in the innermost depth of the rim to protect spoke ends from chafing the tube.

Any decorative stripe should be applied after the last paint has dried thoroughly. Use a thicker paint that is made for striping and a striping brush. Since the stripe will follow the circumference of the wheel, it's easier to apply if the wheel is mounted and spun. Hold the brush at the place you want the stripe and increase pressure on the brush only if you feel it's running low on paint. Some restorers have found it easier to concoct a simple wooden holder for the brush, rather than trust a shaky hand.

Separate wheel rims were almost always black or natural aluminum color. They were very seldom painted car color, but there's no reason why you can't paint them any color you like. They will require a thorough sanding and there may be a few dents to straighten out on the edges. Give enough primer coats, lightly sanding between coats to provide a smooth base for painting.

You should treat the spare wheel or rim the same as the road wheels. Spares were either side mounted in a well in one or both front fenders, or mounted in the rear. Usually one spare was standard; a second spare was an optional extra. Side mounts were an option at additional expense.

If the car carried only a rim and tire for spare purposes, these were usually at the rear. The holder was a triangular or Y-shaped brace, attached by a bracket to the chassis. A few cars held the spare in shallow tire-shaped holders with a strap over the holder.

Cars that carried fender-mounted wheels and tires had a simple hub on a brace that attached to the frame; the wheel was bolted to this hub. Some carried a clamp that fitted over the top of the wheel and tire, mounted on a post that was attached to the frame or cowl. A threaded decorative nut held the clamp tight. These were normally plated, but can be painted if desired.

It's a good idea to refinish the spare holders and brackets when you do

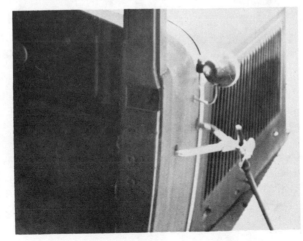

Side-mounted spares were firmly mounted, with a brace from side of cowl through fender to frame. Additional brace was usually fitted to bottom of fender well, as on this '30 Pontiac.

the wheels. If you're going to repaint the fenders or entire car, however, you may want to include these parts at the same time.

Remember to paint the rims before mounting tires. Enamel is best, as it's more durable and doesn't chip as easily as lacquer. Paint the inside of the rim with at least one coat of primer paint. When mounting tires, a little soapy water on the outer bead will help ease the tire on the rim or wheel and protect your new paint.

BALANCING

It is more difficult to balance the wheels on old cars than on later models. To begin with, balancing wasn't as crucial for yesteryear's slower speeds. It's a good idea, though, to balance the wheels as accurately as possible to give better road handling and longer tire life.

Some wire and disc wheels had three or four short studs up through the rim. These were about two inches long, equally spaced around the wheel; lead washers were added for balance. The washers were held in place by a nut on the top or a cap that fitted over them, with a nut holding the cap in place. Additional lead washers can be easily procured.

To balance wheel on older cars with balancing weights, remove weight cover, spin wheel and make chalk mark on spot that ends on the bottom. Repeat several times. If same spot ends on bottom, either remove weights from the down side or add weights to the opposite side.

To balance this kind, you mount the tire and wheel on the car, then jack that wheel off the ground and spin it. With a piece of chalk, mark the spot that stops at the bottom. Do this several times. If it stops repeatedly with the marked spot down, remove one of the washers on the *down* side and spin it again. Do this until the wheel doesn't stop in the same spot each time. You may find that you need to compensate for the *down* side by adding one or more washers to the stud opposite the *down* side. Admittedly, this is a trial and error method, but it's the way it was done. It works surprisingly well if you have patience.

Some drop-center wire wheels can be balanced by adding clip-on weights to the rim; these can be found at almost any tire store. This is easy, inexpensive and well worth your time.

Wooden spoke wheels are balanced in the rim: these are held in place by bolts that go through the tire rim and rim of the wheel. With the tire in place and the wheel jacked up, spin the wheel. Mark the spot that stops at the bottom. Do this several times. If the mark continues to stop *down*, that's the heaviest spot. Usually there's enough length to the rim holding bolt to add a washer or two for balance. While spinning the wheel, also check rim alignment: you can do this by holding a piece of chalk against the rim of the wheel while it's spinning. The chalk should mark a steady line all the way around the circumference. If portions of the line are missing, it shows that the rim is not true on the wheel. This could be due to a tire that's improperly mounted or a rim that's not tightened evenly to the wheel rim. This becomes a trial and error method as you balance the rim and tire.

Disc wheels with detachable rims are balanced the same way as wooden wheels, if they weren't equipped with weight studs on the inside of the wheel. On disc wheels equipped with weight studs, spin the wheel a few times, marking the spot that stops on the bottom. If the mark continues to stop down, either remove weights on the down side or add weights to the opposite side. Do this until the wheel doesn't stop repeatedly at the same mark.

Some of the more expensive cars had a built-in lubricating system. This system of tubes leading from a central reservoir allowed the driver to give a shot of oil to many of the joints and moving parts. These were operated ei-

Lubrication System

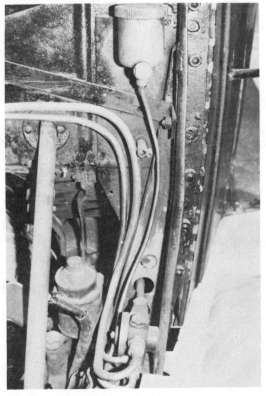

Oiling system used on more expensive cars. Reservoir on firewall holds oil and plunger shoots a measured amount to various joints through small tubes.

ther by a plunger knob on the dash or a foot pedal. An oil reservoir was mounted on the firewall and could be easily refilled when necessary. From this reservoir, a system of tubes ran to the various joints. By operating a plunger, a measured amount of oil could be sent into the system to lubricate parts.

About the only thing that could go wrong with these systems was a broken oil line or a loose fitting. Occasionally the plunger mechanism would need tightening and the washer on the plunger replaced. A clogged tube could be easily cleaned out by running a soft wire through it.

To check such a system on your car, trace out the tubes so you know where they go. Perhaps you have a manual that shows this; if not, just follow each tube to its end. Disconnect the end of each tube and fill the reservoir with oil—or oil diluted with kerosene—to clean out the lines. Put a piece of newspaper under each disconnected line. Push the plunger to see if oil is expelled from each tube. Sometimes a second push on the plunger will be necessary. If any tube doesn't spout some oil, trace the length of this tube to see if it is bent or broken. If not, then disconnect the offending tube and clean it out with a wire. Occasionally a tube gets clogged, more often bent or flattened by a stone the tires turn up; it could have been chaffed as it went through the frame, if the protecting rubber bushing was worn or lost. These were simple and dependable systems that contributed greatly to the longevity of the car. You may find that the system only included the front suspension system or just the spring shackles. Most, however, carried oil to any parts the manufacturer felt needed careful and thorough lubrication.

Depending upon the manufacturer you'll find some systems used grease rather than oil. Some companies made their own systems, others bought them from suppliers. The greasing system worked on the same principle as the oiling system just described. A container, either on the firewall or on the frame under a floorboard, held grease. From this container or central reservoir, tubes ran to the fittings that were to be greased. A plunger sent grease along these tubes to the fittings. Usually one push on the plunger did it: you could tell by seeing the new grease appear in the crevices of the fittings, and the old grease, often a different color because of dirt, push out or fall to the driveway.

You can test this the same way as the oil system. Disconnect the fittings, and with newspapers in place to catch the droppings, push the plunger a time or two. Because of the consistency of grease, it sometimes congealed in the tubes, especially during winter, if left unused. So you may want to clean out the system with a solution of light oil and kerosene. After it is flushed out (with the tubes disconnected, as you don't want kerosene in the joints), drain the tubes and reconnect. Fill the container with new grease and pump till the lines are full and new grease appears in the fittings. If you find a fitting that isn't getting grease, examine its tube to see if it is bent or pinched or broken. You may need to remove a tube like this and get a replacement if you can't straighten it yourself. Also, look at the washer or packing on the plunger in the reservoir. This should not let grease bypass it when pushed. The plunger linkage was quite simple and direct, so if it works the plunger arm as it should, there's nothing to do. A spring pulls the plunger back into position after use.

If you've discovered a broken, crimped or bent tube that will need replacement, a machine shop can usually furnish tubing in the correct diameter and will attach a fitting to the ends. In some cases these were threaded, in others soldered, and a hollow bolt went through into the area to be lubricated. When installing a new tube, be sure it is protected from chaffing against the frame. Clips similar to those holding hydraulic brake lines held the tubes secure and rubber bushings protected them through holes.

If your car came equipped with either an oiling or greasing system, you'll want to be sure it's operating properly, as the components receiving this lubrication couldn't be lubricated any other way. Be sure to check the last fitting or nipple on each tube to be sure the opening isn't blocked, and nothing keeps the oil or grease from reaching its goal. The reservoir should be checked periodically to be sure it has enough lubricant to operate properly.

CHAPTER 6

Top Engine Repairs

The thought of rebuilding an engine often makes the beginner–restorer unnecessarily uptight. It's not as tough a job as it sounds. I've done them all and so can you. But it does take care and thought, as it's nothing you can buzz through in a hurry. There are some frustrations that may crop up as you work on the motor—when they do, go ahead and cuss. You'll feel better!

Engine Operation

Just in case you've never given it any thought or aren't sure how the engine works, here's a simple blow-by-blow explanation. It's basically simple, so don't be in awe of an engine, no matter how big it is. Refer to a physics book if you feel you want or need more technical information.

If gasoline and air are mixed, the combination is highly combustible. When the mixture is compressed and exploded in a controlled container, it produces a power impulse. If the power impulse is controlled and directed, it can cause a revolving movement. As the revolving movement is controlled and directed, it can cause the vehicle in which the container is installed to move.

These basic principles were known for many years. Finally someone put it all together to produce an engine. The engine was fitted into a buggy and the automobile came into being.

Most gasoline engines in cars built since 1900 are four-cycle engines. This means there are four recurring successions of events in the engine's operation.

The container in which the air–gas mixture explodes is called the cylinder. A piston within the cylinder compresses the mixture and is forced downward as the mixture explodes. The downward movement of the piston—which is attached to a crankshaft—causes the crankshaft to rotate. The rotation of the crank on its shaft turns a heavy flywheel; the momentum of the flywheel keeps the crankshaft turning. The turning shaft drives the piston up in the cylinder again. The piston makes four trips in the cylinder to complete its operation.

On the first stroke or cycle, the piston moves down in the cylinder to

74

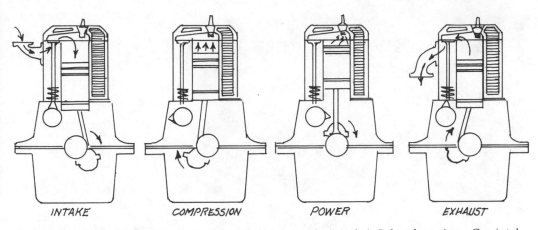

INTAKE   COMPRESSION   POWER   EXHAUST

Simple sketches show operation of typical four cycle (stroke) L-head engine. On *intake* stroke, piston goes down in cylinder and draws in air–gas mixture. Intake valve is open, exhaust valve closed. On *compression* stroke, piston comes up in cylinder, compressing the air–gas mixture. Both valves are closed. On *power* stroke, sparkplug fires, igniting mixture and sending piston down in cylinder. Both valves are closed. On *exhaust* stroke, piston moves up in cylinder, forcing out burned mixture. Exhaust valve is open, intake valve is closed. Gear at end of crankshaft meshes with gear on camshaft to operate valves at proper time.

draw in the air–gas mixture: this is the *intake* stroke. The second stroke is back upward, to compress the mixture: this is the *compression* stroke. As the piston reaches the top of the second stroke, the sparkplug ignites the mixture. This explosion forces the piston down on its third stroke: this is the *power* stroke. The fourth stroke or cycle is back up the cylinder to force out the burned air–gas mixture: this is the *exhaust* stroke.

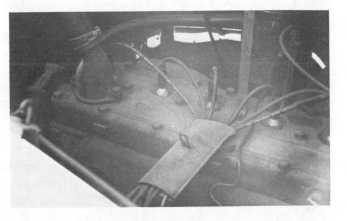

Simplicity of GM's six-cylinder L-head motors of the Thirties make adjustment and repairs easy for the beginner–restorer, as on this '38 Pontiac. Downdraft carburetor has cable-controlled choke. Fan belt drives water pump at front of block. Thermostat is in casting for radiator hose. Sheath protects wires from distributor to plugs.

All other parts of the motor are designed and attached to aid in these four cycles. The carburetor mixes the air and gasoline, and controls the amount admitted into the cylinder. A gear on the crankshaft operates the camshaft, which opens and closes the valves. The intake valve lets the air–gas mixture into the cylinder. Both valves stay closed during the compression and power cycles. The exhaust valve opens on the exhaust stroke. The distributor, operating off the camshaft, times the electric current to the sparkplug to ignite the mixture.

To increase the power impulses, giving more power to the motor, cylin-

Small gear is on end of crankshaft and drives large "timing" gear on camshaft to operate valves. Water pump has been removed, showing water passages around cylinder.

ders were added. These additional cylinders caused some complexities in the design and operation of the engine's supporting parts. They all perform their interrelated functions and the interrelation is easy to understand and follow.

Checking Engine Components

Generally you can tell if an engine needs rebuilding by the way it runs. Hard starting, lack of power, uneven running, etc., all indicate that attention is needed. Heavy blue exhaust also indicates engine wear. Any knocking or grinding noise when the engine is running can indicate mechanical problems. But hang loose on repairs: don't do anything until you know what's necessary, then do only what's necessary.

In order to repair or rebuild the engine, you must know what's in need of repair. From your work on the chassis you should have a good idea of the real mechanical condition of the car. Use your best judgment in diagnosing the real condition of the motor. Careful thought here can save you some hairy moments later on. Remember, it's far less expensive to buy oil for a car that's only used occasionally than it is to pay for a ring job. But if lack of compression indicates a ring job is necessary, then don't put it off.

You'll want all available information on your particular motor. If your clean and search operation turned up any factory material, study it carefully. Refer to any information you were able to get from the manufacturer, car clubs, or owners of similar cars. Get all the information possible and digest it thoroughly before tearing into the motor. You'll be glad you did!

Engine repairs are commonly divided into two classifications.

Top engine repairs. These include the parts of the cooling system attached to the motor, the electrical system, carburetor and fuel system, valves, and carbon removal.

Bottom engine repairs. These sound more gruesome, but they're really not. They're more exacting and require more care. Repairs include main bearings, rod bearings, piston or wrist pins and piston rings. In short, any job which requires removal of the engine pan to perform.

I will cover repairs for the top of the engine in this chapter. Repairs and adjustments to cooling, electrical and fuel systems are covered in Chapters 10, 12 and 13, respectively. Bottom engine repairs are covered in Chapter 7. There are differences in motor construction which may require some variance from the procedures described. However, they are basically the same: the directions will generally apply, so don't come unglued if you find a few bolts or clips I haven't mentioned.

REMOVING CARBON

Cleaning the carbon out is one of the most common jobs on an old motor. It's relatively easy, but will require a bit of muscle. Before you start, however, be sure you have the necessary replacement gaskets. You cannot reuse the present gasket. If your motor is constructed with the intake and exhaust valves in the cylinder head, you may have to get a set of manifold gaskets, too. The normal L-head motor has the valves in the motor block and you won't need other than the cylinder head gasket.

This '41 Chevrolet used six-cylinder valve in-head engine. Be sure to provide lateral support when resting engine on the pan so it won't tip.

Start by cleaning off the cylinder head, paying attention to the bolts that hold it in place. Usually, the nut will be on the top with a washer under each nut. These must be clean and free of grease so your wrenches will fit snugly. You must remove anything that is bolted to the cylinder head. This can mean a horn bracket, a bracket for the coil or harness guides for the wiring system. Disconnect the wires from the sparkplug (not from the distributor) and *tag the wires*. Remove each sparkplug and inspect the inside of the plug as you take it out. It should contain a slight amount of evenly burned carbon. If the plug is filled with a gummy looking substance, that's an indication that the cylinder is pumping oil or that the plug has been improperly gapped and isn't firing.

Sparkplug at left is oil fouled and has gummy deposit on electrode. Plug at right has carbon buildup that also prevents proper firing. Sparkplugs are inexpensive and usually need replacement on old cars.

Disconnect and remove the radiator hose after draining the radiator. You'll probably want to replace the radiator hose, as old ones often crack and leak. They're inexpensive and easy to replace.

Once the hose has been disconnected and the plugs removed, you're ready to start cylinder head removal. With a carefully fitted socket wrench, start to break loose the nuts on the cylinder head. This will require pressure for the initial quarter turn. Start at one corner and take one quarter turn only. Do not take any one nut off at this time. The second nut you loosen should be diagonally opposite the first. For example, if the first nut loosened was the left rear, the second nut should be the right front. What you must do is break loose every nut in such a pattern that you'll be *evenly removing the pressure on the cylinder head.* You could cause it to crack otherwise. Once you've given each nut a quarter turn, repeat the process—giving each nut a half turn. By this time the pressure should be relieved so you can start the third round, removing each nut and washer as you go. Don't worry if one or two of these are very difficult to turn and you find the stud turning out with the nut. Occasionally this will happen: you can loosen the nut from the stud in your vise, but be sure to put a piece of cloth into the threaded hole. This will prevent it from becoming filled with carbon as you work on carbon removal.

Remove head bolts by giving quarter turn to left front, then to right rear, working opposite nuts in order. After a quarter turn each, give each a half turn in same order. After one turn each, remove nuts in any order you want.

When all the nuts are off, try lifting the cylinder head. It's probably not going to budge. One way to get it loose is to replace the sparkplugs (do not connect the wires) and turn the motor over a few times. Compression should break loose the sticking head. Another way is to work your putty knife around the edge of the gasket between the head and the gasket. Other restorers have bought two long bolts with the same thread as the sparkplug at a hardware store. With these bolts screwed into the plug holes, they act as handles to lift off the head. *The cylinder head must be kept level* as it's lifted straight up. Any binding will be caused by the head scraping against the threads on the studs. Handle the head very carefully, being sure not to drop it. Once removed, place it on your workbench.

Next remove the cylinder head gasket. You may have to ruin this completely to get it off, but you're not going to use it again, so do any necessary prying against the gasket—not the block. Take care not to gouge the block in this operation.

It's best to clean the carbon deposits from the cylinder head on your workbench or any flat surface. Use a wire-bristled brush for most of this. Be

With cylinder head removed, scrape carbon off with putty knife and wire brush: be careful not to gouge metal. If water passages are badly blocked, have head "boiled" at radiator shop.

careful not to gouge any part of the head if you have to work on stubborn deposits with a putty knife. While you're at it, clean out the water passages: these are the rusty looking holes around the head. Since these allow the coolant to circulate, it's important they be clear of scale and obstructions.

If there appears to be an excessive amount of scale, or if any of the passages are completely blocked, you should take the head to a radiator shop and have it "boiled out." This costs very little and will allow the engine to run cooler. However, if water passages in the head are clogged, chances are the passages in the block are clogged too. Work loose what scale you can, but plan to have the block flushed out after you've completed the carbon removal job and have the car back in operation. A properly circulating cooling system is important to the efficient operation of the engine.

With the head removed and the gasket out, you're looking at the top of the pistons and valves. Depending upon firing order and number of cylinders, only one or two pistons will be level with the top of the block simultaneously. Also, some valves will be lifted above the block and others flat against it.

Cylinder head on valve-in-head engine is heavy, so handle it carefully. To remove carbon deposits, scrape with putty knife and use wire brush. Be sure water passages are free.

Use your putty knife to scrape off the black deposits that will be on the piston tops and valves. Scrape flatly so as not to gouge anything. Also scrape off the block in such a manner that the carbon doesn't drop into another cylinder, valve opening or water passage. Clean each piston and valve top and the small areas in between. You'll have to turn the motor from time to time, either with the starter or a crank, to rotate the cylinders.

This is the time to assess wear on the cylinder walls to determine if rings are needed. Feel for a ridge at the top of each cylinder when the piston is

Reaming tool attaches to electric hand drill. Abrasive bars remove glaze on cylinder walls. Spring provides pressure.

down. A ridge indicates cylinder wall wear, since there was no ridge originally. Don't get uptight over a slight ridge if there's only a light deposit of carbon on the piston top. The engine may have had replacement piston rings installed to take up for this wear. It will be only the combination of a ridge you can feel, plus really gummy deposits on the pistons and valves, that indicates excessive oil being pumped past the rings into the combustion chamber.

Though this photo shows block removed from car, you can easily feel ridge indicating amount of cylinder wear at top. After scraping carbon deposits from top of pistons, remove ridge, making sure to get grindings out of cylinder.

However, if you find one or more pistons that are much different from the others in the amount of carbon deposit and the composition of the deposit, it indicates these pistons weren't firing properly. The problem could be as simple as faulty sparkplugs or badly worn rings on the pistons letting an excessive amount of oil into the combustion chamber. If, after you've cleaned the carbon and valves and installed new sparkplugs, you still have firing problems with these cylinders, you'll have to consider installing new piston rings: a ring job.

Inspect the cylinder head and blocks for any cracks. Cracks in the water jacket portion of the head can be easily welded. However, any cracks in the block will require disassembly of the engine and removal of the block to a

Examine cylinder head for cracks. Notice crack at valve port on middle cylinder, making replacement necessary.

welding shop, where it can be repaired in all but the most severe cases. In these few instances, you'd have to locate a replacement block. Directions for engine removal are covered at the end of Chapter 7.

GRINDING VALVES

It's a good idea to grind the valves while you have the head off. Before you grind them, be sure you have the recommended valve tolerance information for adjustment after reassembly.

Properly ground valve, ready to be installed in engine. Grind valves in the same valve seat to get closest fit. Clip attaches to ridge near the bottom of valve stem to control valve motion.

Crank the engine over a few times to see that each valve opens and closes. Any cracked or pitted ones should be replaced. The valve cover plate(s) are on the side of the block, between the banks on a V type. Small bolts or knurled nuts hold these in place. A cork or fibre gasket prevents oil leaks. Get replacement gaskets, if possible, or cut your own from sheet gasket material. With the plate removed, you'll see the valve stems going through the guides and springs, and the adjustment bolts on the lifters. The lobes on the camshaft lift the intake valve when each piston is to receive its air–gas mixture, close it for compression and firing, and open the exhaust valve to expel the burnt charge at the beginning of the exhaust stroke. Before removing any of the valve mechanism assemblies, you'd be wise to examine the operation of the valve opening and closing mechanisms. Notice the valve guides, springs, lifters and adjusting nuts: study the whole assembly carefully before you dismantle anything, so you'll know how it goes back together. You may want to make a simple drawing of an intake exhaust valve, noting the sequence of/the retainers, springs, washers, shims, etc.

Work on the valves one cylinder at a time. This may take slightly longer, but it's easier for the beginner, as you'll have a complete valve assemble as a guide. However, if you decide to remove all the valves at one time, make certain you have a method of identifying each. You should replace every valve in its original position when you're through cleaning and grinding. A handy identification method is to cut a piece of cardboard the length of the block: mark the front. Punch a hole in the cardboard for each valve; as you remove a valve, put it in the corresponding hole.

You can remove valve guides yourself or have the job done at a machine shop. Valve stems must be completely clear of sides on valve guide tubes.

Before removing any valves, look for broken or noticeable weak valve springs. Each spring on intake valves should be the same height and tension. The same applies to each spring on exhaust valves. However, the springs may be different for the intake and exhaust: be sure you keep track of which is which.

To test the valve springs, crank the motor over until each piston comes to the top four times. Check between each cranking to be sure all springs compress and expand identically. Weak springs must be replaced for proper operation.

A small clip fits in a slot near the bottom of each valve stem. Remove this clip and you can lift the valve out. Be sure to catch and keep any washers or shims that may fall loose along with the valve spring. Note the order in which they come off, as they must go back the same way.

The purpose of grinding valves is to get as close a fit between the valve head and valve seat as possible to eliminate any leakage between them. Usually the valve seat, located in the block, will be of different metal than the rest of the block or even the valve itself. This is so the wear will come in the valve seat instead of the valve itself or the engine block. You'll find replacement valves and valve seat inserts are usually available. For some orphan makes, you may need to take the old valves to a supply store where replacement valves of the same specifications can be secured.

To grind the valves, buy a valve cleaning abrasive compound. You can rent a valve grinding tool, but it's not necessary, just easier. Rub some abrasive compound on the edge of the valve and place it in the correct valve hole. Using either the valve grinding tool or a wide screwdriver if the valve has a slotted center, press down and turn it back and forth. This pressure and movement makes the compound smooth the metal edges of the valve and the valve seat for a close fit. The amount of abrasive compound you use and the extent of grinding you must do depends upon the condition of the valves. You can tell as you go along how much grinding each valve will require. Any replacement valve must be ground in to fit the corresponding valve seat.

Be sure to clean all the valve springs with kerosene to remove grease. Clean out the valve guides to assure free movement. Clean clips and washers so everything goes back together easily. While the valves are out, look for excessive wear on the lobes of the camshaft: these will become worn after a great deal of use and need replacement. Usually there's a provision for shims to be added which will take up for all but extreme camshaft wear.

Lobes on camshaft operate valve lifters. These are usually short rods, though some cars used a hydraulic lifter. Center gear on the shaft drives vertical distributor shaft to coordinate sparkplug firing sequence with valve openings.

When reassembling the valves, place each valve down through the hole in the block, then through the valve guide and spring. Be sure that each washer and shim is replaced in the same order it was originally. Do not put the valve cover back yet.

Note the provision made for adjusting valve tolerances. These short threaded rods are usually "double nutted" to prevent the adjustments made on valve openings from changing during operation of the motor. After you have the motor running, you'll need to adjust the valves to the proper tolerances. This may vary between the intake and exhaust valves. With small wrenches or screwdriver and wrench, depending upon differences in individual makes, you can raise or lower the amount of valve stem travel. The less it moves, the closer the tolerance. A thickness gauge (listed under suggested tools) will allow you to set the valves to the correct tolerance.

With valve cover (or plate) removed, it's easy to adjust valve clearance. Set up carburetor to slightly above idling speed. Adjust valves while motor is warm. Use thickness gauge and set to recommended clearances.

Nut on washer holds cap in place on valve springs in overhead valve engine. Valve stem fits through guides which occasionally need replacement.

With the valves back in place and the top of the block, as well as the cylinder head, cleaned of carbon, you're ready to reassemble the parts. Place the new head gasket so the holes line up with the studs. Some people like to soak the head gasket in water before installing it, as the water will soak into the asbestos filling and swell the gasket slightly. You must place the gasket over the studs absolutely level; *do not bend or force the gasket to fit*. Properly aligned, it'll slip easily into place. Normally you won't need to use a gasket sealing compound, but if you do, use it sparingly—you don't want any excess forced into combustion chambers around valves or into water passages.

With the gasket in place, slip the head over the studs. This must be properly aligned and lowered in a level position. A drop of oil on each stud is a good idea. Start replacing the washers and nuts, turning each one down as far as you can with your fingers. Using a wrench, tighten each one a little at a time using the same pattern in tightening as you did in removing them. You must eventually get all the nuts tightened to the same degree. Some restorers may want to rent a torque wrench for this. If renting a torque wrench, tighten the nuts to about 90 pounds pressure unless your owner's manual recommends otherwise. It's only necessary to use a torque wrench on an engine with a high compression head. After the motor has run enough to warm up, you'll need to tighten all the nuts once more whether you used a torque wrench or not.

It's wise to install new sparkplugs—use your thickness gauge, set to the recommended gap. New plugs are not expensive and help greatly in the overall operation of the engine. Be sure to use new plug gaskets.

Connect the appropriate wire to each sparkplug, replacing any bad wires. Make sure each wire has a good contact at both ends. Remount any part that was attached to the cylinder head. Fit the new radiator hose, using a bit of gasket compound on the outside of the pipe the hose fits over. Don't use so much of the gasket compound that excess can get into the cooling system. Tighten the hose clamps and fill the cooling system. Be sure there's oil in the base before you try to start the motor. After a few turns on the starter, the motor should fire. Let it run to warm up, then look for any leaks around the cylinder head bolts. Tighten all bolts one last time.

You'll need to adjust the valves with the motor running. Most valve tolerances are given for a warm motor. Look up the tolerances for the intake valves and adjust these first. (You'll get a little oil thrown at you as you work on the valves with the motor running; there's no other way.) Use small wrenches, a screwdriver and thickness gauge to set the tolerances. This may require your going over each intake at a slightly faster than idle speed for valve adjustments. Replace the valve cover gasket and plate; the job is done.

VALVE-IN-HEAD MOTORS

The valve grinding and carbon removal job is somehwat different for a motor in which the valves are located in the cylinder head instead of the block. These valves are operated by long pushrods that ride on the lobes of the camshaft. These rods actuate rocker arms, which in turn open and close the valves. In a few cars, the camshaft was located in the cylinder head and the valves operated directly off the lobes on this overhead cam. Usually in this design the camshaft was chain driven, though some were gear driven.

The F-head type of motor located the exhaust valves in the motor block and the intake valves in the cylinder head.

F-head engine has large intake valves in head, and exhaust valves in block. Both operate from the same camshaft.

To grind the valves on anything other than the valve-in-block motor, you must remove the cylinder head; this usually includes the manifolds. The procedure is the same as described for the valve-in-block motor. However, you'll find the cylinder head much heavier on these motors, as it contains the valves and valve actuating mechanism.

The intake and exhaust manifolds must be disconnected or removed from the cylinder head, depending upon the design of the motor. Usually the exhaust manifold needs only to be disconnected from the exhaust pipe at the first flange and can remain with the cylinder head.

The carburetor is bolted to the intake manifold and must either be removed or the linkage disconnected and removed as a unit with the cylinder head. A little study beforehand will tell you how to handle the exhaust and intake manifolds on your motor in order to remove the cylinder head.

With the cylinder head removed, you'll see the valve lifter rods. There may be two sections per valve in some motors. These rods ran vertically from the camshaft to the cylinder head, either inside or outside the motor block. They were usually outside the water jacket area, protected by cover plates that were held in place by small bolts.

There is a rocker arm for each valve: it's a short piece running crosswise and rides on a shaft. As the lifter rod pushes up against it by fulcrum action, it pushes down on the valve stem, opening the valve. The valve spring closes the valve as the rocker arm moves back to its normal position.

Twin cam overhead valves, as on this XK Jaguar, look complicated but are simple and easy to adjust. Because of costs, not many cars used this feature.

Adjustment of overhead valves can be made at the point where the valve lifter or pushrod acts on the rocker arm. At this joint, the rocker arm contains a short threaded rod that meets the push rod. A lock nut holds this threaded rod at the desired position. You can adjust the valves to their specified clearance here, using small wrenches and a thickness gauge.

You must grind the valves and the ports into which they fit, just as in the valve-in-block motor. Disassemble the valve operating mechanism once you have the cylinder head removed. To remove each valve, hold it seated with a small block of wood. Compress the spring and remove the valve spring washer retainer and clip: the valve is then free to be lifted out of position.

It's suggested that the beginner–restorer work on the valves one cylinder at a time, so there's a completely assembled valve mechanism as a guide. If you are sure you won't be confused, you may want to work on all the intake valves at one time, then all the exhaust valves. In any case, each retained valve should be returned to its original position. If you're using a replacement valve, it should be ground into its valve seat to assure a proper fit. Remember not to mix intake and exhaust valves.

Clean and check the valve springs, washers and retaining clips. All intake springs should be the same size or height to assure equal pressure. The same applies to exhaust valve springs. However, the intake and exhaust valve springs may be made to different specifications. Don't mix them.

In reassembling the valve operating mechanism within the cylinder head, be sure all pins, springs and washers are clean and securely in place.

You can adjust valves without removing the cylinder head if a valve adjustment is all you believe necessary. Remove the valve cover plate on the block for valve-in-block motors. The pushrods have a threaded adjustment that lengthens or shortens them, causing them to change the amount they lift each valve. Some times there will be provision for additional thin washers and shims to be inserted between the spring and spring retainer. These change the tension of the spring and should only be used when a spring isn't doing its job properly. Use your thickness gauge to adjust the lock nut on the short valve-actuating rod that rides against the camshaft. Adjust the valves with the motor running just above idle speed: first intake valves, then exhaust valves. Be sure oil is circulating on the valve operating mechanism when the motor runs and that the gasket between valve cover and block is in good condition to prevent oil leaks.

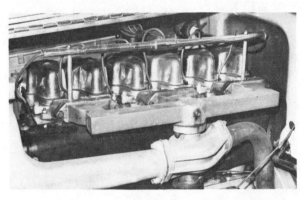

Individual valve cover for each cylinder is held in place by clip, as on this side-draft air cooled motor, a '30 Franklin. Earlier Franklins used down-draft air cooling.

To adjust the valves on a valve-in-head motor, remove the valve cover at the top of the engine. This is usually held in place by two or more wing nuts. They are easily removed, as they have no function other than holding the cover tight against a cork or felt washer. The valve rocker arms run perpendicular to the motor and operate on a shaft that runs lengthwise along the motor. This is often called the valve walking beam or rocker arm shaft.

Early Ford V-8s didn't include oil filter. Filters are easily installed and give protection to engine. With air filter removed, it's easy to adjust the carburetor and to check connections in fuel line from fuel pump to carburetor. Center-mounted generator bracket adjusts to keep fan belt tight.

On the side opposite the valve, a short threaded rod fits into the rocker arm. The length of this arm controls the amount of valve opening. Loosen the lock nut and increase or decrease the length of this threaded rod to provide the specified valve movement, using your thickness gauge. Tighten the lock nut to hold the proper adjustment.

Set the engine at just above idle speed: adjust the intake valves first, then the exhaust valves. It's not unusual to have to regulate these two or three times if the valves were badly out of adjustment. A sticky valve can often be freed by squirting a few drops of light oil on the rocker arm or valve spring.

Oil should circulate on the walking beam and rocker arms as the motor operates. If you find any oil holes or lines that are plugged, clean them out. When replacing the rocker cover on top of the motor, be sure the gasket is in good shape so you won't have oil leaking around it when the motor is in operation.

STARTER

There can be several reasons why a starter won't work: a dead battery is the most obvious. Other common causes are a dirty or malfunctioning solenoid switch; dirt in the starter motor; loose electrical connections; or a broken starter drive. The strictly electrical causes for starter malfunction are covered in Chapter 12. A broken starter drive can be considered a top engine job, since you won't have to remove the oil pan to get at it.

Three bolts hold the starter motor casting to engine. Strong spring forces spiral starter-drive gear back from flywheel when motor fires.

The starter drive mechanism, sometimes called the "Bendix drive," activates automatically when the starter motor is put in operation. The starter shaft rotates and the screw shaft on which the driving gear is mounted throws the gear in mesh with the teeth on the flywheel. When the engine fires and the flywheel starts to turn under engine power, the impulse throws the starter drive gear out of mesh. At this point the starter switch should be released. A strong coil spring on the screw shaft pulls the drive gear back. Occasionally this spring breaks and must be replaced.

The starter drive mechanism is easy to get to: remove the starter motor by first disconnecting the electrical connections. There were usually two to four bolts holding the motor to the flywheel housing. A bearing inside the housing supports the end (not visible) of the starter drive shaft. You may want to put some blocking under the starter motor as you remove the bolts to avoid putting strain on the starter drive shaft. The starter assembly will pull away from the housing, and the drive gear free of the flywheel teeth, once the holding bolts have been removed. The starter assembly is quite heavy, so have a good grasp on it when lifting it away from the motor.

You'll see the drive mechanism extending from the engine side of the starter motor. You can easily spot a broken spring or chipped or missing teeth on the drive gear. Replacements for both are readily available. The spring is attached to the shaft by a bolt through a crimp in one end of the spring. The other end of the spring is similarly attached to the pinion that rides on the screw shaft. Occasionally these springs break and replacement is simply a matter of disassembling the drive to remove the old spring and install the new.

You may find a tooth missing or some teeth chipped on the small drive gear. You should have no trouble getting a replacement gear. But if you should, the teeth can be rebuilt by welding in new metal and grinding it down. With the mechanism disassembled, be sure the screw shaft is well lubricated so the drive gear turns easily. A light oil on the starter spring is a wise idea. Check the bushing in which the far end of the shaft rotates. It is a simple push-in bushing that can be easily replaced if it's worn.

When reassembling, be sure the shaft is properly seated in the support bushing and that the drive mechanism has cleared the teeth of the flywheel. Line up the holes on the starter motor housing with the flywheel housing and replace the bolts; be sure the weight of the starter doesn't rest on the shaft. Reconnect the wiring and the starter should work.

It's not beyond the beginner–restorer's ability to remove or install an engine. It is, however, a heavy job—one that has to be done very carefully to avoid injury to you and damage to the engine. This is a good time to call on a friend for help.

Removal or Installation of an Engine

In some autos, engines and transmissions were mounted in the chassis as a unit, with the motor supports at the front of the block and the rear supports on the transmission. Others mounted the engine as a separate unit with front and rear supports, then added another support for the bell housing or transmission. Examine your particular car to see where the supports are located: this way you'll know exactly what to remove before you start the disassembly process.

Borrow or rent a chain hoist that has sufficient capacity to handle the weight of the engine. It must be properly secured to an overhead beam that will support the engine's full weight. Don't assume that a 2 × 4 brace in the garage or an ordinary 2 × 6 joist is strong enough for this job.

Either bolt additional braces on existing overhead supports to add required strength or build your own overmotor support. Don't take any chances on a support you add or build: make certain it'll hold all the weight necessary. Some rental places can furnish tubular frames that will fit over the front end of your car with the hoist attached.

Because of the engine's weight, you should plan on moving it as short a distance as possible. If you're going to work on the engine once it's out of the chassis, be sure you have a strong, solid support. If you plan to work on your garage floor, make a solid set of braces to hold it in upright position with the pan on the bottom.

First you must remove the hood, radiator shell and possibly the headlight crossbar, though the latter isn't always necessary. Remove only those parts necessary to give you working room and provide enough space to move the engine forward to clear the firewall.

You'll usually find it advantageous to remove as many of the bolt-on accessories as possible before removing the engine. The generator, carburetor and fan assembly should all be removed to avoid damaging parts when lifting the engine out. Disconnect all wires, control rods and cables, as well as anything connected to the firewall. A reminder here to label all the disconnected parts so you'll know where each belongs.

Before you remove the motor support bolts, it's wise to put blocks under the engine pan and clutch housing to support the weight of these components. Or you may want to loop the chainfall around the engine so it will support engine weight as you remove the motor supports and bolts that connect the flywheel housing to the clutch (bell) housing. In some engines it's necessary to remove the splash pan that fits from the side of the engine to the chassis. Some cars didn't have any.

With the motor support bolts and the bolts that hold the flywheel housing out, you're ready to remove the engine. Be sure the chain hoist is securely attached, cradling the engine in such a manner that it doesn't put strain on any one part. Also be sure the hooks on the chain are secured and any safety bolts you may be using are tightened.

Connecting rod, welded to bolt, screws into cylinder head to provide "eye" for hook. Valve springs are clearly visible with cover plate removed. Fuel pump sits at front of Jeep motor.

Raise the chain hoist just enough so it assumes the weight of the engine. Slide the motor forward a couple of inches, until you know the splined end of the shaft has cleared the splined socket. With this accomplished, you can move the motor up and out of the car.

If the engine and transmission were installed as a unit, you may want to remove it as a single unit. If you do—and it is probably easier—you'll have some additional disconnecting to do. The foot and hand brake connections, the clutch linkage, universal joint, etc., all must be attended to. If you feel you'll have any trouble reconnecting everything as it was, make a simple sketch to jog your memory.

You can, of course, put supports under the transmission and clutch housing and remove the bolts that attach the flywheel housing to the clutch housing. Your biggest problem here will be fitting the splined shaft back into the splined hub when reassembling.

Many restorers prefer to remove the cylinder head, intake and exhaust manifolds, engine pan, and all bolt-on accessories. With these eliminated, they have a much lighter and simpler unit to remove from the chassis. There are also screw-in hooks that thread into the block, as well as brackets that can be attached to studs in the block, so the hoist can attach and lifting is made easier.

If you remove the engine and transmission as a unit, you'll have to move the engine farther toward the front of the car before you can lift it up and out, because of the additional length of the clutch housing and transmission.

It's a good idea to install rings, main bearings, rod bearings, etc., before you install a replacement motor if in the replacement motor, these components are needed. The reason is that it's easier: you can get all around the motor more conveniently and reach parts with less trouble. However, if you're rebuilding a motor to this degree, you'll have the head and manifold off. These can be better installed once the motor is back in the chassis. There's always a risk of damaging a part that's bolted on when you hoist the engine to put it in the car.

Completely rebuilt motor ready to be installed in chassis. It's recommended that the home restorer remove generator, carburetor, water pump and other bolt-on accessories which can be easily damaged by chain hoist.

You must be sure the chain hoist is solidly attached to the overhead support and that the support is strong enough to bear the engine's weight. Be sure, too, that the chain hoist is attached to the motor so it will handle it evenly, without strain on any one part, and the motor can't slip or shift position as you move it.

Lift the motor just high enough to clear any obstructions, then lower it into the chassis. Push it back so the splined shaft will fit into the splined hub without being forced. You may want to turn either the shaft or hub so the splines line up. Sometimes a little powdered graphite on the shaft helps in joining these parts. Once these are joined, bolt the flywheel and clutch housings together. Next come the motor supports. Many cars had rubber bushings between the supports to absorb vibration. You'll probably want to insert new ones, as the old bushings are often deteriorated and can't do their job.

Bolt on all parts that need to be attached, such as the generator, carburetor, manifolds, fan, etc. Join the wires so the electrical system is complete. Attach the gas line and check all connections to make sure there are no leaks. Next connect the carburetor controls, gas pedal, choke rod or cable, etc. You'll probably want to install new radiator hoses. Since the cost is negligible, this is an excellent time to do it. Install a new fan belt now if the old one shows any sign of wear. Fill the radiator and check the cooling system for leaks.

With all wires and other connections tight, fill the base with oil. If your car has an oil filter, it should be clean and tight. If the filter is the kind that holds a replaceable cartridge, install the new cartridge before filling the base with oil. Check all oil lines to be sure there are no leaks.

At this point, if you've done everything right, the motor should start and purr like a kitten.

In removing or installing an engine, the biggest problem will be handling the weight of the unit. The rest is a simple procedure of disconnecting, and later reconnecting, the controls, fuel line, radiator, handling the hood, etc. Work as slowly as you want. Get help for the heaviest jobs. Most of all, have confidence that you can do the job, because you can.

CHAPTER 7

Bottom Engine · Repairs

Bottom engine repairs will take you to the very innards of the motor: this is the Big Time. The very thought of working on main bearings, connecting rods, and piston rings has kept many old car owners from even attempting the job. The lingo used by mechanics, who speak of thousandths of an inch, baffles and scares the average guy or gal. Memories of repair shops with motors suspended on chain hoists and parts scattered all over workbenches can chill thoughts of doing these jobs yourself.

Oil pan removed from V-8 engine shows sturdy block construction. Flywheel bolts to one end of crankshaft. Pulley bolts to other end. Main bearing caps, held in place by two bolts, show clearly.

Bottom engine repairs are not as difficult as they sound. It's true that there are exacting measurements you must adhere to, but there are simple gadgets that make this easy. These are time-consuming jobs, nothing you can buzz right through. They can all be done by a beginner willing to work along carefully. They're gutsy jobs, but hang loose: you can do them.

From your original check on the mechanical condition of the car, you have more than a vague idea of how the motor performs. Your test drive and subsequent trip home in the car should also help you determine the motor's condition. Opinions of knowledgeable friends should also help. But to find out, you've got to take a closer look. Use your best judgment: you don't want to do any unnecessary work; neither do you want to leave needed repairs undone. If there are deep sounding knocks in the motor, pounding sounds as you accelerate, heavy blue smoke from the exhaust, coupled with loss of power, you'd better have a look.

Before you have a go at it, though, make sure replacement parts will be available. You can ask at any good automotive supply store about bearing inserts, piston rings, gaskets, etc. At this point you won't know precisely what you'll need; explain that you're simply inquiring if these parts will be available if you need them. Once you have this assurance, you can start a diagnostic trip through the engine's main parts.

Disassembly

These are "bottom engine" jobs, so you'll have to attack them from underneath the car. Later, some of the actual fitting of parts can and should be done at your workbench.

Start by putting the gear shift in neutral position. Remove the sparkplugs to relieve engine compression. Drain the oil from the base: a large threaded plug at the lowest point of the engine base should be removed. Let the oil drain out into a large flat container. Oil will drain slowly; it never seems to drain completely, so replace the plug when the dripping has become too slow to live with.

Remove the bolts holding the engine pan. If your engine has a cast aluminum base, develop a pattern of quarter turns on opposite ends, as suggested for cylinder head removal.

Start your diagnosis by examining the oil that has drained out of the base. Look for any bits of metal, metal shavings or other foreign matter. If there is water in the oil, that means it's coming from somewhere. This could be as simple as a blown head gasket or it could mean a cracked head or block. Once you've examined the oil, dispose of it.

After draining oil out of base, remove bolts holding it to block. Clean base with kerosene or strong detergent. Remove sludge that may have accumulated under baffle.

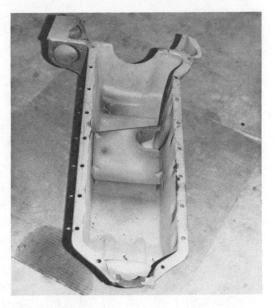

When necessary to cut new gasket for oil pan, trace outline on gasket paper or cork. Mark where holes must be punched for attaching bolts to base.

Examine the engine pan thoroughly, too. Any washer, cotter pin or bit of metal in the base can mean trouble. You should have a replacement gasket for the base. If not, you can trace one from the outline of the pan on sheet cork. Clean the pan out thoroughly and set it aside for eventual reassembly.

Remember this is a diagnostic trip. You want to repair anything that needs it, yet you don't want to do unnecessary work. Because of this, you'll be doing things in a slightly different order than if you knew beforehand exactly what you were going to replace or repair.

Once the engine pan is off, you'll be looking up at the real guts of the engine. The crankshaft, main bearings, connecting rods, cylinder walls, pistons, piston pins, oil pump, etc., will all be in plain view. Don't let it overwhelm you: there are relatively simple checks to detect any problems.

The parts that you're looking up at may be oily, but they should all be clean. Any sign of scorched metal indicates a loss of lubrication. This could be caused by a clogged or malfunctioning oil pump or clogged oil lines. Any broken metal or cracks can indicate serious trouble.

Six-cylinder engine with base removed, showing the following components: *A.* Main bearing cap holds crankshaft in place. *B.* Connecting rod bearings connect piston to crankshaft. *C.* Crankshaft counter balancers. *D.* Timing gear meshes with gear on end of crankshaft. *E.* Camshaft which operates valves.

OIL LINES

If you believe there's been a lack of lubrication to the main parts of the motor, you can clean the oil lines leading to these parts. The number and location of oil lines will vary according to the design of the engine. One way or another, however, they all go from the oil pump to the main bearings. There will be a screen around the oil pump. Remove the screen and clean the mesh. A toothbrush and kerosene do the job beautifully. Disconnect each oil line at the pump end and trace it till you find the other end. Disconnect it at the destination end, being careful not to bend the pipe as you remove it. First of all, blow through it. If there is no problem, run some kerosene through it and let it stand on end to drain. If it's difficult or impossible to blow through, use a little kerosene in the pipe and work a piece of wire back and forth from both ends till it's clear. Rinse the inside of the pipe with kerosene and stand it on end to drain. Do this with each pipe from the oil pump.

The tubes or pipes from the oil pump to various parts only carry oil to that point. Grooves in the bearing surfaces carry the oil to the bearings themselves. With the oil tube off, you can insert a short piece of soft copper wire into the opening and probe for the oil slot. Do not force the wire and don't necessarily expect it to poke through easily to the other end. These grooves may well be narrower in diameter than the wire you're using. If you can work them through the grooves, fine. If not, don't lose any sleep over it.

OIL PUMP

With the oil lines removed from the pump area, examine the oil pump. It is a simple gear-driven pump that forces oil under pressure to the bearings. Oil circulates from the sump or reservoir (engine pan) through the filtering screen into the oil pump. It is pumped through one or several oil lines to the bearings. Systems vary, but in most motors you'll find oil being forced to the main bearings, connecting rod bearings, piston pins and camshaft. Some cars used a splash system, consisting of miniature dippers on the bottom of the connecting rods to splash or scoop oil into moving parts.

Check the gears that drive the oil pump. These may be readily visible, or may require that you remove two or three bolts to pull the pump out of

Oil pump removed from oil pan. Gear-driven pump draws oil in through screened underside of circular intake and circulates oil under pressure to main bearings, connecting rod bearings, camshaft, piston pins and other parts.

location. The teeth on the gears should not be chipped or broken. They may, and probably will, show wear. Evenly worn teeth aren't anything to worry about, unless they're worn so thin it appears they're near the breaking point. Rebuilt oil pumps or replacement gears can usually be located. A chipped or broken tooth can be built up by a machine shop. Usually you'll find there are shims, easily removed, that will allow the driving and driven gear to mesh more closely. Only remove a shim if the amount of wear has allowed considerable play or movement in the pump action.

After the oil is pumped to the bearings throughout the engine, it finds its way back to the base. A tube carries it from the lowest point in the base through an oil filter and back into the pump area. The oil pump does not draw oil from the lowest part of the base, so theoretically it is constantly supplied with oil that has been filtered clean. Some inexpensive cars did not have an oil filter—they relied on impurities settling to the bottom of the oil pan.

On some engines, the oil filter had a cartridge that could be cleaned and reused. It consisted of a series of mesh screens with various sized openings to filter out impurities which collected in a shallow well below the outlet pipe. These can be cleaned with a toothbrush and kerosene and should be cleaned every thousand miles, unless the manufacturer recommended differently. Later cars had disposable cartridge filters that were easily changed. Filter cartridges are inexpensive and should be replaced with every oil change.

When working on the oil pump system, be sure to clean out all oil lines. Do not use a rag or cloth because of the lint. Clean the whole system with kerosene and let the parts drain dry before reassembly. Be careful not to crossthread any of the fittings as you reassemble the system or to put too much pressure on any fitting. You can hold one side of the fitting with one wrench and tighten against it with another wrench. You must have tight joints. Do not use any sort of gasket compound on the joints.

When refilling an oil system that you've completely drained and cleaned, remember to add enough oil to take care of the filter—an additional quart over the capacity of the base. The best way is to fill it till the dipstick shows full. Run the motor a few moments to let the oil circulate, then measure the dipstick again. If the stick shows less than full, add what it takes to bring it up to the full mark. The difference between the first and second filling indicates what's in the oil system. Do not overfill the base with oil, as this will only foul the sparkplugs. Most owners of old cars buy their motor oil in ten-quart or larger cans, and add only the amount they need. This is easier and less expensive in the long run than using quart size cans.

MAIN BEARINGS

The crankshaft is held in place in the engine block by journals and revolves on main bearings within these journals. The number of main bearings will vary. In the more expensive in-line engines, there was one more main bearing than the number of cylinders. In V types, expensive engines had one more than half the number of its cylinders. Less expensive engines had fewer main bearings. For example, a four-cylinder engine could have

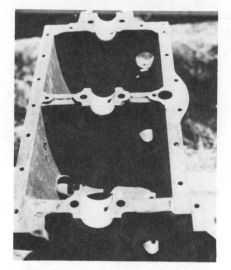

Use soft wire to clean out oil passages that provide lubrication to bearings. Bearing inserts take up for wear and are easy to install.

three or five bearings. Inexpensive V-8s usually have but three main bearings.

If you have a loud knock or thunk in the motor, you'd better check the main bearings. They were usually the first to suffer when an engine got low on oil, either through neglect or excessive oil consumption. To check a main bearing, it's usually best to check the rear one. You'll have to remove it from the supporting journal. Either two or four bolts hold the journal in place. You may find the bolt head exposed or you may find a castellated nut and cotter pin exposed. Remove either the bolt or nut. Break each one loose before completely relieving the pressure. The bottom half of the journal will come off easily when the nuts or bolts have been removed. In this journal you'll see a shiny half circle with some grooves in it. This is one half of a main bearing. Usually, the bottom half of the bearing will take the most wear, as it supports the weight of the crankshaft.

If the bearing you're looking at is smooth with the little grooves and tiny hole in the middle clear and clean, chances are it's OK. The oil grooves will barely show on a bearing that is worn or burned. Looking at it in profile, it will be more worn in the bottom of the half circle than on either side. It will be scorched—the metal will be streaked in a different color—if it's burned out.

When you removed the journal that held the bearing, you may have found several shims or very thin washers between the two halves of the journal. These were included as a provision for taking up wear. If the bearing is smooth and clean, but thin, you can remove a shim from each side to tighten the action of the main bearings. However, if you do it on one, you must do the same on the other main bearings.

If you found the bearing was badly worn and burned, it should be replaced. If one bearing is bad, chances are others will need replacement too. Bearing replacement is covered later in this chapter.

If the main bearing you inspected appeared satisfactory, you can replace it and consider yourself lucky. When reassembling the bearing into the journal be sure it is clean, that the oil grooves are wiped clean and any tiny hole in the bottom is clear. Insert the journal in such a manner that you don't injure any threads on studs that may extend down through the jour-

If you've removed the engine from car, with cylinder head off, turn engine so main bearings are exposed. Clean out oil lines and grooves after crankshaft is removed.

Bearings come in two halves: side ridges hold them in position. Bad bearings will show scorched or worn spots. Fit replacements to get required close tolerances.

nal. No part should be forced into place: they will all fit easily but snugly back in the right order. Tighten it to the original degree and replace any cotter pins. It's best to use a new cotter pin if there's any chance that the original one will crack or break as you reuse it. On some cars you'll find a thin, stiff piece of wire threaded through the nuts and bolts and twisted together. This is to hold everything in place and takes the place of cotter pins. If you can't reuse the wire, it's OK to use individual cotter pins of the same diameter.

ROD BEARINGS

The next check you make should be the connecting rod bearings. There'll be one set for each piston. You'll see each connecting rod attached to the crankshaft on the "throws" between the main bearings. The connecting rod literally connects the piston to the crankshaft. The bearing at the bottom, or big end of the rod, allows the rod to move as the crankshaft makes its circular movement.

If a previous check has shown you have one cylinder that's misfiring, check its connecting rod. Otherwise, choose one near the front of the motor, as this is usually the greatest distance from the oil pump and would suffer first from lack of oil. Turn the crankshaft so the rod is in the down position. You'll notice that there are two halves to the part of the connecting rod that fits around the crankshaft. To remove the bottom half of the rod, remove the cotter pins holding the nuts. Remove the nut on each bolt and the bottom section of the rod will pull away from the other section. Remove this carefully so you don't damage the threads on the bolts. The rod bearing will be narrower than the main bearing and smaller in circumference. You'll notice

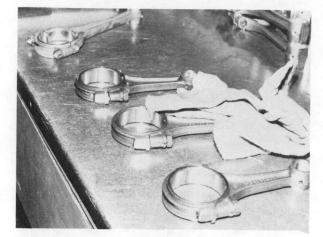

Connecting rod bearings are held in place by two bolts through both portions of rod. New inserts, easily installed, give "like new" performance.

Piston pins take terrific pressure, causing wear. Drive out old pins after removing holding device. Insert new piston pins and secure each so it can't gouge cylinder wall.

Piston, or "wrist," pins fit through top of rod attaching it to piston. Rod is either drilled to provide oil passage or a tiny tube is attached to carry oil to wrist pin.

oil grooves and a small hole; the bearing surface should not look or feel badly worn. It should be very nearly the same diameter all the way around the half you are holding. It must not appear scorched in any place.

It's perfectly possible for one connecting rod bearing to be burned out and for the others to be OK. You can therefore replace only the damaged bearing, but it's a better idea to replace them all. Since you have the base off the engine for this check, you'll save repetitive work. Directions for connecting rod bearing replacement are in later paragraphs.

With bolts removed at bottom of connecting rod and the lower half of the bearing removed, connecting rod will pull down and free of cylinder.

PISTON RINGS

You can check the rings on the same piston simultaneously with the connecting rod bearing. While you have the bottom half of the connecting rod removed for the bearing inspection, it involves only a little extra effort and time. Turn the crankshaft so it pushes the piston you're working on up into the cylinder. As this piston reaches the top, you should be able to hold the rod in place and turn the crankshaft just enough to free the rod. By turning the crankshaft with the connecting rod held still, you can pull the piston down free of the engine block. There are spring expanders behind some rings, so the rings may appear to be of greater circumference than the piston as you get it free from the block. You must compress each ring into its slot when you reinsert the piston into the cylinder.

Take the piston to your workbench and inspect it. The rings fit into grooves in the piston. There will be three or four rings, depending upon the motor. You will find that at least one is an oil ring; it will be slotted to remove excess oil from the cylinder wall, yet allows adequate oil to remain to prevent scorching. On a few autos, the oil ring was near the bottom of the piston. In most cars, the rings were all close to the top of the piston. The others are compression rings. Occasionslly a ring will be broken. Unless it has gouged the cylinder wall, don't get hung up about it, as rings are easily replaced. If the cylinder wall is gouged, in most cases it can be rebored at a machine shop and a replacement piston fitted. Or you can resign yourself to the fact that the piston will always pump a little oil and you need a different sparkplug to handle it. Normally it's better to do the reboring, since the cost isn't prohibitive.

If the rings sprang out a bit as you removed the piston, this is a good sign. It shows the ring has been doing its job, maintaining a tight seal between the piston and cylinder wall. If the ring doesn't even meet or extend beyond the circumference of the piston, the rings need replacement. If you have reason to check more than one piston, do it at this time, using the same procedures. However, be sure to mate the parts properly if you take more than one piston out. You want the same bearings together in the same position as originally and on the same piston rod. Ring installation directions are given later in this chapter.

PISTON PINS

While you have pistons out to check rings, it's the time to check piston pin condition too. Although they're called pins (also known as wrist pins), they are really round shafts. These hold the piston on the top end of the connecting rod. As such, they take the terrific pressure created in the combustion chamber. These fit through holes that line up in the piston and connecting rod. There is a bearing on the small end of the connecting rod that should be checked at the same time as the pin that goes through it.

Drive out the holding pin that keeps the shaft in place. On some cars, there'll be a clip instead of a pin: if so, remove the clip. You should be able to force the shaft out with gentle tapping. Brace a piece of wood against the shaft and tap against the wood. Once the round shaft is out, inspect it for uneven wear. It should be smooth, without ridges or scorched spots. The bearing on the small end of the connecting rod should also be smooth, show even wear, and must not show any scorch marks. The oil groove must be clean. Many connecting rods were drilled so oil could be forced up from the crankshaft or big end of the rod to the bearing in the small end. Other cars relied on enough oil splashing up to keep the wrist pins lubricated. If there is an oil hole, run a fine soft wire through it to be sure it's open. If the pin and bearing show only even wear, they won't need replacement. If they're worn very thin and allow excess play, you should plan on replacing them. Replacement wrist pins and bearings for the connecting rod are readily available. If you feel they need replacement, you can plan on doing it without much more difficulty than you had in inspecting the pin. More detailed instructions are included in later paragraphs.

Reinstallation of Components

MAIN BEARINGS

Putting everything back together again isn't too difficult, but it's one job you must do very carefully. To install main bearings, first disconnect the bottom half of the connecting rod bearings. Place them in proper order for mating in reassembly. If you're only going to replace the main bearings, you do not have to remove the pistons. Leave them within the cylinder walls as you work.

The main bearings sit in journals or holders that are held securely to the engine block by bolts. Usually the bolts are threaded into the block, and will not come out. Remove any cotter pin holding a nut on the stud and break it loose. There will be two or four bolts holding each journal. Break each nut loose before completely relieving the pressure, then remove the nuts. Remove the center bearing or bearings first, leaving the end ones to support the crankshaft as you work. When you get to the end ones, you'll

Worn crankshaft can be turned down, balanced and made as good as new by machine shop. Main bearings form straight line through center of shaft; rod bearings are at end of throws.

need to support the crankshaft with a jack against a piece of wood. Don't use pressure on the jack, just brace the crankshaft in place to take the weight off the journals. On some engines, you may have to remove a covering plate at the front of the engine to remove the crankshaft. Do not remove any gears that are attached to the crankshaft or turn any gears that mesh with them. The crankshaft is heavy, and it may require the assistance of a second person to move it. Be sure not to drop it. Pull it slightly forward after the journals have been removed, freeing the splined end at the flywheel.

V-type motors have wider rod bearing areas in crankshaft throws, since each holds two connecting rods. A few more expensive V-type engines had "blade and fork" rods which meshed, as cylinders were opposite each other.

Engines were designed so main bearing wear would come in the bearings, which are replaceable, rather than wear on the crankshaft itself. Some professionals will occasionally have the crankshaft reground and balanced. These aren't jobs for the beginner–restorer and are seldom necessary. You can have a machine shop do this if you feel it's worth the added expense.

Your goal is to replace the two half bearings that make up each main bearing. On some engines, because of their construction, the main bearings can be removed without removing the crankshaft. In these engines, the journals holding the bearings are so constructed that they can be removed one at a time. If your motor is constructed this way, you don't have to disconnect the rod bearings. Take off the nuts holding the sections of the journals together. As you do this, the two half-circular bearings will also come out. You replace them in reverse order, reassembling the journal and tightening the holding nuts. Do one bearing at a time.

In replacing the main bearings, you're working to remove the up–down, as well as front–back, movement of the crankshaft. The only crankshaft movement should be a spinning motion.

When buying replacement bearings, you'll probably be asked about

Rebuilt crankshaft ready for installation. With new bearing inserts on connecting rods, and main bearing inserts, bottom engine will be like new.

A burned out crankshaft bearing can be rebuilt at a machine shop. New metal must be welded in and the bearing turned down to proper dimensions on a lathe.

"over-size" needed. Over-size refers to the thickness that takes up for wear on the crankshaft itself. Usually if you show one of the bearings you plan to replace to the clerk in the automotive supply store, he can either tell you or find out for you. If in doubt as to the amount of over-size, purchase the largest and plan to file it down to a snug fit. Filing on bearings is always done on the back of the bearing or the edges where the bearing halves come together: *never file the inside of a bearing.*

Automotive supply stores carry a handy product for determining to what thousandth of an inch you're tightening bearings. This looks like a piece of thread, though it's fairly stiff. It is plastic: as you tighten two pieces, you insert the plastic string between the two surfaces. As you tighten, the plastic thread flattens out. You pull it out and measure the flattened piece against a chart that's supplied. The width of the plastic indicates the thickness in thousandths of an inch that you've tightened, taking the guesswork out of this aspect of the job. The plastic threads are inexpensive and easy to use.

You want the bearings to fit snugly and provide enough new metal to replace that which has worn off in use. Start with an oversized bearing and file it slowly and evenly. Use a fine gauge file, taking off but a little metal at a time. File in flat strokes, so you're removing the same amount of metal all the way across the surface you're filing. This is a job which you'll file a little, then try for fit and file again. Working carefully, you can fit each replacement bearing into the corresponding journal. Once properly fitted, they're ready for reassembly. Fit both upper and lower portions of each bearing onto the corresponding area on the crankshaft to assure proper fit.

If you had to remove the crankshaft, use extreme care in fitting it back in place. Insert the upper journals in their respective positions. You may need help in handling the crankshaft. If not, use a wheel jack with wooden block to help support the crankshaft. Slide the splined end into the flywheel opening. Do not force this; if it's level and the splines are properly lined up, it'll slide together easily. You may need to turn the crankshaft slightly to line up the splines.

With the crankshaft sitting in place, held there by the wood and jack combination, start by putting the bottom half of the front journal into place and tighten it just enough to hold it steady. Then do the same with the back journal. With the front and rear journals in a position to give the necessary support, you can remove the jack and wood support and install the other journals. With all the journals in place, tighten the middle one to the de-

Jack shafts fit at end of crankshaft, connecting it to driving plate on flywheel. Undue play in gear teeth or splines can be easily checked.

Pulley attaches to the drive shaft in order to turn fan, generator and other accessories. Some pulleys are finned to help cool the metal.

sired degree. The crankshaft should turn easily, but not spin freely. After the center one, work toward each end till all the journals are tightened. You should be able to turn the crankshaft freely by hand. Too tight, the motor won't turn over. Too loose, you're inviting trouble. Be sure each journal is completely assembled with the necessary washers and cotter pins in place.

CONNECTING ROD BEARINGS

You can replace the connecting rod bearings without removing the rods from the engine, if that's the only job you want to do. Usually a motor is given a ring job at the time the connecting rod bearings are replaced. If that's your plan, the instructions that follow pertain to the rod bearings. Later paragraphs concern the installation of piston rings.

Remove the bottom half of each connecting rod bearing. There will be two nuts you'll need to back off the threaded studs. There will be cotter pins holding these nuts in place. With the bottom half of each rod removed, make sure you have a system of keeping the lower half matched with its mate. I've used colored felt tip pens to do this; other times, string tags marked to show the piston number. Remove the upper half of the rod from the crankshaft by turning the crankshaft by hand, while holding the rod with the other hand. When each rod reaches the top of the turn, hold it steady as you turn the crankshaft beyond the high point. This will free the rod from the crankshaft. You can remove the portion of the bearing that is in this part of the rod, leaving the piston up in the cylinder. Only occasionally will you have to pull the piston down and remove the bearing at a workbench.

Insert the new bearings into their proper holding journals. If you got oversized ones and they need filing, do this as you fit the bearing halves. Only file on the back or outside of the bearing, never in the inner curved portion. You may need to file the flat edges where they meet. Use short, flat light strokes and a fine gauge file. Use the plastic thread mentioned earlier to gauge the clearance in thousandths of an inch. Put each rod back onto the crankshaft to be sure it doesn't bind. With the rod attached, spin the crankshaft; make certain the rod is fitting snugly before going on to the next one. Completely tighten both halves of the rod before working on the next one.

PISTON RINGS

Refer to the earlier section for instructions on removal of the pistons so new rings may be installed. Your dealer or automotive supply house should be able to suggest the over-size rings you'll need. Remember that many cars had the same size piston, so you can order by car make and the dealer can crossreference to find the correct size. The amount of over-size will depend upon the wear the engine has absorbed. Over-size rings can easily be filed down to fit. The amount may vary from piston to piston, as the job must be done one piston at a time. Of course, you must be sure that each piston goes back to the cylinder from which you removed it. You should also get a set of ring expanders, fine springs that fit between the piston and the ring inside the ring groove to hold the ring tight against the cylinder wall.

At this point, you should consider having the cylinders rebored. This inexpensive (about $10 per cylinder) job will make the cylinders perfectly round. New pistons can be fitted and the machinist should have these on hand when he rebores the block. Obviously you have to remove the engine to have this done. A motor that is rebored and fitted with new pistons can run like new.

When fitting rings, file off unwanted over-size at the cut end of the ring. A short flat stroke with a fine gauge file will do it. It doesn't take much to

Clamp will hold piston rings in ring grooves while installing piston in cylinder. A simple twisting motion tightens clamps. Clamp is handy, but not absolutely necessary for ring job.

remove several thousandths of an inch, so don't get hasty. Normally the ring will float in the groove in the piston. This allows rings to rotate slightly and distribute wear. The rings were kept from rotating with a tiny vertical pin on a few makes. You'll have discovered this as you disassembled the piston.

There is a simple, clamp-like tool that you can rent to hold rings in place as you reinstall the piston into the cylinder. It isn't necessary to use one, but it will speed up the job. While reinserting the piston, hold each ring and push the piston up. As it slides up, hold the next ring tightly together so it'll fit inside the cylinder. Do this with each ring until the piston is entirely within the cylinder. The outward force of the rings will hold the piston secure until you're ready to connect the rod to the crankshaft.

PISTON PINS

These round shafts, called piston pins or wrist pins, are not hard to replace. Refer to the previous instructions on removal of connecting rod bearings and pistons if necessary. You'll need to work on one at a time on your workbench. Remove the clip or holding pin and you can tap the piston pin out. Do not hit the metal directly: hammer against a small piece of wood. The pin will slide out of the piston holes and the hole that holds the bearing in the top end of the connecting rod. Be sure oil passages in the rod are clean before inserting the new pin. Install the new bearing in the top end of the connecting rod. This is usually a one-piece bearing that can press in from only one direction. The actual piston pin shouldn't need any filing or fitting. If you feel it does, use a fine gauge emery cloth to file all the way around it. The piston pin should fit snugly in the new bearing and back through the holes in the piston. Any retaining clip or pin should be secured in place and the piston reinserted into the proper cylinder. In fitting the pin and upper rod bearing, you are working to avoid any up–down or back–forth play in the pin. You want only a smooth revolving or wrist action to the pin. You must take care when using emery cloth to apply equal pressure all around the pin. You must not get the pin out of round.

When you're working on bearings or rings—any place where close tolerances are necessary—be sure to work slowly and carefully. A file will cut off a lot of metal in a hurry. This is metal that can't be replaced. You must also take care in filing any curved surfaces to keep the curve the same radius as it was previously, without getting any flat spots.

None of the jobs described in rebuilding an engine are really difficult. These are all jobs the beginner–restorer can do. Only a few may require the help of a friend because of the weight involved.

The more sophisticated jobs of milling down cylinder heads, having a crankshaft reground, cylinders rebored, etc., must be done by a machine shop. The cost for these services is reasonable. Often a second motor can be located, and between this and the original, a most satisfactory engine can be assembled.

The main bearings, upper and lower rod bearings, piston rings and pins, oil pump repair, etc., are all jobs usually necessary to rebuild a motor to where it'll give many thousands of miles of satisfactory service. Remember to work slowly, taking your time with each part.

Engine Removal   There'll be differences in removal procedures because of variations in individual engines. Generally, you remove the radiator, including hoses. Disconnect the exhaust manifold at the first joint. Disconnect fuel lines, wires and operating control rods. Before removing bolts in motor supports, place firm supports under the engine pan. Remove bolts attaching flywheel housing. Using a chain-fall hoist, support the motor weight, move it forward till the splined shaft clears the splined hub. Then hoist the motor up and out. In some cases, you'll need to remove the carburetor, generator and other attached parts. This is a job where it's wise to ask a friend for help.

CHAPTER 8

Drive Train

Drive train is the name the boys gave to the parts that transmit the engine's power to the rear wheels—in other words, what goes round when you press the pedal down! To do its job, the drive train has to make power run at right angles to the source. The system consists of the clutch, transmission, universal joints, differential, rear axles and flywheel (actually, the flywheel is part of the engine; however, I've included it with the drive train since it is more logical for repair and restoration purposes).

Let's make a survey of these parts for diagnostic purposes: some may need replacement, others simply an adjustment, some may need nothing at all. But you won't know until you've inspected everything thoroughly.

FLYWHEEL

Start with the flywheel: that's the big balance wheel at the back of the engine. Its original purpose was to keep the crankshaft revolving between power impulses. Later on, someone decided to put a ring of teeth around this gear, fit a small electric motor, and that's how the starter was born.

You'll need to get in position to look at the teeth that ring the flywheel. On some cars, the housing was left open at the bottom, so you lie on your back looking up. On other cars, there's an inspection cover that can be removed to give you a look-see.

Quite logically, the ring of teeth around the outer edge of the flywheel is called a ring gear. The starter motor drives against these teeth to turn the crankshaft when starting, so you'll want to check for broken or missing teeth. It's seldom you'll find any, as the drive mechanism on the starter motor was designed to protect these teeth. In well over a hundred cars I've worked on, I've only found one that needed flywheel repair—a '37 Terraplane with three broken teeth. Incidentally, Hudson and Terraplane left the bottom portion of the flywheel exposed, as did a few other makes.

Just have someone hand crank the motor for you (*ignition off!*) or run it

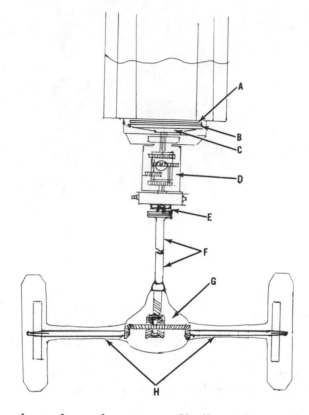

Drive train transmits power at right angles, converting revolving power of engine to forward motion of car. Typical drive train includes *A.* driving plate, *B.* driven plate, *C.* clutch assembly, *D.* transmission, *E.* universal joint, *F.* drive shaft, *G.* differential, *H.* axle shafts.

through on the starter. Chalk mark your beginning spot so you don't spend more than a minute or two on this check.

Broken teeth may make a dentist happy, but you shouldn't have that reaction. If a few scattered teeth are only slightly chipped you don't necessarily have to replace the gear now. Be prepared, however, for eventual replacement of the gear. You'll know when the starter motor meshes with a broken tooth and breaks those next to it. You can find replacement gear rings with little trouble and they won't cost much. They're a bear to replace, though, and I hope you won't have to tackle this job. Directions on how to do this come later. In some cases, the teeth can be rebuilt by welding a small glob

Check the teeth ringing circumference of flywheel, which mesh with teeth on sliding starter gear to turn over the engine. Ball bearing in center of flywheel holds end of crankshaft.

of metal onto the broken tooth and filing this down till it makes a new tooth. You can try to find someone with a portable welding outfit who will do this job in your garage.

CLUTCH

Don't let terms like clutch assembly or clutch action throw you. Actually the clutch (taken as a whole) is a very logical series of parts that connect and disconnect the engine from the drive train. It allows you to apply the engine's power when you want the car to move. It disengages the engine for starting, shifting, etc.

Fulcrum action of six strong springs on pressure plate forces splined clutch plate against engine-driven plate. New facing is easily riveted on clutch plate, correcting slipping clutch.

When you made your initial evaluation of the car through your test drive, you should have noted clutch action. Now comes the moment of truth. You make your check through a large inspection plate at the top of the housing. It's the only inspection plate up front under the dashboard, the same one you used to check the flywheel.

The clutch assembly consists of a drive plate and a driven plate. There's a release mechanism activated by the clutch pedal (the one on the left), that allows for adjustments. There are the necessary linkages and adjustments to keep all the parts working properly.

Remove bolts and slide clutch assembly out of housing to examine clutch plate. Rivets must be at least 1/16-inch below fabric facing.

The drive plate is the last part that is firmly attached to the engine. It's a large disc that revolves with, and at the same speed as, the crankshaft. This seldom needs attention, except occasionally a new facing. The driven plate, more often called the clutch plate, is a fibre-covered disc with a splined hub to fit the clutch shaft. It's the clutch plate that usually gives any trouble you have with clutch action. These babies wore thin and lost their grip. Worn down fibre on the clutch plate would allow slippage and though the motor might race, the car would move slowly or not at all.

Clutch linkage mechanisms vary from car to car. They operate a puller yoke to draw the clutch plate back from driving plate, releasing the clutch. Stiff spring pushes against throwout bearing to operate clutch.

A thrust plate forces the driven plate against the drive plate. The pressure comes from a stiff spring, quite logically called the clutch spring. This spring presses against the hub section of some flexible levers. Via a fulcrum action, spring pressure forces these levers against the outside rim of the thrust plate. The thrust plate, in turn, pushes against the fibre-faced clutch plate. A puller yoke, activated by the clutch pedal, works on the throw-out bearing to release clutch pressure.

You really have four things to check, all quite easy. You'll need your extension light. With the car in neutral and the ignition off, check the amount of fibre on the clutch plate. You'll spot it, as it's easily visible. There'll be a band, or bands, of fibre held in place by rivets, around the outer circumference. If the fibre is worn down so it allows the rivets to rub against the driving plate, you're in for a slipping clutch. The plate must be replaced before the rivets wreck the drive plate, and that'll really cost you money. There should be fibre extending beyond the face of the rivets to give satisfactory service. The fibre may look and feel glazed, but that doesn't matter.

The next check for your busy fingers is the adjustment ring. Remove the locking pin or adjustment clamps. If there is room to move this ring clockwise, you can tighten it to take up clutch action if necessary. You won't need to adjust this unless you felt some slippage in the clutch.

The third check is the throw-out bearing. It should work smoothly when the yoke is pushed against it. (The yoke is the large forked piece activated by the clutch pedal.) The bearing should slide smoothly on its shaft: if it doesn't, it should respond to some lubrication. If that fails, the bearing should be replaced.

The last thing to check is the pedal linkage. This varies somewhat with car make. There may be a height adjustment on the rod that goes through the floorboard. There should be an adjustment where the pedal arm is attached to the yoke shaft. There may be a lever stop adjustment where the shaft emerged from the clutch housing. This controlled lateral movement. Directions for clutch adjustment and repairs are covered later in this chapter.

TRANSMISSION

The transmission is that metal case that sits directly behind the clutch housing. It contains the gears and is topped off by the gear shift lever. To check it, you should remove the inspection plate on the top (occasionally found on the side). If, when you made your test drive, the car went through the gears without any unusual grinding noise or clunking when you slowed down, there is no need to make any additional check on the transmission. But if you weren't satisfied with the transmission action, you can look for yourself. You start by removing the drain plug on the bottom to let the oil drain out. Remember to replace the drain plug before you pour oil back in later to keep from flooding your garage.

The inspection plate is usually secured by bolts: remove these and lift off the plate. If this plate contains the gear shift lever, as is often the case, be sure the car is in neutral and lift the lever straight up. Note the position of the notched or forked end of the shift lever as you remove it. You must make sure the gears are in the same position when you replace the shift lever. Otherwise, you not only change the shift pattern, but you ruin a lot of expensive gears. If it will be easier, you can remove the top shaft of the shift lever. Expose the holding pin by lifting slightly on the shaft to relieve pressure and drive the pin out. This should be done before you remove the bolts holding the plate in position. In either case, you must remember the position of the forked end for future reassembly.

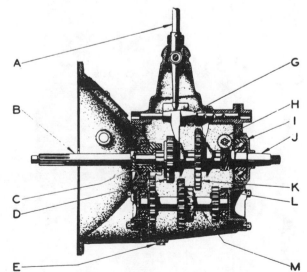

Typical three-speed transmission A. shift lever, B. gear shaft, C. pilot bearing, D. high–second gears, E. drain plug, G. shifting fork, H. speedometer drive, I. sliding shaft shims, J. sliding gear shaft, K. low–reverse gears, L. counter shaft shims, M. counter shaft.

With the top off and the oil drained, you can see the bearings on which the main shaft rides. These should not have much play in them and you can make this test with your fingers. Rotate each gear so you can see or feel every tooth. Any that are chipped or missing will indicate a gear that must be rebuilt or replaced.

The transmission does its job by moving the revolving motion of the engine-driven clutch gear shaft through a series of sliding gears on a counter shaft. These gears either increase or decrease the speed of the final shaft connected to the universal joint. An increase in engine speed through a smaller gear gives added power for starts, steep hills, etc. Be sure there are no washers, bits of metal, metal shavings or broken teeth in the bottom of the gear case, indicating trouble ahead. Examine the oil that you drained out of the transmission for particles of metal that indicate breakage.

If you find you have to replace or rebuild any gears or replace bearings, you'll have to remove the transmission from the car to do so. Many cars had transmissions built by the same supplier. It may be to your advantage to locate a replacement transmission rather than spend too much time or money rebuilding a badly worn one. This is a matter of judgment on your part. Directions on how to remove the transmission are given later in this chapter.

UNIVERSAL JOINTS

Universal joints allow the car to go over bumps without breaking up the drive train. They act as hinges between the engine–transmission unit and the rear axle. They allow the axle to remain connected to the transmission, yet move up and down as road conditions demand. Most cars had a universal joint at each end of the drive shaft. Some had but one: the connection between the transmission and the drive shaft.

There are some easy checks you can make. If you found broken leaves in the rear springs or worn spring shackles, these indicate that the car carried heavy loads or traversed rough roads. In this case, there must be wear on the universal joints too, as they had to operate under stress.

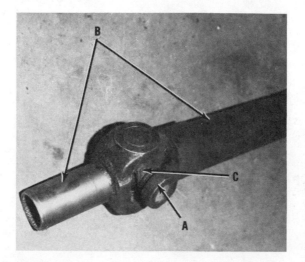

Universal joint: *A.* yoke bushing, *B.* sleeve yokes, *C.* journal. These act together to protect engine and transmission from up–down movement of rear axle.

Some cars had a universal joint where drive shaft joined differential, in addition to a joint at front of shaft. Second joint was usually a ball and socket type, as on this '28 Franklin.

Look back at your initial evaluation sheet on the car. If you noted a pronounced rattle coming from the midsection of the car (light load at low speed) it could indicate a worn universal joint. First check to see if the joint is dry, indicating it hasn't been lubricated. A dry joint can lead to eventual repairs.

About the only real way to detect a worn universal joint is to take it out and have a look. To do this, you'll need to disconnect the drive shaft at the front end. This usually is a matter of removing from four to six bolts that held cotter pins to keep them tight.

With the drive shaft disconnected, you'll expose one end of the universal joint. Some joints were essentially a ball and socket: the socket in which the ball rotated was held together by a series of bolts. Other cars had a joint which consisted of four short shafts which formed a cross and fitted into journals. One set of journals were on a flange yoke bolted to the transmission side of the joint. The other set of journals were on a sleeve yoke. The sleeve yoke was splined to receive the drive shaft end. These four short shafts rotated in bearings. They accommodated the up–down movement of the rear axle.

There is no adjustment you can make to compensate for universal joint

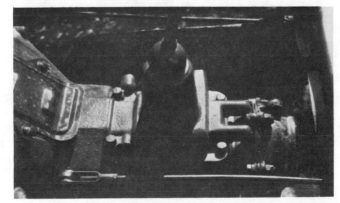

Ford-built cars with transverse springs had only one universal, located where drive shaft attached to transmission. It was a serviceable ball and socket type.

wear. A replacement joint is necessary on the ball and socket type. New bushings can be fitted on the shafts attached to the journal, if you found these worn. If the parts don't appear worn, be sure to lubricate them well before reassembly. If they are worn, replacement of the unit or worn parts is necessary: we'll get into how this is done later on.

DIFFERENTIAL

The differential, that big housing in the middle of the back axle, changes the direction of the engine's power. The engine's power is revolving to the point it reaches the differential. Here that movement is turned at right angles to the direction the wheels are mounted. The differential has a second purpose, too. It allows each rear wheel to rotate independently of the other. This allows the inside wheel to turn more slowly than the outside wheel when cornering. Not all rear axles and differentials are exactly alike. They varied according to the manufacturer's ideas. However, they all function the same, containing bevel, ring, pinion and spider gears to perform their functions.

If your test drive produced a solid clunking or heavy rattling noise issuing from the rear of the car, this indicates play in the rear axle shafts. These can be adjusted. If there's an oil leak from the differential, it indicates the cover plate gasket needs replacement. It also indicates a good possibility that the differential gears aren't getting the protection they need from the oil. If there's an oil leak into either rear wheel, there are faulty oil seals. Oil marks on the tires are another indication of leaking oil seals.

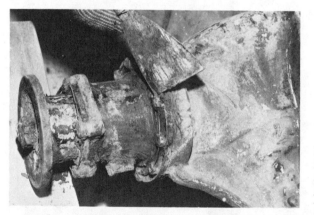

Pinion shaft assembly at front of differential attaches to end of drive shaft and takes up thrust of drive train. Adjusting shims allow take up for wear.

Both rear wheels should be on jacks. Revolve one wheel: the other should either remain stationary or revolve in the opposite direction. If they both revolve in the same direction, the bearings are too tight. These can be adjusted. If one brake drum is closer to the backing plate than the other, this indicates one axle shaft extends farther than the other from the differential housing. This is easily adjusted.

Drain the oil from the differential housing by removing the drain plug at the bottom. Examine the oil for any metal shavings it might contain: these would indicate grinding wear. Remove the plate at the back of the differential case. Take care not to damage the gasket. If it tears apart, you can trace and cut a replacement, as you must keep an oil-tight seal here.

Differential on '28 Franklin with rear plate removed to show bevel ring gear that is adjusted by collars locked in place on each side of bevel gear. Franklin's lightweight rear axle featured rod brace.

Using your extension light, examine the teeth on the gears. Even wear won't mean too much, as there may be shims to compensate. Any chipped or broken teeth will have to be repaired: either a replacement gear or metal welded to the broken teeth and filed to proper size and angle.

The pinion gear is the forwardmost gear in the differential. You check it for wear and possible broken teeth. This gear revolves in the same direction as the drive shaft. On some cars, this must be inspected from the front of the differential. You have to remove a protection dust cap, if this is the case. There are adjustment nuts that allow you to take up any front to back motion in the pinion gear.

The large gear you see as you look into the differential case is the bevel ring gear: this must not have any chipped or broken teeth. The position of this gear is usually controlled by shims in the pinion shaft housing and axle gear case. You can compensate for even wear on this gear. Adjustable bearings allow you to remove noticeable end play.

Bearings support the rear axle shafts so they don't bear the weight of the car. These mesh with other gears in the differential housing. Check the teeth to be sure none are broken. The bearings should not be worn: they won't give the support necessary and hamper the axle shaft from turning

Rear axle shafts, showing beveled gears that drive from large bevel gear in differential. Worn teeth can be built up and ground to size if replacement shaft can't be located.

freely. Worn bearings have to be replaced. You'll probably see felt washers that act as oil seals to keep oil in the gear case from running out the axle shaft housings. Worn bearings put an extra strain on the axle shaft and can cause the shaft to break. When the axle shaft breaks, the wheel can slide outward on the stub that's attached to the hub. I had this happen on a Lincoln Zephyr once; it's an unsettling experience at best.

After checking the differential, inspect the rear wheel bearings. This you do by removing the hub, which usually is a part of the rear brake drum assembly. The axle shaft is supported at each end by a bearing. You'll have to remove the cotter pin and nut on the shaft. You'll notice a tapered slot into which a key fits to keep the axle from spinning without turning the hub. There should be only very slight in–out play of the axle shaft. Adjustments should take up the play on all but badly worn shafts.

Repairs   If, when making the checks outlined on previous pages, you find repairs and adjustments are indicated, there's no sweat. You can make all but a very few yourself. Make certain that replacement parts are available. Also check on available rebuilding services.

FLYWHEEL

If you have to replace the ring gear on the flywheel because of missing or broken teeth, first see if someone can bring a portable welding outfit to your garage. If so, they can weld on small lumps of metal over the missing or broken teeth. These you can file down to shape and size. If this service isn't available to you, you'll have to remove the old gear ring.

You've got a lot of disassembly work to do to even get at the flywheel. Don't remove the engine from the car to get at this, though that's how a garage would do the job. The average gal or guy will find the following method easier. Disconnect the universal joint where it connects the driveshaft to the transmission. Use a piece of light rope to hold the driveshaft in place when removing the bolts; later, let it rest on the garage floor. You've got to move the transmission back, so will need the driveshaft out of the way.

Remove the clutch housing and transmission as a unit. You start this by removing the bolts that hold this housing to the rear of the engine. They'll form a half circle at the top and another half circle you'll have to attack from underneath. On some cars you may have to disconnect the clutch pedal linkage. You may also have to remove the emergency brake linkage on cars with the brake to the left of the driver. With this disconnected and the bolts in the housing removed, you should be able to pull the whole assembly back. It will be necessary to use some blocking under the transmission or clutch housing as you loosen the bolts. This will keep undue weight and pressure off the splined shaft, which will slide back much easier.

The flywheel will now be exposed. You may find a series of bolts holding the flywheel to the flange on the back of the crankshaft. You won't see the crankshaft from this position. These bolts may have a stiff piece of wire threaded through each bolt to keep them in place. To get at the ring with the teeth on it, you may have to remove the flywheel. On other cars this will not be necessary; the slot-headed bolts holding the ring gear in place can be removed, allowing the gear to come off. You'll find any bolts in these inner sanctums will be tight. They'll be finely threaded and will require plenty of pressure to break loose. They will come out, however, so don't get uptight at the effort required. If you had to remove the flywheel, you'll find an oil seal to keep the engine oil from leaking into the flywheel housing. It's a good idea to install a new seal when you reassemble these parts.

Once the old ring gear has been removed from the flywheel, install the new one. Be sure all bolts are in as tight as you can make them and that any bolt head that was originally countersunk is back in the same manner. Be certain no extra washer or old cotter pin is left in any housing.

When reassembling these parts, be certain to replace everything in the right order, tightened as it was before. Reassembly requires the splined shaft to slide easily into its mate. The weight of the bell housing, clutch assembly and transmission must not rest on the short splined shaft. Keep supports under it as you bolt the housing back on the motor. Line up holes with a punch, if necessary, so you won't damage the threads on the bolts.

With the bell housing and transmission back in place, reconnect any pedal or hand brake linkage that you had to disconnect. The last step is to reconnect the universal joint between the back of the transmission and the front of the driveshaft. You may want to support the driveshaft by blocking or tying it in place as you line up the bolt holes. Be certain all washers are in place and all cotter pins securely bent into position.

CLUTCH PLATE

We can cover clutch adjustments and repairs at the same time, but perform your adjustments first. Remove the large inspection plate so you can get at the clutch adjustment mechanism. To stop the clutch from slipping, cut a piece of wood to hold the clutch pedal down while you're working. Some cars had a number of clamps holding the thrust plate against the clutch plate. Others had a locking pin that allowed the adjusting ring to be moved. With the clamps loosened or the locking pin turned to the *in* position, insert a large screwdriver in the ring hole and turn the ring one or more notches clockwise. This should take up for normal clutch wear. Pedal linkage adjustment will vary, but there will be some adjustments you can make. The pedal arm may have a holding nut that will allow you to lengthen or shorten the shaft that holds the pedal through the floorboard. Adjustment here depends upon the length of the driver's legs. Another pos-

Remove clutch inspection plate to reach adjusting ring locking pin. Pull out locking pin and turn it to hold it in position. Move adjusting ring clockwise one or more notches to compensate for clutch plate wear.

sibility is where the pedal arm is connected to the shaft that runs crosswise. Adjustment here changes the back to front movement of the puller yoke. It should be regulated so you get clutch action when the pedal is released an inch or two. On this crossshaft there will also be a set screw on each side: make these both the same to assure even pressure when you press the pedal. It's a good idea that the springs inside as well as outside the clutch mechanism be well oiled. Some powdered graphite in splined shafts is recommended. However, be sure not to get any oil on either the drive or driven plate. Be sure everything is tight as you replace the inspection plate and your clutch adjustment is done.

If you're going to replace or resurface the clutch plate, you'll find that you can usually do this through the inspection plate. On some cars, however, you have to remove the bell housing surrounding the clutch assembly. On these cars you'll have to remove the transmission to get the bell housing off. If this is the case with your car, the transmission bolts onto the back of the bell housing; usually four or six bolts are all that need be removed to allow you to take out the transmission. Be sure to support the weight of the transmission from underneath if you have to remove it. There may be some pedal linkage you need to disconnect to get at things. The clutch plate slides off the splined shaft easily. The new one will slip on easily; remember to use a little graphite on the splines when you do this. However, you've got to get to the clutch plate first. This fibre-lined plate is in front of the throwout bearing, puller yoke and adjusting ring. The direction from which you remove these depends upon how much you had to remove to get at them. If the design of your car allows you to remove the clutch plate by pulling it forward off the splined shaft, you do not have to remove the other parts. However, if you had to approach it from the rear, these parts must be removed first. They will all slide off the shaft easily. The main thing to keep in mind is the progression in which they fit together so you can reassemble them in the right order.

When replacing the clutch plate, check the throw-out bearing. This is normally at the back of the clutch. It's activated with a puller yoke by clutch pedal action. It helps the main coil spring compress and release clutch pressure. If the bearing is worn, you'll have to replace it. Since many clutch assemblies were made by outside suppliers, you shouldn't have any trouble in locating the right replacement. When installing a new throw-out bearing, grease the splines and the shaft on which it rides. You'll never get the chance to lubricate things this easily again.

It's a good thing to remember that on some old cars that aren't driven very much and are left in gear when not in use, the clutch plates will tend to freeze together, making it almost impossible to release the clutch. I had a 1928 Franklin that had acquired this problem before I bought it and it gave me fits to free the friction plate. An easy prevention is a board, cut to length, to hold the clutch pedal to the floor when the car isn't in use.

TRANSMISSION

Transmission repairs are probably something you'll want done at a garage or machine shop, as about the only thing that can go wrong with them is broken teeth on the gears. The bearings that support the shafts can only be replaced if they're worn. However, you can replace the bearings yourself and you can remove the transmission from the car should it be necessary to replace any gears.

To remove the transmission, you should first drain it. Once that's done, block some support under it so there'll be no weight on the shafts. Remove the front holding bolts. Usually there'll be cotter pins to remove first. Disconnect the universal joint at the rear and let this rest on the floor. If your car's hand brake works on the transmission, there'll be some linkage to disconnect. Do this at the point closest to the transmission. You may need to remove the brake band: if you do, there should be two or more guides that hold it in line. With these out of the way, you should be able to pull the transmission back—freeing the splined shaft—and lift it out of the car.

This '39 Chevy originally had column shift, now changed to floor shift. Column linkage should have been removed. Cars with electric column shift provided emergency shift stick.

Some makes mounted the transmission, clutch assembly and engine as a unit. They are bolted together and the rear engine supports are at the back of the transmission. (On other cars, the rear engine supports are at the back of the engine.) If your car has rear motor supports at the back of the transmission, be sure to support the back of the engine on blocks before removing the rear engine mounts. Then remove the bolts holding the transmission housing to the bell housing. Once you have these out, the transmission will pull backwards and you can lift it out. It won't be too heavy for one person to handle.

If you plan to install new bearings in the transmission to take up for end play in the sliding shaft or countershaft, you'll need to remove the gears to get at them. Most transmissions had shims behind the rear bearings to take care of adjustments. End play shouldn't be over .008 inch; measure this with your thickness gauge. The shafts with the gears on them can be pulled out of the bearings once the case has been completely disassembled. Remember to clean everything as you reassemble the parts. Lubricate the shafts so everything slides together as it should. Nothing should be forced together. The case must be reassembled so it's perfectly tight. It's a good idea to wash the gears and shafts with a mixture of half kerosene and half oil before reassembling the transmission case. Be sure the gear selector yoke is back in the proper location so you can shift gears when you're ready. Give the outside of the transmission case a spray coat of black paint before putting it back in place in the drive train.

UNIVERSAL JOINTS

It's easy to replace universal joints once you locate the necessary replacements. You may need to take the original parts with you when you go to an automotive supply store, as the clerk may not know any more about parts than you do. With the original in hand, you can at least see that it looks right, the bolt holes line up, etc.

Be sure to put some support under the driveshaft as you remove the bolts holding the universal in place. Disconnect it from the driveshaft end first, then from the transmission end. On most cars you can do this job from the inside. On some later models, you'll have to work from underneath. Once disconnected from the transmission and the driveshaft, the universal joint will be in your hands. Replacement is simple: just be sure it's well lubricated before you bolt it in place. Once in place, be sure all the holding bolts to the transmission and driveshaft are tight, and the job's done.

You may also find some fabric rings that go between the end of the universal joint and the front of the driveshaft. Other cars had these fabric rings where the driveshaft joins the differential. These were usually about a half-inch thick and acted as an additional cushion to protect the drive train from jackrabbit starts, jerks, jolts and bumps. Usually four to six bolts fit through holes in flanges to hold these in place. Replacement rings are readily available should you need them.

DIFFERENTIAL

Adjustments and repairs to the differential are not hard to make. Neither are part replacements difficult, although they usually require that you lie on your back under the car with the work above you. When you start this, hang your extension light in such a position that you don't have to stare into it as you work. Also, place the cord so you don't roll over it when you move. It's wise to position yourself so that you don't get dirt in your eyes and mouth as you work.

Adjust the pinion shaft at the front of the differential by removing the protective dust cap, if there is one. This will let you get at the bearing adjustment nuts. You tighten these nuts to tighten the bearing. The adjustment should be made so the pinion turns freely, but with no appreciable end play. There are pinion adjusting shims just before the pinion gear. Removal of these shims lessens the distance between the gear and the housing; add shims to increase it. After eliminating excess play, be sure the lugs on the lock washer are bent down in opposite directions to keep the two nuts from moving. To prevent the washer from cracking, never crimp it in the same place. Use a new washer if you need to.

The bevel ring gear (large gear) and the pinion gear mesh. This meshing is usually controlled by the shims in the pinion shaft housing already mentioned. Remove or add shims till this gear meshes perfectly with the smaller pinion gear. If you damaged the felt washer or if it was already damaged, replace it with a new washer to prevent oil leaks.

Bearings support the bevel ring gear: these are adjusted by a threaded collar on each side. Any adjustment should be made to allow the gear to turn freely, but with no noticeable end play. After you've made any adjustments, be sure to lock the adjusting nuts.

The rear axle shafts are supported by bearings and retaining washers keep the oil in the differential case. The axle shafts are tapered where they fit in the rear hubs. They're slotted so a tapered key holds the shaft tightly in the hub. There is no adjustment to the bearings that support the axle shaft. If they're badly worn, they have to be replaced. You remove them by pulling the shaft out through the hub end. With the shaft out, you can remove the old worn bearings and insert new ones. At this time you should replace the felt oil seals. You do not have to remove the bevel or pinion gear to replace an axle shaft.

In–out movement or end play of the rear axle shafts is adjustable. This is controlled by adding and removing shims in the back of the bearing retainer at the hub. The same number of shims should be used on each shaft so that each shaft will extend into the differential end hubs the same amount. If one shaft is a different length than the other, the longer shaft can cause binding on a brake. This is because the longer shaft will push the backing plate of that brake to rub against the rim of the brake drum. While working on rear axle shafts, be careful not to get any oil or grease on brake drums or linings, as this will cause them to grab.

Aside from some individual variances in design and assembly of clutch, transmission, universal joint, drive shaft, differential and rear axle assemblies, the procedures for adjusting, repairing and replacing parts are the same. There are no big secrets to repair or adjustment of these parts. I've done them all successfully on many different cars; you can, too.

CHAPTER 9

Steering System

Aside from the brakes, there's nothing more important to your safety when enjoying your old car than the steering system. From the wheel in your hands to the wheels on the road, it's important to have it working properly. The system of joints, gears, shafts and rods that make up the steering system is very simple to understand and repair. If the steering system is working right, it helps you appreciate those curves!

You should check the entire steering linkage: it's not difficult to figure out. If you were able to make a test drive before you bought the car, you've got a good idea how it steers. You may not need to make adjustments or repairs.

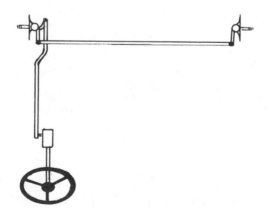

Schematic drawing of typical steering system. Arm from gear box pulls or pushes rod connected with left wheel spindle. As left wheel turns, tie rod moves right wheel in same direction and same amount.

You should have about one eighth of a turn of play in the steering wheel. Much more than that indicates some attention is required. Remember that irregular steering can be a result of worn or improperly inflated tires, out-of-balance wheels, different size tires, worn spring shackles, etc. In other words, just because it steers like a truck doesn't necessarily mean the steering system is shot.

As engines were moved forward and independent front suspension became popular, many cars adopted a center-pivoted steering system as shown in this schematic.

Since you have the car on blocks with weight off the axles your checking job is easy, because all the joints in the system will be hanging loose.

STEERING GEAR BOX

The only gears in the steering system are contained in a box or case at the bottom of the steering column; the steering wheel is at the top. There is a worm gear on the steering column and a sector gear with which it meshes. Usually there's a plate on the top or at the side of the gear box: after removing this, you can see the gears involved. Look for broken or missing teeth on the sector gear. Usually there's a provision for taking up wear on this gear by adding or removing shims; these allow adjustment of the gear so it fits or meshes closely with the worn gear on the steering column. Normally this case is filled with grease. If your car has been properly lubricated over the years, you won't be apt to find any trouble with these gears.

STEERING COLUMN

Make sure the bottom of the steering column is securely bolted to the chassis–frame. You'd have some hairy moments if this were ever to work loose. I have come across at least a half dozen cars over the years, wherein the steering column had worked loose from the frame. It can happen on a Packard or a Whippet. Check the brace on the firewall or dashboard that helps support the steering column. On some cars, the steering column is adjustable for rake, allowing it to accommodate different sized drivers. On cars with this adjustment, you're more apt to find a steering column that's not tightly bolted in position.

Steering column bolts to chassis, with a brace where it passes through firewall and usually a second brace at the dashboard.

Yours may be a car that has the rod connecting the wheel with the gear box contained inside another column. This doesn't change its steering in any way, but does protect the inner shaft from damage.

Since the steering system is a series of joints with various length steel rods between these joints, you'll have more to check than you can see by opening the hood. Most of the unseen parts of the steering system will be pretty well covered with road grime, so you'll need to do some scraping and scrubbing with a putty knife and wire-bristled brush before you can check everything. On the more expensive and better engineered cars, there were provisions for taking up wear in many of these joints. Other cars made no provision for adjustments and simply relied on rubber bushings or washers between the joints.

STEERING ARM

The short shaft that extends down from the gear case at the bottom of the column is the steering arm. This is firmly attached to the shaft on which the sector gear turns. Check here to be sure that the arm is firmly attached to the shaft. There may be a tapered key on the shaft, as well as a spring washer and nut with cotter pin. There will usually be a ball joint at the bottom of the short arm that allows flexibility in its connection with the drag link. The bushing in this joint may be worn.

DRAG LINK

The drag link is the rod that extends from the steering arm to the tie rod, running parallel to the frame of the car. It has a joint on each end. In most cars you'll find a provision for taking up wear at one or both ends of the drag link. If the steering wheel spokes don't seem to line up properly when the wheels are pointing straight ahead, the correction is made on the drag link. It needs to be lengthened or shortened to turn the spokes of the steering wheel. Play in the drag link indicates worn bushings at one or both ends.

Gear box on bottom of steering column contains gears which transfer turning of steering wheel to push–pull motion of rod to front spindle.

TIE ROD

The tie rod runs parallel to the front axle, about six inches behind it. It keeps both front wheels pointing in the same direction. As the drag link pulls or pushes the short arm connected to the steering yoke, one wheel turns. The tie rod which runs between and connects the steering yokes makes the other wheel turn the same direction and same amount. Most cars had provisions for adjusting the tie rod at each end. These keep the front wheels in alignment. Excessive play in the joints connecting the tie rod to the wheel yokes indicates worn bushings.

Front axle of '28 Franklin shows connecting arm to gear box arm and tie rod. Toe-in adjustment is at ends of tie rod.

FRONT AXLE

The front axle connects and supports the front wheels. It is fitted with a yoke on each end. Wheel spindles, sometimes called king pins, fitted through the axle yokes and the end of the wheel spindles. This combination made a hinge at each front wheel. The spindle bolt or king pin acted as a pin in each wheel hinge. The short arms (mentioned in the paragraph about the tie rod) connect the wheel spindles through joints to the tie rod. Front wheel shimmy and poor steering are the result of really badly worn systems.

There is a silicone product that comes in a tube with a needle on the end. You insert the end of the needle into the joint and squeeze. The liquid silicone will flow around the parts: when this has hardened, it sets just like a new rubber bushing and you've installed it without taking anything apart. This is great for replacing worn bushings. I can tell you that it's easy to use; if you follow the directions on the tube you'll have no trouble.

There are spring attachments you can buy to fit at the end of the tie rod. These take play out of the tie rod–spindle arm joints. On most cars there's nothing to disconnect before clipping these in place and they'll do a great job, especially on Ford-built cars.

There is another device that clamps to the front axle. It has two spring arms that push against the tie rod to take up play. Get the style that fits your axle and mount it in the center. Be sure the stiff spring arms are pushing against the tie rod. This will stop a lot of cases of wheel shimmy. I've used this on a Rolls Royce, as well as Model A Fords.

With cars that made provision for adjustments on the various joints in the steering linkage, you first try to make these adjustments. In many cases the drag link and tie rod were made of tubular steel. A plug was threaded into the ends of these. These plugs usually pushed against a stout coil spring. The spring in turn pushed against a convex washer. This washer fitted in the end of the tie rod.

There can be excessive wear at any of these joints and an inspection of each will tell you its condition. Steering systems varied by make and size of car. Consequently, the provisions for adjusting and compensating for wear also varies. On some cars you can add or remove shims at these joints. On those makes which have a ball and socket joint, you can usually tighten the socket by screwing in the threaded rod that pushs the sides of the socket closer around the ball. Some cars relied on the resiliency of a rubber bushing to keep the joint tight.

CHECKING SPINDLE BOLTS

To check for wear on the spindle bolts (king pins), grasp the front wheel housing or brake drum. Try moving it back and forth, as well as up and down. This will tell you the amount of wear. You should find only a slight amount of movement if the spindle bolts are in good condition. Usually any wear will be in the spindle bolts. However, some cars used a softer metal in the bushings in these joints: in this case, the bushings would have to be replaced.

System Repairs   Before getting too involved with adjustments and replacements in the steering linkage, you might be wise to consider some time and money saving products on the market. These will correct many of the problems that exist in worn steering systems. They are not a replacement for new parts and shouldn't be used on steering systems that are badly worn. On cars that had provision for adjustment of the various joints on the steering linkage, first try to make these adjustments. In most cases the drag link and tie rod were tubular steel. A plug threads into these. The plug usually pushed against a coil spring that in turn pushed against a convex washer. This washer fitted against the ball that was attached to the part mating with it. There was a similar convex washer solidly fixed in the rod, and this was not adjustable. Pressure from the threaded side of the joint formed a socket

Wooden wheels in common use in the Twenties often suffered from weather in open cars. This wheel can be rebuilt and refinished to give additional service.

around the ball. The take-up provision consisted of either screwing the threaded side of the joint in farther or adding shims or washers between the end of the threaded part and the coil spring. A cotter pin was usually fitted to hold the threaded piece in place. In most cases, tightening these joints does the job.

Some cars had threaded ends on the tie rods. On these threaded ends, the socket part of the joint was screwed. The inside of the socket usually contained a washer which pushed against a spring which pushed against a convex washer. This pressure held the washer against the ball, which was attached to the part mating with it. To tighten these, you must remove the cotter pin on the end and turn out the threaded plug. This will allow you to take the ball part of the joint out of the slot. Tighten the threaded receptacle a sufficient number of turns to take up any unwanted movement; then slip the ball end of the joint back into the slot and insert the threaded plug and cotter pin.

On some cars the socket end of the joints was held on the tie rod or drag link by a bolt. This allowed the socket to be removed, and shims added, after the socket was dismantled. On those cars that depended upon rubber bushings alone, there is no adjustment. Worn bushings will have to be replaced, unless you use the silicone injection I mentioned. As you know, silicone injections have gained favor in other applications. They'll work on your car, too.

If you decide you want to replace the rubber bushings, disassemble the joints and remove the old ones. When you have the joints apart, clean them thoroughly with kerosene. You may need to take the old bushings with you when you go to purchase new ones. Many times a similar bushing that was made for a different make of car can be found.

REPLACING SPINDLE BOLTS

Since there is no way of adjusting the spindle bolts, if you find them badly worn you'll have to either replace the spindles or bushings. Don't let the thought of this throw you: I've done it many times, with the simplest tools. Depending upon how your car was designed, you may need to install only bushings through which the spindle bolts fit, or you may need to replace the spindle bolts, or both. To find out, you'll need to disassemble these joints.

Start with either front wheel. If your car has front brakes, remove the bolts holding the brake backing plate on. You'll find the long pin threaded on one or both ends. There will probably be a cotter pin through a castellated nut with a washer that must be removed. With all nuts and washers removed, you can easily tell if the pin is tapered. You must drive the pin out. If tapered, drive from the small end. Do not hit the pin directly. Use a piece of wood to protect its end. Even though you won't be using the pin again, if you batter the end of it you won't get it out of the holding yokes.

In some cars you can get to the pin without removing the backing plate for the front brake. If this is the case on your car and you have room to work on the pin, don't remove the backing plate—there's no use in making extra work. In either case, you'll have to provide support for either the brake or the hub as you drive out the old pin. If you don't, they'll bind and make the pin more difficult to remove.

With the pin out, you can easily tell if the wear is on the pin, the bushings, or both. Look for ridges where the axle yoke and wheel yoke fit together. If you can see or feel ridges, they need to be replaced. If they're perfectly round and show no wear, they'll be OK and only the bushings will need to be replaced. Since the cost of pins and bushings isn't high, you may want to replace the entire spindle bolt and bushings group while you're at it.

The old bushings can be driven out of their yoke. You can tell if the outside measurement of the bushing is greater at one end than the other. If so, drive from the smaller end. Again use a wooden block between the bushing and the hammer.

There are tools you can rent if you feel you'll need them to install new bushings. Normally you can fit them in place by tapping on a piece of wood on top of the bushing. Occasionally you'll find you'll need to remove a little metal from the outside of the bushing. Emery cloth or a fine gauge file is all you'll need. Use caution in filing the outside circumference, being sure you remove the same amount of metal all the way around. I've ruined more than one bushing by filing it out of round.

In some instances, you may find a large thin washer between the yokes on the axle and wheel spindle. If these appear worn, you'd better replace them. However, the replacement washer may need a bit of filing to make it fit snugly; it shouldn't be driven in.

To install new spindle bolts, line up the axle and wheel yokes. Lubricate the new spindle bolts with graphite or light oil. They must be driven into place, but this usually requires only a light tapping. Remember to use a piece of wood between the pin and the hammer. Lubricate the nut threads before replacing the bolt. Be sure the washers are in place and tighten the nut, lining up the holes in the nut and bolt so you can insert the cotter pin. Be sure the cotter pin is securely bent into place. If you had to remove the brake backing plate, attach it in the proper position.

Remember that the spindle bolt acts as a pin in the wheel–axle hinge. It should allow the wheel to be securely attached to the axle and must turn easily. There should be no play in the joint with the new pins and bushings in place.

Note that there is a set screw and lock nut on each steering knuckle, acting as a stop to prevent the wheel from being turned far enough to hit the frame of the car. Adjust these stops on each side to give about an inch and a half of clearance between the tire and frame.

ALIGNING FRONT WHEELS

When the front wheels are properly positioned, they toe-in slightly, are slightly off vertical, and are tilted slightly backward. Toe-in controls the parallel position of the wheels. Axle tilt controls the caster, or backward tilt. Camber, or vertical position, is controlled by the positioning of the axle yokes and wheel spindles.

If you don't want to take your car to a garage offering wheel alignment services, you can check the axle tilt and toe-in yourself. Before you do, however, check the tire sizes, wheel balance, and air pressure in the tires. You may save some work.

Wheel Toe-in. Wheel toe-in controls the direction the wheels point. They actually should point slightly toward each other. The distance between the wheels at the back should be up to a quarter of an inch more than at the front when they're carrying the weight of the car.

To check this, jack up the front end of the car. Hold a piece of chalk or a Magic Marker against the middle of the tire and spin the wheel. Hold it steady, so it makes a line around the circumference of the tire. Remove the jack and lower the wheels. At a point about ten inches from the floor, make a cross mark and measure the distance between the marks at the front. Move the car ahead till these cross marks are the same distance from the floor but at the back of the wheel. The measurement should be up to a quarter inch more at the back. Alter this distance, if necessary, at the ends of the tie rods by adding or removing shims.

Axle tilt. If, when you took your test drive, you noticed that it took constant effort on your part to keep the car going straight, this could be caused by incorrect tilt of the front axle. Also, if there was little or no tendency for the wheels to return to the straight-ahead position after cornering, this could indicate too much axle tilt. There is an easy test you can make at home, if you don't want to have the front wheels aligned at a garage specializing in front-end alignment.

First, be sure you've checked the size and pressure of each front tire. Axle tilt controls the caster action of the wheels: the yoke at the end of each front axle that holds the wheel spindles should be tilted one degree forward of vertical. This doesn't seem like much and you may wonder how you can check it.

Tack a yardstick to a short piece of 2 × 4 lumber. Be sure the stick is perpendicular to the lumber. Check this with a carpenter's square. The 2 × 4 lumber will give sufficient weight at the bottom to hold the yardstick vertical.

Jack the front wheels off the floor, but no more than a quater inch. You want them where there is no weight on the tires. Place the yardstick against the center of the axle hub. With a piece of chalk or a felt tip marker, mark the top and bottom of the tire at the outside center. After doing this on each tire, lower the wheels back to the floor so they're bearing the full weight of the car. Place the yardstick at the original position, centering through each axle hub. If the tilt is correct, the bottom mark will be about a half inch behind the vertical stick and the top mark about a half inch ahead of the vertical. Both wheels must be the same.

If you find correction is necessary, it's made at the point where the axle crosses the spring. This flat spot on the spring is called the axle chair, as it's where the spring sits on the axle. Metal shims can be inserted from the back side to correct insufficient tilt or removed from the back side to lessen the tilt. Loosen the bolts holding the spring to the axle to work with shims.

Wheel camber. This is the angle of the wheel spindles to vertical. It was engineered into the positioning of the axle yokes so they would hold the spindles away from vertical. With the car's weight on the front wheels, the wheels should be about two degrees closer to each other at the bottom than at the top. On most old cars this was not adjustable. The only correction was new spindle bolts and bushings.

Once the front end is properly aligned, keep it that way with attention to tire pressure, wheel balancing and occasional checking of the nuts at the axle seat. Proper lubrication of the steering and spring shackles helps. If you have to patch a tube on a front tire, change the tube to a rear wheel, as even a patched tube can change the balance of a front wheel.

CHAPTER 10

Cooling
System

The cooling system in a water-cooled motor consists of the radiator, upper and lower hoses, fan, fan belt, water pump, water passages in the head and block, thermostat and temperature gauge. In an air-cooled motor, it consists of a large fan, possibly a fan belt, air passages and ducting, and cooling fins on the cylinders.

The purpose of either type of cooling system is to keep the motor operating at its most efficient temperature and to prevent overheating. The enemy of the water-cooled system is vibration that causes leaks and resultant loss of coolant. In cold weather, the possibility of a freeze-up is also a danger. The enemy of the air-cooled system is dirt accumulation in the air ducts and cylinder fins, preventing the air from circulating. There is no danger of freeze-up.

In a water-cooled motor, the water pump—usually located in the motor block and driven by the fan belt—circulates water. There are water passages in the motor block and cylinder head through which water is pumped. The pump forces the water up to the top of the radiator. There is a tank across the top of the radiator which allows the water to filter down through tiny tubes or water passages to a tank across the bottom of the radiator. The fan

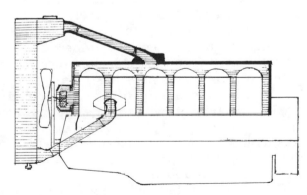

Typical cooling system. Coolant circulates in block and head, then is pumped to top of radiator where it cools as it flows through radiator and back into block. Fan draws in air through radiator and drives water pump.

draws outside air in through the radiator, cooling the water in the radiator core. An overflow pipe from the top radiator tank protects the radiator core from bursting as water is forced into the top tank faster than the core can handle it.

The water circulates back through the lower radiator hose into the engine block, where the process starts again. In addition to air drawn through the radiator core by the fan, the forward motion of the car also pushes air through the radiator core. This air escapes either through louvres or vents on the side of the hood or out the back of the engine compartment under the floor of the car.

There is usually a thermostat located in or near the upper water hose. This will stay closed until the water inside the motor's water passages has reached a predetermined temperature. It will then open and allow the water to start circulating through the radiator. Most thermostats were set between 160° and 180°. Some of the lower priced cars did not include a thermostat; more expensive cars sometimes had shutters over the front of the radiator core that were opened or closed by a thermostat.

A few manufacturers saw no necessity to provide a heat gauge or thermometer as standard equipment. Others had a gauge located at the top of the radiator filler cap: this indicated the temperature of the water in the top radiator tank, slightly hotter than the rest of the system. Other cars had a thermometer in the motor block connected to a dashboard gauge. This gave a truer reading of the cooling system. On cars where no gauge was included as standard equipment, one could be added as an accessory at additional cost.

Throughout the cooling system there are gaskets, the main one being between the engine block and cylinder head. This keeps the coolant from getting into the cylinders and down into the oil in the engine base. This gasket also keeps the coolant from getting into the valve system and eventually into the base.

Usually there's a gasket if the water pump housing is a separate casting added to the engine block. There may be gaskets where the base connections are attached to the cylinder head and motor block.

There will be clamps at each end of the hoses. Some V-type engines had two upper and two lower hoses, along with two water pumps. Other V-type engines had two outlet hoses at the top, but only one inlet hose at the bottom.

Air-cooled engines had no gaskets to contain the coolant between the cylinder head and block, since there was no coolant. In fact, most cylinders and heads are a single casting on air-cooled motors. In some cases, the cooling fins are cast on the cylinder. Others had a different metal, attached after the casting and machining process. The "radiator" is a dummy, provided to allow air to enter the engine compartment and fan area, as well as to give the appearance of a water-cooled car. There were no hoses for clamps and no water pump. The cooling fan was attached either to the front or rear of the crankshaft, or was driven by a fan belt if placed in a different location. Air was ducted to the individual cylinders, then forced through the cooling fins on the cylinders and out underneath the car. Air cooling was simple and dependable.

Checking the System   The cooling system must be clean and tight: this applies to both water- and air-cooled systems. A water-cooled system must be free of leaks.

If your test drive indicated that the car overheated, if you found signs of the coolant leaking into the oil or oil in the coolant, you'll have to check the various components. This also applies if you find any signs of the coolant leaking out of the car. You can make the following checks with no problem.

RADIATOR

You can tell if the radiator is leaking by a puddle under the front of the car, if you're sure your pup hasn't been around. If you see wet spots on the radiator core, they indicate leaks. If there are wet spots where the header or lower tanks join the middle or core sections, these too indicate leakage. If the leaks appear to be few and small, you can add an antileak compound—either powder or liquid; the directions on the label tell you just how to use them.

If the radiator seems clogged, forcing water to stream out of the overflow pipe, it'll need to be flushed out. Open the bottom petcock and run water through the radiator from a garden hose. If a reasonable amount of water will flow through the radiator without backing up, the radiator is clear. Too much pressure, and the hose may flip out drenching you and everything around. You can easily tell what amount of water to run through the hose. If the radiator is clogged, there are excellent radiator flushes on the market. Just follow the directions on the label. If flushing results in a small leak or two, use the antileak compound I mentioned.

In some cases you can "back flush" the radiator: this is sort of like an enema for the radiator and can be a messy job. To do this, you remove the filler cap. Remove the lower hose—either from the block or radiator, whichever makes it easier for you to insert the hose at the bottom. You'll have to make as nearly a watertight connection for the garden hose as possible: wrap some rags around it before inserting it in the radiator. Clamp it as tight as possible to keep the water from running back out. Turn on a moderate amount of water, forcing it up through the core and out the top. This isn't a hard job, just kind of messy.

Never, but never, try to force a wire or rod down through the radiator core to clean it out. A friend of mine who tried this ended up buying another radiator. You can run a fine flexible wire through the overflow tube, but don't try to ram it through.

Use caution with either a radiator sealing compound or radiator flushing compound: some are injurious to aluminum. Read the label very carefully and follow the manufacturer's directions. There are many fine brands on the market and they're inexpensive.

If the radiator leaks badly, you'll have to remove it and have it repaired at a radiator shop. If this is done, have it flushed at the same time. The radiator is attached at each lower side of the frame and held in position at the top by a rod or rods to the firewall. Remove the nuts holding these and you can lift the radiator up and out of the car.

FANBELT

One of the most common causes of radiator overheating is a loose or broken fan belt. The belt drives the water pump as well as the fan, so if the belt is broken, obviously you have no fan or water circulation. A belt is inexpensive; you should carry a spare one in the car at all times. If the fan belt is loose, it may not turn the water pump or fan at the required speed. It must be tight enough to turn the fan and water pump, but must not be so tight it puts pressure on the water pump pulley shaft, etc. It'll squeak if it's too tight. Check the lubrication on both the fan pulley and water pump pulley. Check the pulley on the generator, too, if the fan belt drives the generator: it did on many cars. If these are properly lubricated, you won't use excess motor power overcoming friction.

FAN

There's little that can go wrong with the fan, unless the car has had a front-end accident and the blades are bent. Bent blades can damage the radiator core and cause a vibration at moderate to high speeds. If you can see a bent blade as the fan turns with the motor idling, remove the fan and straighten the blade at your workbench. Remember that the blades are meant to be set at an angle to draw in air. Do not make them flat as you straighten. If the fan is badly bent, try to locate a new one with the same number and size blades and the same hub diameter as the original. The fan was usually held to the hub by bolts or rivets, easily removed and replaced.

Shroud can be removed from radiator to repair core. Use vacuum cleaner on blowing cycle to force dirt out of core fins. If you must paint the core, use a thin coat on outer surface only to preserve cooling capacity.

WATER PUMP

To check the operation of the water pump, remove the radiator filler cap and run the motor at idling speed. When the motor heats to operating temperature, water will swirl through the top radiator tank if the pump is working. You can usually spot a leak around the water pump housing (maybe a gasket). There may be a leak around the water pump shaft: in most older cars, the packing was a treaded string that was forced around the shaft where it entered the housing. Some cars had a washer-type packing. The string type can be repaired without removing the pump; simply force replacement packing string into the opening around the shaft. The washer type, like a faucet washer, requires that the pump be removed and the new washer pressed into place.

Probably the biggest source of water pump failure is lack of lubrication. Once you've got it operating, be sure to keep it properly lubricated to avoid future problems.

If, when you check the upper radiator tank with the motor idling, you do not see any movement of water, this indicates the pump is not circulating water. Check the fan belt first to see if it is turning the pump properly. If it is and no water circulates, you'll have to remove the pump and check the vanes or impeller. Usually the pump was a simple affair, just vanes on an impeller shaft. Sometimes the vanes will wear down or rust away. Sometimes you'll find the vanes eaten away by an additive that has been used. You should be able to buy a replacement pump, either new or used; if not, a machine shop can weld new vanes on the shaft. Be sure to lubricate the pump and use a new gasket and gasket compound when reinstalling the water pump housing. Repair kits are usually available.

RADIATOR HOSES

Worn or rotten hoses will allow water to leak, especially when under pressure. Hoses cost so little and are so easy to apply that you have no excuse for relying on an old one. If you replace a hose, take a section of the old one with you to match for proper diameter. You can measure the length if necessary, allowing enough to fit over both house mounting tubes so the clamps will fit. If the hoses are missing, measure the outside diameter of the hose mounting pipes, but remember this will be the inside diameter of the hose. Sometimes the lower hose will be a different diameter than the upper one. Use gasket cement on the hose mounting pipes, but not so much it'll get inside the cooling system. Be sure all hose clamps are tight.

THERMOSTAT

As the engine warms up, if the thermostat won't open and allow the water to circulate, it may need replacement or repair. Remove the thermostat: you may see that it just needs cleaning to remove rust accumulation. You can check its operation by placing the thermostat in a pan of water at the temperature it comes from the tap. Heat the water on your stove. As the water gets hot, you should see the spring compress and the diaphragm open. If the water boils, yet the thermostat doesn't open, throw it out and

Radiator shutters were a popular feature on many cars. The more expensive cars controlled shutters thermostatically. Others were hand controlled from dashboard, as on this Essex.

get a new one. They're inexpensive and easy to replace in the hose or head. If your car has a hot water heater or if you intend to install one, you may want to consider putting in a "hotter" thermostat. This will require a higher temperature before opening to allow water out of the block. Do not exceed the manufacturer's recommendations if you have them available.

HOT WATER HEATER

If your car is equipped with a hot water heater, it automatically becomes a part of the cooling system. As the coolant circulates, it passes through the heater core. Check the hose attachments, both on the engine side and on the heater itself. These must be leakproof. You can test the core of the heater by removing it: put a cork in one of the outlets and fill the other end with a hose or pour water in through a small funnel. Don't spill any water while doing this, at least not on the heater core. If you see a wet spot on the heater core, this indicates a leak. Better get it repaired at a radiator shop to keep from drenching the interior of your car sometime with hot water from the heater. Check where the hoses go through the firewall to be sure they're not chafed or worn thin at this point. There should be a rubber gasket protecting the hoses from the metal edge of the holes. Be sure to check the clamps on both ends of each heater hose. Make sure the heater hoses aren't crimped, restricting circulation. Attention to the electrical portion of the heater is covered in Chapter 12.

HEAT GAUGE

If your heat gauge is radiator mounted, it will require but little attention. Check to be sure the tube at the bottom of the top radiator tank is clean and that the washers are tight. Occasionally you'll need to replace the fluid in the tube. Sometimes the figures or markings on the dial face have lost their legibility and must be remarked.

If your car has a dash-mounted gauge, be sure the wires are tight at the terminals. Check where the heat plug is located in the block or head. Some of these had a string packing like water pump shafts. More string may be packed in if necessary. The screw-in type won't require anything unless there's a sign of a leak. Sometimes a bit of gasket compound on the threads will remove a leak around the heat plug. Unless the glass over the face of the dash gauge is broken or the needle is bent, you won't normally have to touch the gauge. There are places that specialize in repairing dash gauges of all types. If there's not one listed in the Yellow Pages for your town, you'll find ads giving locations in many of the motor magazines.

FREEZE-UP PLUGS

Most water-cooled motors had one or more small round plugs in the block or head, designed to be forced out by the expanding pressure of water as it froze. Sometimes these worked, more often they did not, and the freeze-up resulted in another portion of the cooling system splitting. Look for this plug, usually the size of a nickel. It may be on the side of the cylinder head or low down on the block. It must be perfectly flat and fit in the hole without any signs of a leak around it. Replacement plugs are available; if you have to put one in, be sure to clean the area in which it seats and use some gasket compound. Usually these tap into place.

SOLUTIONS

Maintenance

Once you have the cooling system on your water-cooled car in proper condition, it's a simple matter to keep it that way. Your old car may not be driven too often and you may overlook adding antifreeze at the proper time. I know one man who forgot to add antifreeze to his Rolls Royce and had an expensive repair job that could have been prevented.

It's a good idea to use a fifty–fifty solution of water and a good grade of permanent antifreeze. Occasionally, the permanent types will search out leaks that water won't find. However, the newer types also contain a sealant if they do find a tiny leak. The mixture of permanent antifreeze and water is actually a better coolant than water alone. It's a good idea to add a can of water pump lubricant for the internal parts. Normally, a rust inhibitor will be contained in the antifreeze. If not, a can of rust inhibitor may be added. Any linkage, either manual or thermostatic, to radiator shutters should be checked for tightness and easy movement. It may require a drop of oil occasionally. Be on the lookout for any pools of the coolant that may have come from the car. A check on the dipstick from time to time will assure you there's no water in the oil.

AIR-COOLED SYSTEMS

Once you're sure the air ducts and baffles that deflect the air within the ducts are clean and tight, there's little more to do. Fins around the cylinders must be clean so air can be forced through them. The joints between air ducts must be tight so there's no air loss.

You can clean the fins or air passages with a jet of air blowing from the exhaust cycle of a vacuum cleaner. If you have access to an air compressor, it's a good idea to clean these out from time to time. I got a face full of dirt one time using an air hose on a Franklin motor that hadn't been run in over ten years, so use goggles if you're bending over the engine and using a strong stream of air.

If the fan on your air-cooled motor is belt driven, be sure the belt is in good condition. Keep a spare belt in the car. You may need to lubricate the pulleys through which it passes. Make sure there are no obstructions over the intake for the air that will cool the motor. Also, make sure there is provision for the air to escape quickly and easily after it has done its cooling job.

If air can enter freely, circulate without obstruction in and around the system, and be exhausted properly, there is nothing more you need do. Just don't lose your cool by ignoring the cooling system.

CHAPTER 11

Brake System

By current standards, the brakes on many old cars are inadequate. These autos didn't have to attain or maintain today's average speeds. The slower speeds, along with far less traffic on the roads, didn't require brakes with contemporary stopping capabilities. If you're not used to driving an old car frequently, you may find yourself going faster in traffic and closer to the car ahead than you should be. It's a helluva feeling to have the car ahead stop suddenly and find yourself plowing into its rear end with your painstakingly restored beauty.

These comments apply pretty much across the boards, especially on brakes that were mechanically controlled. With hydraulic brakes, if there are no leaks in the system, you can pump the pedal for more stopping ability. With mechanical brakes, once you've hit the bottom of the pedal travel, you can only hope you'll stop in time. You may want to drag your feet or throw out an anchor, but it won't help.

Many states require an inspection of the brakes and other components in order to license the car. Whether or not this is required in your state shouldn't matter. You'll want and need the maximum stopping power the

External contracting front brake on '25 Buick shows activating arm, brake shoe guides and adjusting nuts. Tighten nuts on brake shoe guide to take up for wear.

original system can offer. Remember that the life you save (when you apply the brakes on your old car) may be your own.

If you drove the car before you bought it, you should have a good idea of how the brakes worked. Even if they seemed OK, you ought to make a complete check of the system to avoid future brake failures.

Actuated by the brake pedal, the brakes apply pressure through a series of jointed rods or cables or hydraulic pipelines to stop the car. Generally up until the mid-Twenties, cars had either two-wheel brakes or a brake that worked on the transmission. By the late Twenties, all cars had four-wheel brakes. Some were mechanically operated through cables or rods. Others were operated hydraulicly. In the Thirties, a few of the larger, more expensive cars had a vacuum booster to give added braking power.

TWO-WHEEL MECHANICAL

Inspecting Brake Systems

If your brakes are the external contracting type, the brake bands and linings are on the outside of the brake drum. Pedal pressure through rods or cables tightens the bands against the outside of the brake drum. If the brakes are the internal expanding type, pedal pressure pushes the brake shoes and lining outward against the inside of the brake drums.

A. Simple arm action activates two-wheel external contracting brake, which clamps against drum when applied. Many cars used two shoes on each wheel, coupled by pin at back.

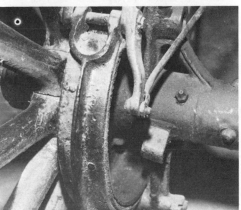

B. Detailed viewing of the mechanism.

To check the external type, remove the pins that hold the bands together at the back and disconnect the brake arms from the bands at the front of each brake shoe. If the bands show uneven wear, they can be reshaped and the linings replaced. The rivet heads on the brake linings should be at least one-sixteenth of an inch below the surface of the brake lining. Any less than that and they'll need relining.

To check internal expanding brakes, remove the wheel so you can remove the drum. On some cars, especially those with wooden wheels, the wheel may be attached directly to the drum. With the wheel and drum removed, the brake shoes and backing plate will be in plain sight. Look first for uneven wear on the lining: this can indicate warped brake shoes which must be replaced. Again check the amount of lining above the rivet heads. There should be at least one-sixteenth of an inch of lining above the rivet heads. Check the actuating arms that move the brake shoes when pedal pressure is applied. These should be secure and move freely. Check the springs that contract the shoes when pedal pressure is released. These should be clean, have adequate tension and be firmly attached.

Be sure rivet heads are evenly seated and well below surface when installing lining on brake shoes, as on these two-wheel internal expanding brake shoes.

On both internal expanding and external contracting brakes, check the brake drums. They should not have any deep scratches nor gouges in them caused by exposed rivet heads. The drums should be perfectly round.

If the brakes are cable operated, check the cable ends and any cable attachment points. It must not bind in any part and the cable must not be frayed, especially where it goes through the frame. On rod operated brakes, check the rod connections and pins to be sure they're not worn.

Check the linkage on both types of brakes from the pedal to the cross member that applies the braking force evenly to the wheels. Linkage must be secure and worn pins or bolts replaced. The rods or cables that extend from the cross member to the rear wheels are connected by pins through yokes or eye bolts. None of these should show wear, if you want the best that the system can provide. Check the shaft on which the brake pedal is mounted. The supports must be solid and the connection from pedal to shaft secure.

TRANSMISSION SERVICE

Transmission service brakes were discontinued in the mid-Twenties. With this type of brake, force is applied to a wide drum at the rear of the transmission. Pedal pressure, connected by a simple linkage, is applied to force an externally mounted band and lining to close around the drum. It slows and stops the car by action through the drive shaft, differential and axle shafts to the rear wheels.

To check this type of brake, disconnect the clamp and holding pin from the brake bands at the rear of the transmission. Usually you can do this from inside the car with the floorboards removed. This will allow you to inspect the bands to make sure they're evenly worn. If not, they must be reshaped. Also check the thickness of the lining and the distance above the rivet heads. If the lining is worn or rivet heads are near the surface, replacement is necessary. Check the linkage connecting the brake bands to the pedal. Pins in the linkage must not show wear. The mounting of the pedal on the shaft must be secure. The shaft mountings between the transmission case or clutch housing and the frame must be secure. The shaft should move freely, yet have no play in it.

FOUR WHEEL MECHANICAL

Four-wheel mechanical brakes were either rod or cable controlled. Pedal pressure was transmitted to a cross member, called the brake actuating rod, which had a connection for each of the four wheels. On some cars the rear brakes were larger than the front brakes. Others had the same size brakes on all four wheels, but applied more pressure to the rear brakes with a longer arm on the brake actuating rod. Some cars had external contracting brakes on the rear wheels and the internal expanding type on the front wheels. No matter which system your car had, you should inspect the brake linkage for worn pins or eye bolts. Be sure any springs in the system have retained their tension and are securely attached. Cables sometimes ran partially through tubes. If your car has this type of connection, be sure the cable can move freely within its protective tube.

Inspect the brake shoes, bands and linings. Any that are out of round must be reshaped or replaced. Lining that does not extend at least one-sixteenth of an inch above the rivet heads must be replaced. The actuating levers and springs within internal expanding brakes must be examined for wear. On external contracting brakes, the hinge or joint at one end of the brake band assembly must be checked for wear. Look for worn pins or springs that have lost their tension.

FOUR-WHEEL HYDRAULIC

Four-wheel hydraulic brakes comprise a simple and dependable system. Pedal pressure operates a plunger in a central cylinder or reservoir which exerts pressure on fluid-filled tubes to a cylinder in each wheel. This fluid forced opposing pistons within each wheel cylinder to push outward against the two brake shoes in each wheel. When pedal pressure was re-

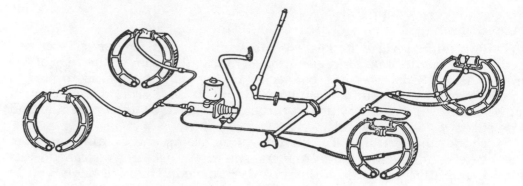

A typical hydraulic brake system: pedal activates plunger on master cylinder, sending fluid through brake lines to cylinders in each brake. Fluid forces arms in each brake cylinder to push brake shoes against drums. Springs draw shoes together when pressure is released. Hand brake operates through cables to rear shoes.

leased, strong springs between the brake shoes brought the pistons in the wheel cylinders back to their normal position. This forced the fluid back into the lines and reservoir.

In addition to checking the brake shoes and linings—as in the mechanical system—you must check the system of tubes, cylinders and plungers in the hydraulic system. Press the brake pedal down as far as it will go and hold it there. The pedal should not creep or settle as you apply pressure. If it does settle slowly, this indicates a leak somewhere in the system. It could be in the plunger attached to the brake pedal at the master cylinder; in any of the fittings and joints along the tubing; or in the individual wheel cylinders.

To search out a leak, first make sure the fluid in the master cylinder or reservoir is up to the mark indicated. Each fitting in the tubing must be checked for leaks. Cut a stick to hold the pedal down. The tubing runs from the master cylinder to a cross pipe: this tube feeds two back brakes and one front brake. A second tube usually feeds the other front brake. In some systems, one tube goes to a small holding tank and a tube runs from this to each wheel. You must check each connection in the system of tubes. Also check for any spots along the tubing which may have been damaged and would allow fluid to escape. Check the holders through which the tubes run, attaching them to the frame. You should spot any leaks in the tubing easily.

There are short flexible lines to each wheel to compensate for up and down wheel movement. These were often rubber and cracked with age, causing leakage.

Often the plunger packing in the master cylinder will have deteriorated, allowing the fluid to bypass the plunger and not forcing the fluid in the

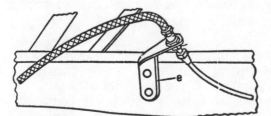

Hydraulic brake systems have flexible brake hose from end of stationary tubing to wheel cylinder. With age, these tubes sometimes developed leaks. Avoid cross-threading when installing new hoses.

tubes into the wheel cylinders. You can spot this with the filler plug removed from the cylinder or reservoir: the fluid will churn in the cylinder as you move the pedal-operated plunger.

If you see a drop in the fluid level after filling the reservoir and operating the brakes several times, you know there's a leak. If it's not in the master cylinder nor in the lines, it has to be at one or more of the wheel cylinders. You'll have to remove the brake drum on each wheel to inspect these, though you may see evidence of fluid leaks around the bottom of the brake backing plate if the leak is severe enough.

If the pedal can be pushed to the floor with some effort but the brakes don't hold, it indicates there's air in the brake tube lines, caused by fluid that has leaked out. If the pedal cannot be pushed to the floor and the brakes don't hold, it indicates there is grease or oil on the brake linings which must be removed.

Brake adjustments are simple, so don't let the thought of rebuilding the brake system throw you. Directions are given by type of brake system.

Adjustment and Repair

TWO-WHEEL MECHANICAL

To adjust external contracting brakes, jack up each wheel so you can spin it easily. The two brake bands on each wheel were secured at both ends. The holding mechanism at the back contained one, in some cases two, bolts. When the nuts on these bolts were tightened, they drew the ends of the two brake bands closer to each other. On the front a bolt(s) with a lock nut could be tightened so the bands would have less distance to travel when pedal pressure is applied. The object in adjusting this type of brake is to get the bands as close to the drums as possible without causing any dragging when the brake is released. The clamping action of the band against the drum, actuated by the short brake arm, is the only adjustment at each wheel. The spring that spreads the bands when the pressure is released should be cleaned and oiled so the components work correctly.

If, when you examined the bands, you found excessive lining wear in one or more spots, this indicates the band is out of round. A simple way to correct this is to place a large screwdriver between the drum and band at the low spot. With this in place, push the brake pedal hard a few times. This should reshape the band. The thickness of what you put between the drum and band determines the degree to which you'll change the band's contour.

On mechanically operated brakes, the rods or cables connecting each brake with the brake actuating rod also had provisions for adjustment. Loosen the lock nut holding the yoke or eyebolt in position and screw the end further into the rod or cable end. This shortens the rod or cable and gives more leverage. When doing this, get each side exactly the same length to avoid unequal brake pressure which can cause skids. On some cars the rod connecting the pedal to the brake actuating rod had a similar adjustment. You may want to take up on this too.

When adjusting brakes and shortening rods and cables, be sure that all pins are in securely, lock nuts tightened and any cotter pins solidly spread. Remember, terrific pressure is built up on the rods or cables and connections can snap. So don't make the mistake of trying to force rods or cables to do the job the brake linings should do.

Cables controlling mechanical brakes often stretched during years of service. If there isn't sufficient adjustment left in the original provision, don't think all is lost. Auto supply stores sell cable tighteners: these are made to fit on the existing cables. By attaching and tightening these little devices, you can force a permanent shortening of the cable. These are inexpensive and easy to use: be sure you take up the same amount on each cable for equal braking pressure. It sure beats buying new brake cables, if the original cable is basically sound.

To adjust internal expanding brakes, jack up each wheel so you can spin it easily. There were usually two brake shoe pivot bolts on each wheel. These move a cam which regulates the position of the brake shoes to the brake drum. Turn the pivot bolts counterclockwise to push the brake shoes toward the drum. To move the shoes away from the drum, turn clockwise. Adjust each wheel by turning these pivot bolts until the shoe binds against the drum. Turn the bolt back one quarter turn. You can usually feel the ratchet motion of the cam as you do this. This releases the pressure of the brake shoe against the drum. Do this on each wheel. Usually these pivot bolts are self-locking and will hold their position. If not, a jam nut was provided to be tightened against the pivot bolt. Strong springs contract the brake shoes when the pedal pressure is released.

Adjustments to brake linkage, whether rods or cables, follow the same procedure as for external contracting brakes. You must remember to equalize all adjustments. Also keep in mind the terrific pressure put on shortened cables or rods. I've had the yoke connections on Model A Ford brake rods snap when I made the rod too short. You can't make the rods do the job the brake lining is designed to do.

INSTALLATION OF NEW BRAKES

It's usually easier for the beginner–restorer to remove the brake shoes and take them to a place that specializes in relining. However, if for some reason you want to do this yourself, don't hesitate. Before you start, be sure that replacement linings for the brake shoes or bands are available.

When installing brake linings, it's usually easier for the beginner to do one wheel at a time. This gives you an assembled brake as a guide in case you forget the order in which you removed the parts.

On external contracting brakes, remove the brake bands by disconnecting the brake rod or cable connection at the front. Disconnect the holding device at the back so there's nothing holding either top or bottom band

You may find brake linings that are rotten and unevenly worn. Remove old lining and thoroughly clean shoes before attaching new linings. File down any high spots before installing new linings. Set rivets squarely to get proper holding.

together. This will relieve pressure at the front and the bands should be disconnected from the clamping device. Usually a cotter pin will hold a castellated nut on the bolt holding each band to the clamping mechanism. Each band should pull away from the drum easily. In some cases, there may be guides around the circumference of the bands to keep them from moving sideways. If so, remove these to free the bands.

It's best to work on the bands at a workbench. Remove the old linings and clean the bands thoroughly with your wire-bristled brush to remove any grime or scale. The new linings fit inside the bands and replacements must be the same specifications as the original. Rivets must be countersunk so they're absolutely tight and even. A handy hand rivet tool makes this job easy. They don't cost much and you should be able to borrow or rent one for the short time you'll need it. As a suggestion, rivet the lining on both ends of the brake band, then work toward the center. Use a small punch to line up the rivet holes in lining and brake band. You may need to file off any high spots on the ends of the lining when reassembling.

Once the new bands are on all wheels, you may find some high spots that will wear off as the wheels turn a few miles. You'll have to make a take-up adjustment to compensate for these high spots after the car has been driven awhile.

When installing relined bands, make sure each part is replaced in proper position: this is why it's a good idea to have an assembled brake as a guide. Clean and lightly oil all moving parts. Be careful not to get any grease or oil on either the drums or linings. Adjust the new bands to the point where you can't turn the wheel, even before you apply pedal pressure. Then back the bands off to where the wheel will turn, yet the lining doesn't drag. Any high spots should show up in this operation.

When operating the car, you can tell if a brake is dragging because of too tight an adjustment or high spots in new linings, by feeling the brake drum. It should be warm, but not hot.

When installing new linings on internal expanding brakes, you have to remove the brake drums to get at the brake shoes. Usually you must remove wheel and drum as a unit on wooden wheels. To allow the brake drum to come off, back off the pivot adjusting nuts so each shoe is as far away from the brake drum as possible. Remove the springs that connect the shoes. Brake shoes are usually held in place by a pin. Remove the cotter pin holding washers and the shoe will slide off over the pin or the pin will pull out.

If this is your first brake job, it's wise to do one wheel at a time in case you need a completed brake as a pattern when starting reassembly.

You can reline the brake shoes yourself or take them to a shop that specializes in relining. If you want to do the job yourself, be sure the replacement lining is to original specifications. If you fit new linings yourself and they aren't already preshaped, fit the ground surface next to the brake shoe. Rivet each lining, starting at the ends and working toward the middle. Get each rivet tight and flat. Buff off any high spots on either end of the lining with a file. Be sure to keep grease or oil off the linings and drums. A little graphite or light oil on the springs, pivot bolts and ratchets is a good idea before reassembling the brake.

It costs very little and is a good idea to have a brake or machine shop put the brake drums on their lathe to be sure they're not warped or worn out of round, as sometimes happens. This is something you can't do yourself.

When you've put each brake shoe back in place and secured the springs and pins, back the pivot bolt all the way back so the drum will slide over the shoes easily. With the drum properly secured, turn the pivot bolt counterclockwise to force the new linings against the drums. Tighten them till you can't turn the wheel, then back them off to where the wheel will turn and the linings do not drag. You'll need to make an adjustment to compensate for high spots on the linings after you've driven the car a few miles.

To reline a transmission service brake, first locate the correct brake lining. In some cases you may need to take the old bands with you when seeking replacement linings. If the new linings are without holes, most places selling linings will punch holes for you. This is far easier than attempting it yourself.

The relatively small braking area of the transmission service brake has to do the job of stopping your car, so it's essential that it be in top operating condition. If you find you have a choice in the quality of replacement linings available, always take the best quality lining.

Removal of the bands requires that you disconnect the brake linkage at the connection with the bands. You may need to remove some guides around the circumference of the band that keep it in place. The brake mechanism is similar to that of any external contracting type of brake. The two bands force the lining against the drum in a clamping action.

Disconnect the pins at the hinged end of the bands. There may be springs at this end that must be removed now. With the hinged end disconnected, the pressure will be relieved from the clamping mechanism. The pins and springs that comprise the caliper can be easily removed. Give a little thought to the arrangement of the pins, washers, springs, etc., as you won't have an assembled brake as a guide. You may want to make a simple sketch showing the relationship of the various parts. Lift off the old bands and plan on doing the relining on your workbench.

When installing new linings, try not to force the bands out of shape. Start riveting from each end and work toward the middle. Get each rivet flat and tight. Buff off any high spots at the ends of the linings.

When reassembling, be sure the parts are clean and free of grease and oil. Any guides or holding brackets should be cleaned; springs that release the band pressure should be cleaned and lightly lubricated. If springs appear weak, a washer at one or both ends should help restore any lost tension. Back the adjusting nuts all the way back, so the bands will be as loose as possible when first in place. Tighten them till they bind, then back off just enough so the drum can rotate freely. Lock this adjustment in place. Tighten the hinge end so it will flex but have no play in it; be sure all washers, lock nuts and cotter pins in the claming caliper are in place. Like any other brake, this will require an adjustment after a few miles of driving to remove any high spots on the lining.

If the bands appeared to be out of round or if you made them out of round while installing the new linings, you can restore them to shape quite easily. Place a thin screwdriver or rod in the area between the drum and brake lining. Apply the brake a time or two to change the crimp in the band. A slight tap with a hammer while doing this may help. Do not hit with any force, as you might cause more damage than good.

With the new bands and lining in place, check the connecting linkage, making any take-up adjustments you feel necessary. You must remember that the braking action should come from the new linings, not from increased leverage by shortened connections.

FRONT WHEEL BRAKES

Essentially the same methods are used to install front brakes as rear brakes. There are slightly different procedures for removing front brake drums. Usually you have to remove the cotter pin, axle nut, washer, retaining rings and bearings on the front hub to remove the brake shoe. This isn't a tough job, but you should note the order in which you remove the parts. Also, when reassembling these parts, you must take care to repack the front wheel bearings just tightly enough to remove side-to-side movement, as well as up-and-down movement. Don't tighten the nut holding the bearing in place until the bearing binds.

The rods or cables connecting the front brakes to the brake actuating shaft have take-up adjustments, just like you found on the rear ones. Each must be taken up an equal amount to prevent one brake from grabbing before the other. Because of the extra space allowance required to turn the front wheels, the actuating shaft on each front wheel extends farther out than on the back wheels. This length puts extra strain on the shaft, so you must not place additional stress on it by shortening the rods or cables to any great degree. Make the linings stop the car, not the brake linkage.

First, secure a brake and master cylinder repair kit before starting to work on a hydraulic system. If you can't locate one, you can disassemble the parts and take them to an automotive supply store, where they can undoubtedly be matched up with similar parts. Hydraulic systems were the same on many cars: you should have no difficulty obtaining replacements, even though they may come to you under another car's name.

Start with the master cylinder. This is located close to the bottom of the brake pedal. Disconnect the linkage to the pedal. Also disconnect the fitting that connects the tubing to the cylinder. The brake cylinder is normally bolted to the frame or cross member and can be easily removed after taking out the holding bolts. It's not absolutely necessary to remove the master cylinder to repair it: this will depend upon the amount of room you have for your hands while working. On some cars, you'll notice a separate reservoir for the brake fluid. If you plan to remove the master cylinder, remove the fitting connecting the reservoir to it. Some cars had the reservoir made as a part of the master cylinder. There's no difference in the repair procedures, either way.

Assuming you removed the master cylinder, work on it at your workbench or a table. Disassemble the cylinder carefully, noting how it was put together. The piston within the cylinder may have a rubber ring or a seal: this must be a tight fit so the fluid won't bypass the piston. The replacement is installed by removing the nut and washer that hold the seal to the piston. When activated, the piston pushed the fluid against a spring-loaded piston cup. There is an inlet port between the piston and the piston cup that lets the fluid in from the reservoir. It must be clean and free of obstructions so the fluid can pass through it easily. The piston cup has a rubber ring or seal. This is replaced by removing the holding nut and washer. The action of the piston, pushing against the spring-loaded cup, forces the fluid

Hydraulic Brake System

through an outlet check valve to the tubes leading to the brakes. There is also an inlet check valve at the same end of the cylinder. Both must be clean, so there's nothing obstructing the fluid as it moves in and out of the cylinder. The spring seldom requires other than cleaning. When you've cleaned every part and opening and replaced the rubber seals, the cylinder can be reassembled. Clean out the reservoir, whether attached or as a separate unit. Don't use any rags that might leave strings, lint or threads in the cylinder. Don't refill the unit at this time, but attach it back into place in the car. Reconnect the pedal linkage.

Check each fitting on the tubes; if a fitting shows no sign of having leaked, there's nothing you need do to it. While tracing the lines, it's wise to check the little clips or fastenings that can vibrate or chafe the tubes. These can eventually cause a leak and consequent brake failure. If any of these are missing, you can easily make a replacement out of light metal. If you make a replacement clip, it's wise to insulate it from the tube by wrapping the adjoining portion of the tube with rubber or plastic tape.

Pay special attention to the short flexible lines that lead to the wheels. If there's any sign of cracking or deterioration, they should be replaced.

When threading connections together on hydraulic lines, take care not to get them cross threaded. This can happen easily and will make a fitting that is bound to leak eventually.

Each brake line leads to a wheel cylinder, bolted to the brake backing plate. To remove the cylinder for inspection and repair, disconnect the springs holding the brake shoes together. In some cases, you'll have to remove the pivot pins on the opposite end of the brake shoes. Disconnect the arms, or shafts, that extend from the wheel cylinder to the brake shoes, leaving the arms as a part of the wheel cylinder. Take off the wheel cylinder and arms that extend from it as a unit.

On your workbench or at a table, disassemble the cylinder by removing the rubber cups at each end. There shouldn't be more than a teaspoonful of liquid in the cylinder, if there's any at all. You'll find rubber seals or washers on each of the two pistons; these can be replaced by removing the holding nut and washer. Clean the cylinder thoroughly, being sure there's no lint left from your cleaning rag. The small threaded plug at the top of the cylinder should be removed for cleaning, then replaced and tightened.

When reassembling, be sure the piston can move freely and that the rubber cup is firmly attached. The securing bolts must be tight against the backing plate and the tubing joint tight. Don't use shellac or gasket compound on any brake line fitting; you must make them tight without these liquids.

The remaining item to check, after reworking the master cylinder and the wheel cylinders, is the linkage between the pedal and the master cylinder. Location of the provision for adjustment may vary, depending upon the make of car. Usually there was an eye bolt on at least one end of the rod. Check the pins for wear, replacing them if necessary. There must be about a half inch of movement in the pedal before the connecting lever engages with the piston in the master cylinder: this is necessary to ensure that the piston moves enough to uncover the small port from the fluid reservoir. If this port is clogged, the brake fluid will have no way of getting back into the reservoir from the pipelines. The fluid will expand because of the heat generated in use. Pressure can be built up which will apply the brakes.

When you release the brake pedal, the fluid will be trapped in the system. The next brake application tries to push more fluid, with no release back into the reservoir. This causes "brake lock" and you'll have to "bleed" one brake to release the pressure and open this tiny clogged port.

FILLING THE SYSTEM

There's no problem in refilling a hydraulic system, but it does take a little time and patience. First, be sure to get a high-grade brake fluid. If you know the brand recommended for your car, use that. In any case, since so little fluid is required, don't try to save a few cents on bargain fluid. Remove the filler plug or cap in the cylinder or reservoir and fill the reservoir to the line or mark indicated.

Your objective is to completely fill the master cylinder, brake lines and wheel cylinders with brake fluid. All air must be driven out of the system. The hydraulic brake system will not work with air in the lines. Air is compressible, while brake fluid is not. If there is air in the lines when a pedal is pressed, the air simply compresses and does not force the fluid to do its job.

Open, but do not remove, the bleeder valves on the wheel cylinder on all four wheels. There may be threaded caps over these valves. Pump the brake pedal a time or two until fluid squirts out all four valves; then close three of the valves. Add fluid to the reservoir to replace that which filled the lines and squirted out. Have someone press the brake pedal while you attend to the wheel on which you left the bleeder valve open. As the fluid is squirting out, close the valve tightly. This is called "bleeding" the lines. There will be no air in the line or cylinder at that wheel: do the same on each of the other wheels. Halfway along, check the fluid level in the reservoir and add some if necessary. When all four wheels have been "bled" and the bleeder valves tightly closed, there will be no air in the system.

Make a last inspection of the fluid level in the reservoir and replace the cap or plug. Make sure the vent in the reservoir is clear. It's wise to make one last check of the system by holding the brake pedal down and making sure it doesn't creep slowly toward the floor. If the system is tight, once you've pressed the pedal down as far as it will go, it should stay there and not creep down farther. If it does, you've got a fluid leak and you'll need to check all the connections in the system. Once properly repaired, the hydraulic system requires little attention. Check the fluid level occasionally, depending upon usage. As long as the pedal doesn't "creep," you've got no problems.

REPLACING LININGS

To install a set of linings on hydraulic brakes, the procedure is essentially the same as for mechanical internal expanding brakes. Remove the brake drum, exposing the backing plate on which the brake mechanism is mounted. Remove both the pins holding the shoe to the backing plate and the springs connecting the shoes. On some cars the piston arms extending from the wheel cylinder will be attached to the brake shoes; on other cars, these simply fitted into a slot in the shoes. Mark each brake shoe with a pencil so you can put it back into its original position.

If you're going to replace the lining yourself, drive out the old rivets. Clean the surface of the shoe and remove any trace of the old lining. Do not file the shoe or do anything to alter its shape. When installing the new lining, if it is not already preshaped the ground surface must fit next to the shoe. Rivet each end and work toward the middle. Rivets must be countersunk below the surface. The head must seat firmly before you crimp the other end. File off any high spots on the leading or trailing edge of the lining and any visible high spots.

Before replacing the shoes, clean any grime or dirt from the backing plate. Check around the hydraulic wheel cylinder to see if there are signs of fluid having leaked. Do not press the brake pedal while you have the brake shoes and connecting springs removed. This can make the brake fluid force pistons out of the wheel cylinder, causing loss of fluid and letting air into the system.

Wipe a light oil or graphite on the springs and pins before reassembling. Take care not to get oil or grease on the linings or inside the drums. As with mechanical brakes, it's wise to get the drums checked for roundness at a brake repair or machine shop. It costs very little and is well worth the money.

With the new shoes in place and pins, washers and springs all replaced, turn the pivot adjusting nut clockwise all the way. This will draw the brake shoes in toward the hub and prevent jamming or forcing the drums over the shoes. The drum should fit easily over the new linings if you got the proper size and installed them properly. With the drums secured in place, tighten the pivot bolts counterclockwise until the wheel binds. Then back it off just enough so there's no binding as the wheel turns. This should give you plenty of braking surface. After driving the car a few miles, you will need to readjust the brakes to take up for any high spots on the linings.

Emergency Brakes   While rebuilding the service brakes, you should include a thorough check on the emergency or hand brake. You should have some idea of this brake's efficiency from your initial test drive.

There are two basic types of emergency brakes and some variations within these types. All are mechanically operated; none are complicated.

The most popular brake system works on a drum attached to the end of the transmission, just ahead of the universal joint. When applied, it holds the rear wheels, acting through the drive shaft, differential and axle shafts.

The other type of brake operates on the rear wheels. It may be operated by cables or by rods. Some operate on external contracting bands on the same drums as the service brakes. Others operate on internal expanding shoes against a separate brake drum. Some cars utilize the regular rear service brake shoes, but have a separate linkage for the hand brake. In the latter case, some apply only one shoe on each rear wheel, while others apply both shoes on each rear wheel.

Regardless of which type your car has, you can check the lining and linkage. Check the lining first, as it's the lining that should do the braking.

Transmission Hand Brake. Remove the wing nut or holding pin at the movable end of the band. There may be a pin in the joint or a hinge on the opposite side that holds the two bands together. Remove the brake link connection, cap screw or pin. This will allow you to lift off the bands, if yours is the two-band type. If it's the one-band type, you can easily pry it off with a screwdriver.

Check the lining for thickness and even wear. If the lining is worn or any rivet head is exposed, it should be replaced. If the lining shows uneven wear, indicating out of round bands, the bands should be made round before reassembly.

If the linings are OK, and don't need replacement, they can usually be adjusted or taken up by a wing nut or clamp. This should be tightened so that it does not cause friction when the drum turns, but holds firm when the hand lever is in the vertical position. There are also take-up provisions in the brake linkage; the rods are threaded so the linkage can be shortened. If the brake bands were out of round, yet without appreciable wear on the lining, this can usually be corrected by inserting a screwdriver or rod under the spot closest to the drum and applying the brake firmly a few times. Occasionally a light tapping with a hammer during this operation will help. In some cases, it may be necessary to reform the bands over a similarly sized drum where you can pound it to shape.

External Contracting Emergency Brakes. By disconnecting the brake linkage from the bands you can give these a thorough inspection. Remove the wing nut or pin and any rear pin or holding device. Disconnect the release spring. If this appears complicated, leave the other wheel as it is so you'll have an assembled one as a guide. You can lift the bands off for inspection. There should be at least one-eighth of an inch of lining above the rivet heads. If there is any less or if the bands show uneven wear, they should be replaced.

Adjust rear external contracting bands by tightening the wing nut or bolt in the clamping mechanism to bring the bands closer to the drum. They should not drag when the brake is released, but should hold firm when the hand lever is in the vertical position. Do not get oil nor grease on the drums or linings. You should, however, lubricate the clamping mechanism, pin or hinge and any release springs and connections with a light oil.

Check the take-up provision on the ends of the cables or rods. Usually there will be threaded eye bolts with lock pins. Be sure the pins aren't worn and the cotter pins are properly installed. Check the connections at the bottom of the brake lever. Usually there is a ratcheted or notched arc at the bottom and the brake lever usually operates over or through this arc. A notched or pointed rod holds the lever in position. This rod may extend down through the hand brake lever and it releases the lever from the notched arc when pressed. A few drops of oil on the top of the release button may be helpful if it's slow to move. On some cars, the rod is outside the brake lever and there is a squeeze-type handle at the top. In either case, you must be sure this rod seats firmly in the notches and that the release spring is firmly in place and has retained its tension. Make sure the notches are cleaned out. Also be sure the bolts or brackets holding the lever mechanism to the frame or transmission are tight. Because of the leverage in this type of brake, everything in the linkage must be tight and strong.

Internal Expanding Emergency Brakes. You must see the lining to adjust these. This requires removing the drum as previously explained. There should be at least one-eighth inch of lining above the rivet heads if you're to make any adjustments. If the shoes shoe uneven wear, the lining must be replaced and the drums checked for roundness.

If, while reading the previous material on internal expanding brakes, you wondered how a brake drum could get out of round, it's because of the hand brake operating on the same drums as the service brakes. If the drum is hot and the hand brake set firmly, in time the drum can warp.

If your car has the system which uses one or both of the service brake shoes for hand brake application, you've already made the adjustment at the wheel when you adjusted the foot brakes. Any additional adjustment must come through the hand brake linkage. Check for wear in connections and joints. Check the lever and attachments holding it to the frame or transmission case. Remember that in this, as in all braking systems, the braking force should come from the linings, not from extra pressure on the linkage.

If yours is the internal expanding system that operates against a separate drum, you'll find this drum attached to, or part of, the main brake drum. Remove the brake actuating arm, and disconnect the brake rod or cable. Back-off any adjusting nuts and remove the cover plate bolts. This will expose the brake shoes. Disconnect the holding pins and springs; the shoes should lift out. There must be at least one-eighth of an inch of lining over the rivet heads. Check for uneven wear.

If there is sufficient lining, you can adjust the brake shoes like any other internal expanding brake. Turn the adjusting nut till the wheel holds firm, then back it off just enough to allow the wheel to move without binding. Lock the adjusting nut to hold the shoes in position. Do this on each wheel before working on the linkage.

To sum up the important points in emergency or hand brake adjustments: be sure there's adequate lining; tight, but freely moving linkage; equal linkage to each wheel; clean, firmly mounted brake lever; and a freely moving ratcheted release mechanism.

CHAPTER 12

Electrical System

The electrical system isn't hard for a beginner to understand if you'll take a little time to learn a few simple facts about electricity. Your first look at the car's electrical diagram—if you're lucky enough to have one—could blow your mind. Once you learn the fundamentals, however, things fall into place. The system becomes quite simple. In fact, its simplicity is shocking, if you don't watch out!

It's a simple truth that in older cars insulation on wires and cables wasn't what we're used to today. Over the years, insulation became oil soaked or brittle, cracked and frayed. Short circuits resulted. Sometimes fires were the end result.

You'll need to make a careful inspection of the electrical system. In order to do this properly, a basic knowledge of electrical principles is essential. You should also have a copy of your car's electrical system for reference. If you don't already have one, they're easily obtained. Ads in old car magazines tell how to get a copy for a couple of bucks or less.

Inspecting Circuitry

Just remember these basics: electric current will flow through metal if it's forced to. In a car, the force comes from the battery. Force is measured in *volts*. Most old cars had six-volt systems; only a few had twelve-volt systems. The amount of current in motion is measured in *amperes:* a gauge on the dashboard indicates this amount. How much current moves is dependent upon the voltage or force. Resistance to this movement is measured in *ohms*. Now, wasn't that simple?

Your car's electrical system is a series of circuits. A circuit is simply a route of wires that the current travels through to perform certain duties, including operation of the starter, horn and headlights.

In order for electric current to perform these duties, as well as others, it must have a complete route or circuit. It must start from the battery, lead to whatever it's to operate, and return to the battery. The earliest electrical systems did just that. Shortly, however, someone had the idea to ground one terminal of the battery to the frame of the car. From then on, each circuit

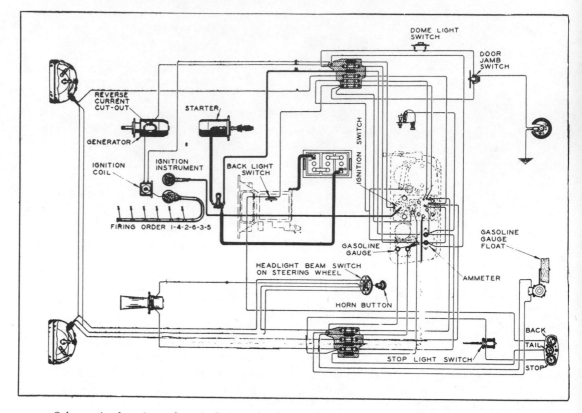

Schematic drawing of typical six-volt electrical system. Note heavy (low resistance) cables from battery to starter, through starter switch and heavy battery ground. Some cars use only one fuse panel.

was grounded, or completed, when it reached its destination. This simplified the system.

STORAGE BATTERY

Technically, the battery is called a *storage battery*. It is a storage reservoir for chemical energy. This energy becomes electric current when a circuit is completed. The battery has a positive and a negative post. Depending upon the make of the car, one of these posts will be grounded—or connected to the frame. The other post becomes the power outlet. Positive posts are marked with a plus symbol, negative posts with a minus symbol. The positive post is the larger of the two. If the negative post of the battery is grounded, the negative pole of the generator will be grounded too.

So that there will be a continuing source of energy, a generator was added to the circuit and is driven by the engine when it's in operation. The generator replaces into the battery the current used for various electrical operations.

CIRCUITRY COMPONENTS

Resistance cuts the amount of current to fit the requirements of its intended operation. It doesn't take as much current to light the headlights as it does to operate the starter. The smaller the wire through which the current travels, the higher the resistance to the movement of the current. So headlight wires, for instance, are smaller than the large wire or cable leading to the starter. Also, current tends to lose power proportionate to the distance it has to travel. For this reason, you'll usually find the battery located fairly close to the starter motor.

Considering a circuit as a route of wire through which current travels, there has to be some means of stopping this travel when necessary. Technically, a switch is a circuit breaker. There will be several switches in your car, each connecting or disconnecting a circuit at your command.

The route of most circuitry is from the battery through the ammeter gauge to the switch, then on to its destination (horn, headlights, etc.) before being grounded to the frame.

To protect the individual circuits, fuses are added. These are thin pieces of metal enclosed in glass. They're inserted at certain locations along each circuit to protect the circuitry. If current exceeds the correct amount, it will melt the metal in the glass tube. This is commonly called "a blown fuse."

GENERATOR

As stated, the purpose of the generator is to put back into the battery the electric current or energy that has been used by operation of the various electric circuits. The generator is contained in a round steel housing, about six inches in diameter and up to ten inches long. It's operated mechanically by the engine. Some cars operated the generator via a pulley on the fan belt, others by a gear operating on the timing chain from the crankshaft. Dodge cars—before joining the Chrysler Corporation—combined the generator and starter into one device: as it turned one direction, it became a starter; rotating in the opposite direction, it became the generator.

The generator is made up of wire coil. The *armature* is the part that rotates

Remove generator from mounting bracket on engine for repair. Nut holds pulley on shaft; cutout is held in place by screws. Movable brush adjusts to change charging rate.

Remove armature by disassembling case. Be careful not to break any insulation on wires. Oil shaft only through slot so you won't cause any shorts.

within other wire coils called the *field*. Three brushes, or contacts, ride on the rotating armature. One brush delivers electric current into the circuit to the battery. A second brush is grounded the same way as the ground terminal of the battery. The third brush is movable to regulate the amount of current or amperage sent to the battery. In operation, current flowing through a coil has a magnetic effect. Coils rotating through this magnetic field produce electric current.

To keep the generator from drawing power from the battery at slow driving speeds, a "cut-out" or *reverse current relay* is located in a small housing on top of the generator. It's an automatic contact switch. The contact remains open until the generator is running fast enough to charge the battery. This is usually between five and ten miles per hour, without the lights on. At this point, a voltage coil magnet closes the previously open contact, then the generator begins to send current to the battery. This circuit goes through the ammeter gauge and will show as a charge on this gauge.

STARTER

The starter motor is located in a round steel housing about the same size as the generator. It drives against a toothed ring on the flywheel. (The starter drive mechanism is explained in detail later.) The circuit from the battery to the starter motor is different from the other circuitry: because the starter motor requires a lot of current, the wire from the battery to the starter has to be of low resistance. This means very thick, comparatively short, heavily insulated. On some cars the contact, or closing of the starter motor circuit, is direct, by means of a pedal. On other cars, where the starter motor is at a distance that won't permit direct closing of the starter motor circuit, a separate circuit is provided. This contains a solenoid or electromagnetic switch that closes the starter circuit. In either case, the circuit goes through the ignition switch to control the firing of the sparkplugs. In most cars the starter motor can be operated to turn the motor over without the ignition being turned on; in this case, of course, the engine won't start. A fuse in the circuit prevents overloading.

FUSE PANELS

To protect each circuit, there's a fuse. These could be located almost any place in the circuit, theoretically; but for simplicity, most fuses are located on a *fuse block* or *fuse panel*. This may be positioned on the engine side of the firewall or inside the car behind the dashboard. Some fuse panels have a cover over them for protection of the delicate glass fuses. Since the circuits vary in the amount of current they carry, fuses vary in capacity. Arranging all circuits so fuses can be in one location makes wiring diagrams appear overly complicated. In some cases, there are *main fuses* that control several circuits, each with its own fuse. These main fuses have a higher current capacity than the other circuits they control. One of the main causes of fire in old cars is insertion of a higher capacity fuse to correct a blown fuse problem. This higher capacity fuse allows more current to pass through the circuit wire than it can handle: this results in overheating and possibly fire. So never replace a blown fuse with a higher capacity fuse to correct a problem.

SWITCHES

Switches are circuit breakers: when open they break or stop the flow of current; when closed or on, they allow current to flow through the circuit. Some switches control more than one circuit. In most instances, switches are located after the circuit passes through the ammeter gauge: this shows the amount of current the circuit draws when the switch is on. However, there are some switches on circuits that do not go through the ammeter gauge. In these instances, the gauge doesn't show the current used. The starter switch is an example—it uses a lot of current, but for a short time. The ignition switch is usually operated by a key for protection against car theft. If it is not key operated, there usually is a main switch which is key operated (this takes its place in protecting against car theft). Circuits in some cars operate aside from the circuit controlled by the ignition switch. These are for operations that the driver may want without the motor running: horn, parking lights, dashboard and starter motor can be examples of this circuitry.

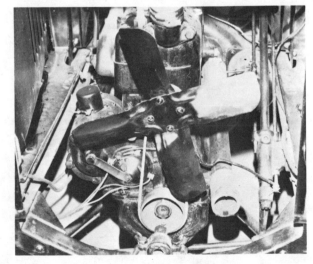

Model Ts had a magneto to furnish spark, as did some foreign cars. Generator as mounted on this '25 T was added late in model production run. Note that it is not belt driven.

MAGNETO

Some old cars had a magneto circuit. A magneto is self-sufficient and doesn't require current from a battery. The magneto generates its own current. It's different from other circuits in that if grounded, it stops producing current. Therefore the switch on a magneto grounds, or ungrounds it, to control the ignition. Some cars used a battery only to activate the starter and depended upon a magneto to provide current for the motor's operation after ignition. The Model T Ford is an example.

IGNITION SYSTEM CIRCUIT

An ignition system circuit operates to distribute electrical current from the battery through the ignition switch to the coil, on to the distributor and condenser, and then to the sparkplugs. At the sparkplugs, the current ignites the combustible mixture of air and gasoline in the cylinders. Each part of this circuit is very important and plays a separate role in the ignition operation. Let's consider them individually.

GM mounted the distributor low on the block on valve-in-head engines. Vacuum control advanced or retarded spark. Clips release distributor cap for inspection of points.

With the ignition switch on (in the closed position) the circuit is completed. Current flows through high tension wire from the center of the coil to the center of the distributor. Coils vary in appearance and location: the most common type is round, about the size of a small beer can. It may be located on the firewall or on a bracket over the motor. Some are square and are attached to the distributor. There is a high tension wire plus two low-resistance terminals.

Coil is mounted either on firewall or on the cylinder head near distributor. If manually controlled, a cable or rod moved distributor to advance or retard spark.

The current coming from the coil to the distributor makes contact with the rotor, which turns in a complete circle. There is a contact point for each cylinder. A high tension wire carries the current from the distributor to the sparkplug in each cylinder. The rotor in the distributor sits on top of a shaft which is timed with breaker points. The breaker points operate from a cam or high point on that shaft. The engine is designed and assembled so that the rotor on the distributor shaft delivers the electric current passed through when the breaker points open and close for one cylinder at a time. This corresponds to the time when the piston within that cylinder is at the top of its compression stroke. The sparkplug ignites the air–gas mixture, forcing the piston down. The cycle starts over again in another cylinder.

In the ignition system, the coil builds up the tension of the current from the battery and sends it to the distributor. The condenser holds or stores the electrical charge constant till needed. The rotor cap in the distributor closes the circuit to each cylinder, depending upon the firing order of the cylinders. Breaker points within the distributor open and close in conjunction with the rotor, admitting current to the rotor at the proper time. High tension wires carry the current to the sparkplug. When the current hits the sparkplug, it "jumps" from the electrode in the center through an air gap to another electrode connected to the side of the plug. This jump is a spark that ignites the air–gas mixture.

Look for cracks or chips in distributor head and for worn points in distributor. Be sure wires to plugs and coil have proper connections to make contact.

Electrical Circuit Inspection

Ordinarily you won't have to check all the electrical circuits in your car. However, it's a wise precaution to inspect the wires, giving special attention to the insulation. Some small cracks or bare spots can be repaired with plastic or rubber tape. However, if the insulation is badly oil soaked, cracked or frayed, you'd better replace the worn wires. Unfortunately, the risk of a fire is the alternative. In many instances, you can substitute a new piece of wire for a worn one. There are handy pinch-on terminals now available so you won't have to bother soldering terminals on wires.

It will be very handy in running down shorts and open circuits if you either buy or make a test lamp. This is simply a well insulated car bulb and socket with two lengths of insulated wire connected to it. A clip should be crimped to the end of each wire for testing purposes. Unless this is heavily insulated, don't use it while the engine is running, or you'll get one helluva shock. There can be no shock when the engine isn't running. This is a good time to mention that no matter how stiff a jolt you get from the car's electrical system, it isn't the kind of electric shock which can electrocute you.

TROUBLE SHOOTING

If a circuit, such as a headlight, horn, etc., is inoperative, first check the device itself. It may be a burned-out bulb or horn motor that needs attention. However, if the device seems OK, then look at the fuse. If the fuse is blown, insert a new one of proper size. Try to operate the device with the new fuse. If the new fuse blows, then you must inspect the circuit. The first check is to see if the circuit is grounded properly. Sometimes rust and corrosion had a habit of interrupting the grounding of a circuit. Check to see if the circuit is broken or grounded ahead of the device. This means tracing the appropriate wire from beginning to end. If the wire runs along the frame or other metal, be sure there are no bare spots in the insulation. If it goes through any metal panel or hole in the frame, be sure insulation hasn't worn off. Usually a careful search of the wire will locate the trouble. If not, then give up on that wire and insert a new one. Remove the old wire so it won't cause more problems or confusion. In many instances, as much to protect the wires as to make a neater wiring job, wires ran in conduits or sleeves. These include wires from several circuits, wrapped together for a part of their route. It isn't worth your while to try to insert a single new wire in a conduit. You can, however, often pull out a defective one that you've replaced. If not, and you must leave a wire you've replaced in a conduit, tape the ends.

Often a wire will be shorted where it enters or leaves a conduit because of vibration or stretching. Usually the exposed part can be taped sufficiently to work satisfactorily. New wiring conduits or harnesses can often be bought complete for some makes of cars. If you've got a lot of bad wiring and a new harness is available, it's a good idea to install one. Harnesses sometimes look very complicated. They are a bunch of separate wires of differing lengths, usually color coded for identification. A portion of the group of wires will be bound together inside a heavier insulation with portions of the individual wires sticking out each end.

If you can obtain a new wiring harness for your car—provided you need one—you can replace the wiring system quite simply. You'll either need a wiring diagram so you'll know where each wire must go or you must lay the new wiring harness out and tag each wire when you disconnect the old one, so you'll know how to connect the new wires. This isn't as difficult as it may sound. For instance, disconnect the headlight wires and tag the corresponding wires in the new harness: "headlight, R," "headlight, L," etc. Do this for each wire you disconnect, marking the corresponding wire on the new harness. When the old system is completely disconnected and the new harness tagged, there should be no leftover wires in either system.

Remember that the old system you're removing may have had many splices and repairs over the years. Additional electrical accessories may have been added and the current for these taken from a wire attached to another wire. If this is the case, the new harness may not have enough wires to replace every wire you disconnected. Make note of added accessories such as extra lights, heater or cigarette lighter. For these you may have to run extra wires outside the harness you bought.

You install the new harness by putting the cable-enclosed part in the same position as the original one. Use any holding clips that may be present to hold the new harness in place. Connect the main current connection last, as you don't want wires sparking while you work. Connect each tagged end to the proper terminal. Connect the fuse panel and switches. Connect the power terminal last. Insert one fuse at a time, using the proper switch; test each circuit as you go along. Check the switch terminals, if the current goes through a switch. These should be free of rust or corrosion and the wires firmly attached.

Using your test lamp, ground one terminal. Be sure the switch is closed or on. Touch the contact point of the other wire to the point where the current enters the device being checked. If the light lights, current is going through the circuit and the trouble is in the device itself. If the test light won't light, touch the end of the switch terminal. If it lights, the switch is bad; if it won't light, touch the ends to the ends of the fuse holding clip. If none of these work, look at the final ground on the circuit. Corrosion may have made a good grounding of the circuit impossible. Sometimes grounding with a short piece of wire will work for you, if you can't seem to clean the grounding surfaces properly. If none of these work, replace the circuit.

REPLACING A CIRCUIT

Use the same size and thickness of wire as the one you're replacing. Run it from the power source through any switch and fuse. You don't have to go through the original fuse panel if this is going to be difficult to get at. In a replacement circuit, the fuse can be located anywhere along the line that seems a convenient spot. However it must be insulated by plastic or rubber tape or a rubber sleeve. Run it to the device intended, connecting the wire to the contact point and grounding the other connection. If you're going to replace very many circuits, try using a different colored wire on some of them for easy followup checks. Also run the wires in logical patterns, so there is no strain on them. Be sure the new wires don't come in contact with any moving parts. Any clips used to secure the wire along its route must be insulated so you don't chafe or bare any insultation. Insulated tape is usually the easiest to use for this purpose.

CHECKING GENERATOR OUTPUT

The ammeter gauge on the dashboard will indicate if the generator is charging and register the amount of the charge. With no electrical load other than the ignition system, the gauge should show a charge when the engine reaches an equivalent of five to ten miles per hour. It will probably show a charge as high as twenty at about twenty miles per hour. At higher speeds it will probably show a lower charge. The reduction of the charge rate is controlled by the third brush. This is engineered to give the greatest amount of current under conditions requiring high consumption (slow speeds with lights) and less charge when not as much is required (high speed driving with no lights).

If the generator is not charging, check the fan belt that turns the pulley. It should be tight enough to turn the generator and not slip. You can move the generator to tighten the pulley by loosening the holding bolts and moving the generator against the belt. If the generator is driven by gears, check the gears for excessive wear. To do this, remove the holding bolts and pull the generator back. In some cars, a plate can be removed at the front of the housing to which the generator is bolted. This will allow you to see the generator drive gear and chain. The chain must mesh tightly with the gears: too much slack can make it loose enough to ride over the gears instead of turning them.

Since the generator circuit has its own fuse, check the fuse. It's usually located on the back or along side the generator. If a new fuse blows, there's a short in the generator or in the circuit to the battery or ammeter gauge.

The brushes and commutator are easy to locate in the generator. Remove the band at the end of the generator, and you'll see the brushes and commutator. The armature, as mentioned, spins inside the field. It's supported by bearings in the center of each end of the generator housing. These sometimes need replacement if their lubrication has been neglected over the years. Three brushes, or pieces of carbon, ride on the armature. If these brushes are worn down to less than half an inch, or unevenly worn, they should be replaced.

Brush replacement is simple. Check the screws holding the short wires from the brushes. They must be tight and cannot be corroded. To increase the charging rate, move the third brush clockwise; turn counterclockwise to decrease the rate of charge. Either a knurled nut or screw holds the movable end of the wire to the housing. Be sure it's tight after any adjustment. If you install new brushes, they must be worn in for about a hundred miles before a final adjustment to the charging rate. Do not adjust the brush while the motor is running.

To protect the battery from being drained by the generator at low speeds, there is a "cut-out" or reverse current relay switch located on the top of the generator. Remove the housing that covers it: the contact points should remain open until the generator is running fast enough to charge the battery. A voltage coil magnet will close the contact when the generator reaches this speed. If the cut-out points stick together, sometimes a light sanding or filing will remove corrosion. Don't attempt to work on the cut-out while the motor is running. Replacement cut-outs are inexpensive and good protection. A defective cut-out will discharge the battery into the generator when the engine is stopped and will probably burn out the generator.

CHARGING RATES

High charging rates are caused by a defective battery; loose connections in the generator cut-out external wires; low electrolyte charge in the battery; a cold generator; or a very cold battery. Any of these or a combination thereof can increase the charging rate up to fifty percent above normal, causing extra generator wear.

Low charging rates may be caused by a short circuit or ground in the wiring system, generator or battery; lights or other electric accessories turned on; or low specific gravity in the battery.

Check each of the above, using the test light when searching out a low charging rate. Unless the armature on the generator is badly worn or there's a short in the generator itself, you should be able to locate the trouble.

IGNITION SYSTEM

There are several checks you can make on the operation of the ignition system. Start with the ignition switch: it must be firmly attached to the dash or steering column, so the only movement comes with the key. The wires attached to the terminals must be tight and not corroded. Trace the wire to the coil; part of this wire may be in a metal cable to protect against theft. Wherever the cable or wire goes through the firewall, be sure there is no bare wire that could cause a short circuit. Ignition wiring systems vary somewhat from car to car, but the principles are the same.

The high tension wire from coil to distributor must have secure contacts on both ends. These are usually pinch-on metal clips on the ends of the wires that push into a socket on each end to make contact. It's important that there are no cracks in the insulation. The wires from the distributor to the sparkplugs must also be free of cracks in the insulation and must have solid contacts on each end. Coil and condenser must have tight, corrosion-free connections.

A weak coil can cause hard starting and give a weak spark. It's a good idea to replace a coil that's seen over 50,000 miles service. New coils are inexpensive. So is the condenser. Since there is no adjustment on either coil or condenser, replacement is advisable.

When checking the distributor, remove the top or cap by releasing the clip or clips. Be careful at this point not to disconnect the wires leading to the sparkplugs. The contact at the middle of the top of the cap receives the current from the coil. This contact must not be worn. Each contact spaced around the circumference of the cap must be of sufficient length and width to make contact with the rotor as it passes over. You can spot worn contacts easily. Other than a very light filing if they appear corroded, there's nothing you can do to improve the distributor's performance at this point. Any crack in the distributor cap means replacement, as do worn contacts. The rotor will lift off the distributor shaft. It is notched so it can't be replaced incorrectly. This rotor makes contact at the top, so it can't be pitted, corroded or worn. It also makes contact at the end when it passes over the contact points on the rim of the distributor cap. If the rotor is worn, you'll have to replace it.

With the rotor removed, you have a good view of the breaker points. One of these will be stationary; the other, operating on a spring-like arm, rides on a cam on the distributor shaft. The points should not be burned down. They should be flat on the surface and not corroded. A light filing may help. Also, the gap or distance the points come apart when the cam operates the movable arm can be checked. Use your thickness gauge: the points should open to about .020 inch for maximum results. Check your manual on this measurement, if you have one.

To ensure that the current is coming from the power source to the coil, pull the high tension wire out of the top of the coil. With the ignition switch on, hold the end of the wire about one-eighth of an inch from the contact point in the top of the coil. Have someone operate the starter to turn the motor over. If the wire is still inside the top of the coil, about one-eighth of an inch away from the seat, you'll hear the spark jump. If your car has the type of coil where you can hold the wire a short distance from the contact point, you'll be able to see the spark jump in the same type of test.

To check that the current is coming through the coil to the distributor, remove the connecting high tension wire at the distributor end. Hold it just above, or apart from, its contact point. With the ignition on, again turn the motor over. You'll either see or hear the spark jump.

To check the points, remove the distributor cap. With the ignition on, you should see the points make and break as the motor turns over. The sparking should occur with each movement of the points.

To ensure that the current is getting from the distributor to the sparkplugs, disconnect one plug wire at a time at the plug end. with the ignition on, hold the end of the wire about one-eighth of an inch from the top of the plug. The spark should jump this gap as the motor turns over and it becomes that plug's turn to fire. Repeat this simple test with each plug.

If the current is getting to the plug, the next check is the plug itself. With the motor running, lay a screwdriver with an insulated handle across the plug, about one-eigth of an inch above the motor block. As it becomes that plug's turn to fire, you'll see the spark jump. If you touch the end of the screwdriver to the motor block, it will short out that plug, and it won't fire. While doing this, if you notice a difference in the sound or operation of the motor, it indicates that plug has been doing its job.

Another check on plug operation is to remove each plug from the head, leaving them connected to the distributor. Lay the plugs so the top portions aren't shorted by any metal parts, turn the ignition on, and turn the motor over. You'll see the spark jump the gap at the bottom of the plug when it comes to that plug's turn to fire. You can also learn the firing order of the cylinders that way. However, most cars have that stamped on the cylinder head.

After checking these parts, you should replace any that aren't functioning properly. When replacing sparkplugs, be sure the new plugs are gapped to the manufacturer's recommendations. Use your thickness gauge for this. Be sure the plugs and washers are in tightly and that the wires back to the distributor are tight and free from insulation breaks.

If you're replacing a wire that has the ends stripped and wound around the contact point, you'll get the best contact if you twist the wire in your fingers and bend it around a nail or bolt first. It will then fit easily over the contact point. Bend the wire the same direction as you'll be turning the holding nut. This way, as you tighten the nut you'll be holding the wire even tighter.

If you want to splice wires, the best way is to twist them tightly together. Then if you feel they're not tight enough, you can solder them. Normally, soldering isn't really necessary. If you do solder splices, don't use an acid core solder for the job. Whether soldered or tightly twisted, protect any splices by wrapping them with insulating tape.

If you replace the coil, you would be wise to consider a hotter coil than the original. This is usually a good idea on older cars, as there have been improvements made in coils in the last twenty years.

To replace the breaker points in the distributor, first remove the cap, being sure not to remove any of the wires from their sockets. Next remove the rotor. Remove the small screw on the pigtail fastened to the adjustable breaker point and lift it off the positioning pin. The point attached to the spring-like arm is removed by taking out the screw holding it to the binding post on the outside of the distributor. Be sure that any insulating

Distributor cap and body removed to allow room for installing new breaker points. On some cars, only the cap need be removed to install or adjust points.

washers are in place as you reassemble the parts. Adjust the opening or gap to .025 inch as indicated on your thickness guage. Replace the rotor and cap, again making sure every wire is in place.

Occasionally you'll have to replace the distributor cap on your car. This looks confusing, but really isn't. The hole in the center contains the wire to the coil, so that's no problem. An easy way on six- or eight-cylinder cars is to put a piece of adhesive tape around the bottom circumference of the cap as soon as you remove it from the distributor base, but before you remove any of the sparkplug wires. Starting with the first or front plug, trace that wire back to the cap. Mark a "1" with a ballpoint pen on the adhesive tape where that plug connects into the cap. Once marked, pull the wire out of the cap. Do the same with "2", etc., marking each wire's position on the cap. This way you can make sure the wires are placed in the same position in the new cap. If you get plugs into the wrong position, the engine will misfire. Too many in wrong positions, and it won't fire at all. On four-cylinder cars you should be able to remember the positions without marking the holes, but mark them if you want.

When installing replacement sparkplugs or wires or removing cylinder head, it's wise to tag each wire to avoid mistakes when reconnecting them.

Other than install new brushes on the generator and check the operation of the cut-out, there's little you can do if the generator doesn't work properly. It's a simple matter to remove the bolts holding the generator in place and have it rebuilt. There are many garages that will do this job for you at a reasonable price. In some cases, you may be able to locate a replacement generator that makes rebuilding the old one unnecessary.

REBUILDING THE STARTER

The starter is an electric motor: the circuit that leads to it must be a complete one. It must also be tight in all its connections. If the starter doesn't turn over, check the battery and the connection to the battery. The terminal must be tight. A light tap with a hammer may drive the clamp down the tapered post. But remember, any tap must be a light one. Then tighten the bolt through the terminal clamp. Be sure there is no insulation worn off the cable between the battery and the starter. The grounding cable must be tight at both ends. The attachment to the starter must be clean, free of any corrosion and tight.

Next check the fuse in the circuit. To be sure you're getting current to the starter from the battery, disconnect the cable at the starter end and—holding the insulated part about one-fourth of an inch from the post on the starter—have someone hit the starter button. If the spark jumps, there's current this far.

In some cars, the starter pedal is a part of, or actually makes contact with, the starter. If your car is this type, you can remove the starter switch from the starter motor. Check to see that contact is actually being made when the pedal is pushed. If the trouble is in the switch and you can't correct it by cleaning and bending the contact point, plan on replacing the switch.

If yours is a car with a starter button on the dash or a switch that is not directly a part of the starter switch, you'll have to check the solenoid. This is usually located on the firewall. Check this by turning on the ignition and holding a screwdriver against both contacts. If this operates the starter motor, it indicates a bad solenoid. These are electromagnetic devices not worth monkeying with. They're inexpensive and highly interchangeable among cars.

Should none of the above tests make the starter work, you'll have to remove the starter. There are usually three bolts holding it in place. Disconnect and tape the end of the battery cable. The starter should pull back out of the engine. However, when removing the bolts, support the starter with your hand or a block of wood to keep any strain off the drive mechanism. A bushing supports the drive mechanism at the rear of the shaft. As with the generator, there are many garages that will repair or rebuild starter motors at reasonable cost. You may be able to find a working replacement motor if you don't want yours rebuilt.

REPAIRING LIGHTS

The methods used to check out other circuitry, already thoroughly covered, are essentially the same for inside or outside lights. Any malfunctioning bulb should be checked to see if the bulb is OK. Try it in a socket where you know the circuit is functioning. If the bulb won't work there, replace it with a new one.

Check contact points on the switches, as well as in the lamp sockets themselves. All contacts should be corrosion free and must make solid contact with the bulb base. The fuses involved must seat properly and the connections at each end of the fuse block must be tight.

For stop lights and back-up lights, there are additional switches not with

There were several headlight options offered on cars in the Twenties and early Thirties. These Ryan lights were considered to have superior long-range beam for high speed driving.

You may find that many cars of the Thirties have had conversions to sealed beam lights, added as it became difficult to find replacement lenses.

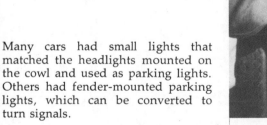

Many cars had small lights that matched the headlights mounted on the cowl and used as parking lights. Others had fender-mounted parking lights, which can be converted to turn signals.

the regular light switches. The stop light is actuated by a small switch connected to the foot brake pedal. When you press the pedal, through a spring connected with this switch, it closes the circuit sending current to the stop light. In some cars, this will only work when the lights are on, though usually the stop light works independently of the other lights. Check the pedal-operated switch and the wiring from it. Back-up lights are normally operated from a small switch that is closed when the shift lever is put into reverse gear. Check the contact points on this switch and the actuating lever on the gear shift. Lastly, check the wiring from the switch.

Starter at right front of flywheel housing. Note heavy cable running from battery to starter switch and on to starter motor. Switch at base of gearshift lever actuates back-up light when lever is shifted into reverse.

After having checked the bulbs, fuses and switches on inside lights that won't work, check the wires themselves. These are relatively lightweight wires and often break. In most cases they'll be between the upholstery and the body or frame. In many cases, it's easier to run new wires. You don't necessarily have to follow the same route with the new wire, if you find it easier to use a new route. Be sure that points at which you secure the new wire are completely insulated so it won't short out. Also, be sure to insert a fuse in the line as added protection.

If, after inspecting the fuse, wires and horn button, the horn won't work, it's probably in the horn motor itself. First be sure that you've checked the point where the horn wire emerges from the tube at the bottom of the steering column. Be sure the insulation is good and there's no short. A dirty commutator on the horn itself will keep it from blowing. Badly worn brushes in the horn motor can also be a cause. If the horn is the vibrator type, check the adjustment screw on the diaphragm. This can also change the sound of the horn. If your car has twin horns, check the relay between them. You can use your test lamp for this. The easiest way to check the wiring system on a horn is to connect the present wires to a horn you know will blow. If it won't blow when connected to your wiring system, that's the cause.

FOCUSING HEADLIGHTS

You can focus headlights yourself, by marking a line about three feet from the floor across one end of your garage. Draw a vertical center line across this mark and to the floor. Position your car about 25 feet back from this wall and line it up so the radiator cap is parallel to the vertical line.

Turn the switch to high-beam position. Cover one light at a time and adjust the other so the top of the beam is about even with the top of the line you've drawn across the garage wall. You adjust the up–down tilt of the lamp either by adjusting the lower screws on the reflector or the ball joint that holds the lights. When the lights are on low beam, they should be slightly above the halfway mark on the horizontal line.

The beam from each light should not cross to the opposite side of the vertical center line, but the left light should point closer to it than the right

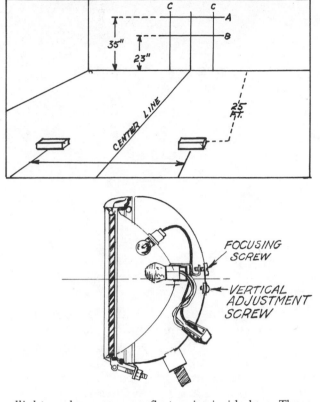

To adjust headlight beams, mark center line on garage floor. Place wheel chocks 25 feet from wall. Draw lines up wall as indicated: line *C* is equal to distance between center of headlights; *A* indicates top of upper beam; *B* indicates top of lower beam.

Focusing screw can be on back of headlight as shown or on reflector rim inside lens. These change vertical adjustment of beams. Bolt-holding headlight controls lateral adjustment. Adjust one light at a time.

Driving lights were usually an accessory that owners added to give extra light for distances. These were in pairs, as on this Rolls, or a single center-mounted light.

light. Side-to-side direction of lights is adjusted by the screws on the sides of the reflector or at the ball joint that holds the light.

Because of the importance of proper focusing of headlights and state inspection requirements, it's recommended that you take your car to a garage equipped with a machine to diagnose the headlight focus. This service costs very little and then you can be sure it's right.

CHAPTER 13

Fuel System

Fuel systems are quite simple, consisting of a fuel storage tank; a means of getting the gasoline from the tank to the engine; and a carburetor. Connecting these are thin pipes called gas lines.

Fuel storage tanks were normally slung between parts of the frame behind the rear axle. Some older cars had the tank mounted under the front seat. Others had a tank mounted high in the cowl between the firewall and the dashboard.

No matter where the tank was mounted, nor the system used in getting the gas from the tank to the engine, you want to use common sense in working on it. Watch the cigarettes, as carelessness here may keep the home fires burning, whether or not you want the heat.

It doesn't really matter where the manufacturer located the gas tank, but location does make a difference in how the gas is fed to the engine. Cars with the tank mounted under the driver's seat or in the cowl depended upon gravity to feed the gasoline to the carburetor. Occasionally, when low on gasoline and going up a fairly steep grade, those cars with the tank under the seat literally ran out of gas. The owner could turn the car around and back up the grade, since this operation kept the level of gasoline above the carburetor.

Many cars with a rear-mounted tank used a vacuum tank on the engine side of the firewall to suck gasoline into a small holding tank. Gravity then fed the gasoline to the engine. Later on, the vacuum tank gave way to a mechanically or electrically operated pump to bring the gasoline from the tank to the carburetor.

CARBURETOR FUNCTION

The function of the carburetor is to mix gasoline and air into a combustible mixture and supply it to the engine. Suction from the piston on the in-

Four-cylinder manifold shows simple two-bolt attachment for carburetor on Model B Ford. Choke rod attaches to carburetor and runs to dashboard.

Typical up-draft carburetor. Gas enters float chamber through screen filter (*A*). Needle valve (*B*) atomizes gas in venturi (*C*), through which air is drawn by piston suction. Butterfly valve (*D*) controls flow of mixture.

take (down) stroke draws the gasoline–air mixture through the intake manifold. It enters the cylinder through the open intake valve.

A pedal called the accelerator or throttle controlled the amount of gas–air mixture allowed to enter the intake manifold. Some cars had a hand throttle in addition to the foot control. A choke was provided to regulate the amount of air let into the carburetor to provide a richer mixture for starting. Shutoff valves and filters were added on the gas line for obvious reasons.

If your test drive indicated the car was running properly, there is really nothing that has to be checked as far as the fuel system is concerned. However, if the engine missed or chugged or if you found any evidence of fuel leaks, you should check the various components of the fuel system. It's wise to check the fuel strainer from time to time. In some cars this was a part of the carburetor. Other cars had a separate strainer with a glass bowl in which sediment or other impurities collected.

Checking the Fuel System

FUEL TANK

Unless the fuel tank leaks, you do not have to remove it. There will be a drain plug located at the lowest point in the tank: you can remove this to

With gas tank removed and flushed with water, remove float mechanism and clean by sloshing with water and gravel to remove scale. Rinse thoroughly with water. If tank has holes, it can be welded at welding shop, never while attached to the car.

drain the gasoline. If your car sat around for a long time, especially if the tank filler cover has been off, it's a good idea to drain the tank. Water, sludge and dirt will settle in the bottom of the tank. These will be the first to come out of the tank when you remove the drain plug, so keep your face out of the way. It's best to remove the filler cover if you're draining the tank so air can enter the tank faster than through the tiny air vent. Remember, *even a tank that has been drained will contain a combustible mixture* and will explode if you're fool enough to hold a lighted match anywhere near the opening. Also, don't insert an electric light bulb through the filler hole to have a look.

Occasionally you'll find it necessary to remove the fuel tank for cleaning or repair. (Not easy to do on a Model A.) There are usually at least two strap iron bands that are bolted to the frame. These support the tank. Before you remove these, be sure to disconnect the gas line from the tank. Also, you should find a wire that connects to a dash-mounted fuel gauge; disconnect it. Place some sort of support under the tank to take the strain off the brackets as you remove the bolts.

It's not uncommon to find holes or rusted out spots in tanks that have been unused for a long time. These can be easily repaired once the tank is removed and completely rinsed out. Remove the gauge float mechanism, taking care not to bend or damage it.

A good way to rinse a tank is to put a couple of gallons of water in it, plus half a pail of pea-sized crushed stone. Put the filler cap on and shake the tank thoroughly. The sloshing action of the stones will loosen any rust. Pour out the mixture and repeat the process if necessary. Finally, hose out the inside thoroughly and let the tank stand with both drain plug and filler cap removed. After the inside has dried thoroughly, the tank can be patched or welded.

Occasionally gas tanks rusted out on the top. I found this on a '36 Auburn and a '32 Marmon. Both cars were convertible coupes with rumble seats. In both cases, the rubber seal around the rumble seat opening had torn or rotted and rain water and melting snow found their way onto the top of the tank. In time, the tanks rusted through and any water on the rear deck quickly found its way into the gas tank. Be sure water draining off the roof and rear sections of your car doesn't collect on top of the gas tank.

Unless you have access to a welding outfit and have had the necessary experience to operate one, take your tank to a shop to have it welded. There are sealants that can be added to tanks to stop seepage and tiny leaks. These sealants also help to prevent leaks from developing. Only use them as directed, with the tank either disconnected or removed from the car. You mustn't let the sealant get into the gas lines which would carry it to the fuel pump or carburetor.

Once the tank is repaired, clean the outside thoroughly and give it a light coat of rust-resistant primer. If the tank shows, you can give it a finish of enamel paint, sanding lightly between coats.

When mounting the tank, use support under it till you've got the holding straps bolted securely in place. Reconnect the fuel line, being very careful not to crossthread the fitting. Reconnect the wire to the gas gauge and you're in business.

FUEL LINES

The easiest way to check the fuel line is to disconnect it where it comes into the vacuum tank or fuel pump. With the gas filler cap removed, blow through the gas line. If the line is clear, you'll hear the bubbles in the tank, just like blowing into a soda straw. *Don't inhale* when you do this, as the fumes or gas could be harmful.

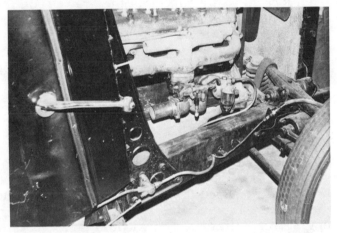

Some cars had reserve section on gas tank and used a second gas line, as did this '33 Mercedes. Control was dash mounted. Other cars used single gas line, with reserve control mounted on gas tank.

The gas line enters the tank (on rear-mounted tanks) at the top, usually near the center. The line doesn't extend to the very bottom of the tank. It usually ends about a half inch above the bottom, to keep from drawing in dirt and water that will settle there. On some cars there will be a reserve valve located on either the tank or the firewall. On the tank-mounted kind with the valve in the normal position, gas will enter the line about the two-gallon level. When the valve is turned to reserve, it will draw down to about a half inch from the bottom. On some cars, a lever under the dashboard switches to a second gas line, reaching lower in the tank when turned to reserve.

On cars with the tank located under the seat or in the cowl, there will be either a drain plug or a shutoff valve on the tank. Gas lines on this type of installation are much shorter. They can be removed easily if necessary. There may be a screened filter where the line enters the tank. This can be cleaned if dirty. All connections in gas lines must be thoroughly tightened after cleaning. Fine threads are on gas line fittings, so be extra careful not to crossthread any fitting. Also, do not use any sort of sealing compound on the joints, as it can get into the lines.

FUEL STRAINERS

A glass bowl attached to the gas line serves as a fuel strainer. Gas will run into the bowl; water or dirt will normally settle to the bottom. By filtering in and out, the strainer will catch any foreign matter and keep it in the unit. There's a thumb screw at the bottom that loosens the spring clip holding the bowl tight against a cork gasket. The bowl should be removed and cleaned from time to time, taking care to clean the screen filters, too. Make sure the cork gasket at the top is properly seated when the bowl is tightened against it.

SHUTOFF VALVES

Some cars had a shutoff valve somewhere along the system. It may have been located at the tank or at the firewall, on the vacuum tank, or near the fuel pump. They usually require only a quarter turn to operate. Unless there is marking to indicate otherwise, the gas flow will be shut off when the handle is crosswise to the gas line. These should be checked to see that they don't leak. Be careful not to exert any great amount of pressure on them, as ordinarily they're supported only by the gas line or the tank to which they're attached.

VACUUM TANK

When the car's gas tank is located below the level of the carburetor, gasoline must be raised to a level above the carburetor to allow it to flow into it via gravity. The gasoline must also be moved from the storage tank to the engine compartment. The vacuum tank works on suction provided by the

Vacuum tank furnishes fuel by syphon principle to float chamber in tank and by gravity to carburetor. Most problems are with leaking or sticky float. Vacuum line from manifold must be airtight and vent free of obstructions.

intake manifold. The tank is airtight when closed. The device is really a tank within a tank. With operation of the engine, the suction created in the intake manifold by the pistons draws gasoline from the rear tank through a filtering system, then into the inside tank or inner chamber of the vacuum tank. A valve is held closed by the suction created in the inner chamber until enough gasoline is supplied to the inner chamber to raise a float. The rising float cuts off the vacuum and opens a valve into the outer chamber or reservoir portion of the vacuum tank.

From the outer chamber or reservoir portion, the gas runs to the carburetor. When the level of gas drops sufficiently in the inner chamber, the float will drop. This opens the suction valve, closing the air valve. Gasoline is again drawn into the inner tank. This process repeats itself as the motor operates, providing a continuous supply of gasoline.

FUEL PUMP

There are two types of fuel pumps: mechanical and electric. Both do the same job, the difference being in the source of power.

Mechanical. This is a simple type of pump. An arm or lever rides on a small cam and the up–down motion of this arm operates a small diaphragm which draws gasoline through the line. On some cars the pump action is through a small plunger operating in a shallow well. The plunger draws gasoline in with one stroke and forces it out with the other stroke. These pumps are usually located near the carburetor. There was usually a screen-type strainer on the intake side of the pump.

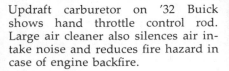

Disconnect fuel line, remove bolts and lift off fuel pump. Rod activates diaphragm to supply steady flow of gas to carburetor. Gas passes through filter to pump.

Updraft carburetor on '32 Buick shows hand throttle control rod. Large air cleaner also silences air intake noise and reduces fire hazard in case of engine backfire.

Electric. Operation is essentially the same as the mechanical type, except that the force that moves the pump is electrical. A small electromagnetic coil furnishes the impulses to move the gasoline. These pumps can be located anywhere along the gas line. They are normally on an electric circuit that operates only when the ignition is on. In most cases you can hear a slight clicking sound as they operate before the engine starts. Occasionally you'll hear this sound at idling speeds. It's normal, nothing to be concerned about. There is usually a screen-type filter at the inlet side of the pump. Some cars had dual electric fuel pumps and a switch on the dash determined which pump operated.

Operational Repairs   You check the operation of either electric or mechanical fuel pumps by disconnecting the gas line at the carburetor. On the electric type, turn on the ignition switch and the gas should soon start to flow. On the mechanical type, after disconnecting the gas line at the carburetor, operate the starter and the gas should soon flow. Do not run the engine with the gas line disconnected, as there will usually be enough gas in the carburetor bowl to run the engine up to a temperature where the gas pouring out of the disconnected gas line could cause a fire.

FUEL PUMP

Depending upon the make of pump on your car, you can usually buy a repair kit. This will contain new gaskets, springs, diaphragm and other parts necessary to rebuild the fuel pump. Don't worry about this job, as fuel pumps are easy to get at and work on. The old pump is usually held in place by two bolts: it should lift out when tilted upward as you remove it. If there aren't instructions in the repair kit, note how things come apart. You want to work toward the diaphragm being flexible, yet airtight. The little coil spring should be properly seated and have sufficient tension to do its job. The arm that actuates the pump must not be worn where it rides on the cam or you won't get full pumping action.

When remounting the pump, be sure the arm slides into place easily. If it's connected to a rod inside the housing, be sure the connection is secure. Line the holes in the pump flange with the holes in the gasket and mounting block. Be sure not to crossthread the mounting bolts. After the pump is securely in place, connect the line to the gas tank. Then connect the line to the carburetor. In connecting these lines, use two wrenches so no tension is on the line or the pump itself as you tighten. Clean the strainers as you reassemble the unit.

To repair an electrically operated pump, first check the fuse to be sure it's getting current. If the fuse is OK, use your trouble light to trace out the circuit. Check the gas line from the tank to the pump to be sure it's open. Also, be sure the filter is clean. Check the line from the pump to the carburetor to be sure that it's free. If you can blow through it when it's disconnected, you know gas can flow through it. Check the ground and the electrical connections at the pump. If all of these are in order, next remove the cover from the small electromagnetic coil, see that the parts are clean and free of corrosion. Check the diaphragm on the pump to be sure it's airtight. Also, check the spring for tension. The movement of gas depends upon the electrical current operating so the diaphragm expands and contracts. Clean out the fuel holding well, if there is one.

After these cleaning and checking operations, if the pump still won't move gasoline, it must be replaced. There is no difficulty in obtaining a replacement, as many pumps are interchangeable so long as the gas line diameters and the voltage requirements are the same. You may have to fabricate your own mounting system if you change the brand of pump.

VACUUM TANK

If the vacuum tank isn't supplying enough gas to the carburetor, you should be able to make some repairs. After you've checked the gas lines for leaks, blockage, kinks or other damage, check for air leaks around the top of the vacuum tank. Check the small air intake vent in the gas tank filler cap. Air has to get into the tank to replace the gasoline used out of it. If this tiny air hole is plugged, it'll cause a counter pressure to build up in the tank and stop the flow of gas. There is also a tiny vent in the top of the vacuum tank: this must be clean to operate efficiently. Check the strainer bowl on the gas line between the vacuum tank and the carburetor to be sure gas can get through it. Also check the strainer at the bottom of the carburetor float chamber. The purpose of all these checks is to be sure that any insufficiency in gas flow isn't caused by something other than the vacuum tank.

Occasionally you'll find that the gas line runs parallel and close to the exhaust system; gas can be vaporizing before it reaches the vacuum tank. You can correct this by wrapping the gas line in asbestos, just as a plumber insulates a water pipe. You can, of course, reposition the gas line if you like.

If you have to remove the vacuum tank, you'll find it held in place by a couple of bolts through a strap into the firewall. With the lines disconnected, you can remove the tank to a workbench. Remove the cap screws to lift off the top portion of the tank. Be careful not to damage the gasket around the top. You can disassemble the tank, noting the relationship of the parts. The most common causes of vacuum tank failure were a leak in the float or a sticking mechanism that operates the float. Once you've removed the float, submerge it in a pan of water to see if any air bubbles come up from it. If so, the leak can be soldered once the gas or water is out of the inside of the float. Usually you should have this job done for you by a tinsmith. The arm that connects with the float and actuates a shutoff valve should be able to move without restriction. The valve and valve seat should be clean. Any spring should be clean and have sufficient tension to do its job.

The inlet into the reservoir portion of the vacuum tank from the float chamber must be clear so nothing obstructs the flow of gas. The outlet at the bottom of the tank must be clean so the gas can flow to the carburetor. Once all the parts are cleaned, the unit should be reassembled: take great care to be sure none of the inside parts bind and that the whole unit is airtight. Once remounted on the firewall, the lines can be reconnected, the unit primed, and it should operate. Use two wrenches when tightening gas lines to avoid strain on the lines.

CARBURETOR

There are several things you can check and repair on the carburetor. In its simplest form, the carburetor is comprised of a bowl that holds gas. A float within this bowl regulates the amount of gas in the bowl. Air is sucked in through the air intake: the intake manifold creates this suction. The incoming air passes over a nozzle(s) which is simply a tiny pointed hole into which is screwed a correspondingly small and pointed needle. These are called needle valves and, by screwing them in or out, they regulate the amount of gas the moving air is able to suck along with it. Essentially they act like a nozzle on a garden hose.

Downdraft carburetor from Ford V-8 sucks air down through venturi, past jet nozzles into intake manifold. Air filter sits on top of carburetor.

Tube on top of '39 Buick downdraft carburetor connects with air cleaner set close to engine to allow low hood line. Filter bowl on gas line can be easily cleaned by loosening thumb screw.

The air–gas mixture goes through a tube or throat. A damper device, controlled by the hand or foot throttle, opens or closes in the throat. When the damper (butterfly valve) is open, a large volume of the air–gas mixture is allowed to enter the intake manifold, when partially open, a lesser amount. There's a set screw that prevents the damper from being completely closed so the motor won't run out of gas. This is the idler adjustment, which controls the minimum or idling speed of the motor.

As carburetors were developed, certain refinements and adjustments were added. But no matter how complicated, they all adjust the ratio of gas to air and the amount of this mixture admitted to the cylinders.

Looking from top down on carburetor bowl with top removed, through twin venturi tubes and needle valves on twin throat carburetor for V-12 engine.

A '29 V-8 Cadillac featured up-draft carburetor placed between cylinder blocks. Vacuum tank is mounted high on firewall and feeds gas to carburetor by pull of gravity.

There were two types of carburetors used. The *updraft* was developed first. This set below the intake manifold and the air–gas mixture was drawn up through the throat of the carburetor and into the intake manifold. The *downdraft* was placed above the intake manifold and the air–gas mixture drawn down through the throat into the intake manifold. Each type of car-

Carburetor sits low between cylinder banks on '39 Cadillac V-8. Huge oil-bath air cleaner almost reaches to fan. Adjustment isn't difficult when air cleaner is removed.

Rubber hose gives flexibility to air cleaner mounted at angle and attached to firewall on '55 Humber. Electric fuel pump furnishes gas to carburetor bowl.

To heat air–gas mixture and give quicker warmups, some cars ran exhaust pipe through heat exchange unit on intake manifold, as did this '28 Franklin.

buretor set at the middle of the front-to-back measurement of the engine for an equal flow of mixture to all cylinders.

Starting with the filter screen where the gasoline enters the float chamber, be sure everything is clean. Usually a fine piece of screen was inserted in the intake flange of the bowl. In some cars you'll need to remove the air

Huge oil-bath air cleaner nearly hides downdraft carburetor on '38 Buick. Oil in base of drum-type container in front is vaporized slightly as air is drawn over it, cleaning and lubricating air mixture.

cleaner to get at this easily. Many older cars had no air cleaner. If your car has one, be sure it's clean and does not choke off the flow of air. Most early air cleaners were a cartridge with copper or steel inserts. They can be cleaned with gasoline or kerosene.

It may be necessary to check the float level: to do so, remove the gas filler line. The gas should be flush with the screw threads. The float controls the amount of gas allowed into the float chamber. It operates in the same manner as the float ball in a toilet tank. Through the arm connected with it, it opens and closes the valve admitting the gas.

Complicated looking, but easy to adjust, updraft carburetor on Rolls features separate starting carburetor, which is controlled from dashboard.

To see if the carburetor float level is correct, remove the float chamber cover. Most carburetors were made of pot metal and won't take a lot of force on bolts and screws, so take care not to damage the thin gasket. There should be a mark on the inside of the float chamber indicating the depth of gas when full. If there isn't, use the guide of the gasoline being flush with the screw threads in the intake line. Bending the float upwards on its shaft about 1/16-inch will increase the gas level by the same amount. Bending the float down will lower the gas level. Normally there will be about 1/4-inch clearance between the top of the float and the float cover.

Most cars with in-line engines had a single throat carburetor. V-type engines had to have one throat for each bank of cylinders to give good per-

It's best to remove carburetor for cleaning and inspection. Usually four bolts hold throat to manifold. Linkage is easy to disconnect. Use two wrenches on gas line to avoid strain on line and fittings.

Complicated intake manifold for V-8 engine uses studs to attach two-barrel downdraft carburetor. Heater hose fitting is at front.

formance. Some V-8s had two carburetors, one for each bank. The trouble was in synchronizing them so both gave the same richness of mixture and the same amount to the manifolds. On today's cars, "throats" are referred to as "barrels." Most V-8s now have a four-barrel carburetor to give a more even mixture flow.

Adjusting needles, or jets, are located in the carburetor throat. Most old cars had two needles: one adjusts the amount of gasoline admitted at idling speeds and is called an *idling jet*. A *high speed or running jet* is a little higher in the throat: this adjusts the richness of the mixture under normal running conditions and takes over at about 15 miles per hour. Some of the more powerful cars also had a *passing jet*, a pump that squirted an extra amount of gasoline directly into the throat of the carburetor when the throttle was floored in a hurry.

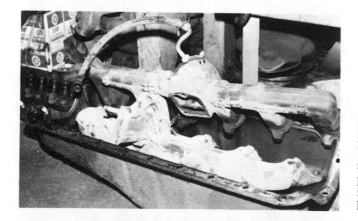

Intake manifold for six-cylinder motor is heavy casting which bolts to block. Exhaust manifold ports fit between intake ports. A single gasket usually includes both intake and exhaust ports.

From the simplicity of the Model A, where you turned the choke rod clockwise then backed off a half turn, needle adjustments varied according to the make of the carburetor. When adjusting the needles, you should adjust the high speed or running jet first. The part of the needle valves you'll see will be a knurled or serrated head screw with a spring between the head and the carburetor. There will be a line or arrow on it; there will be a corresponding mark on the carburetor. A factory engineered stop will prevent you from moving the needle more than one-half turn in either direction. This was determined to be the correct operating range. Backing the needle out allows more gasoline to enter, giving a richer mixture. Tightening the valve into its seat cuts down the amount of gasoline and gives a leaner mixture. Cold weather may require a slightly richer mixture. A slightly leaner mixture may give better gas mileage.

To adjust the high-speed valve beyond the factory limits, remove the little stop device so you can turn the needle at will. Set the hand throttle for an engine speed of about 25 miles per hour. Turn the high-speed needle down into the nozzle; this will decrease the amount of gasoline admitted to the throat. When you notice a difference, or slowing of engine speed, turn the needle back out slowly. This will enrich the mixture. When the engine reaches the maximum speed at the throttle setting, install the locking device to hold it in place.

To adjust the idling needle valve, adjust the set screw on the gas control rod so the engine is idling at the speed you want. This controls engine idle speed only. Slowly tighten (screw in) the idling needle until the engine shows signs of stalling. Back the needle out until the engine idles smoothly. This pertains to the mixture at idling speeds only and has nothing to do with driving speeds.

On cars that are seldom driven, it's a good idea to set the idling adjustment so the motor idles faster than normal. This allows the generator to feed back current more quickly to the battery.

Vacuum-operated windshield wiper motor is easily repaired. Remove top plate, clean all parts. Be sure packing on inner arm prevents leakage. Make new gasket for top if necessary.

CHAPTER 14

Exhaust
System

The exhaust system starts with the exhaust manifold, bolted directly to the engine block. This may appear rusty, but if it is not cracked, there's nothing to worry about. The manifold collects hot gases from each cylinder when the exhaust valve opens. The last stroke of the piston in its four-stroke cycle forces the burned mixture out of the cylinder head, through the open exhaust valve into the exhaust manifold. These hot gases are the living end of the four cycles.

The exhaust manifold is usually the same length as the motor. One end is closed, the other flanged to join the exhaust pipe. On some cars the exhaust manifold empties to the rear of the motor; on others it empties toward the front and may cross the front of the motor before connecting with the exhaust pipe.

The exhaust pipe runs under the floor of the car between the frame and driveshaft. It is usually in at least two sections, though in some small cars it

An accessory item, exhaust manifold combined with hot air heater on Model A. Flexible tube connected it through hole in firewall. In the days before permanent antifreeze, many cars used similar hot air heaters because hot water heaters tended to help boil out antifreeze.

186

was a one-piece affair. The first section runs from the connection with the manifold to the front of the muffler. A second section connects to the back of the muffler and runs to the end of the car. This section will be humped to clear the rear axle.

Unless the motor is extremely loud or you see evidence of exhaust escaping where the manifold joins the block, or unless the manifold is cracked, you won't have to do anything to it. Some of the more expensive cars had a porcelainized manifold; however, most were left as iron casting. If it appears rusty, that's normal. Paint burns off, so don't bother to paint it.

It's seldom that anything damages the manifold itself. However, sometimes the gaskets between the manifold and the block have to be replaced. These are copper and asbestos: if you need to replace them, be sure to locate a replacement before starting.

Check the joint where the exhaust manifold is connected to the exhaust pipe. Normally there will be two bolts through the flanges with a gasket in between: this joint must be tight so there's no exhaust leak.

There is another joint where the front section of the exhaust pipe enters the muffler. Usually this is a slipover joint, the exhaust pipe slipping into the muffler pipe. Be sure the clamp is tight and that the exhaust pipe and muffler are tightly joined.

Flexible tubing welded to original fittings to replace worn original curved pipe. Try to locate solid pipe rather than use flexible tubing. Muffler shops will bend pipe to your specifications.

The pipe that runs from the exhaust manifold to the front of the muffler can be repaired, if there's only minor damage. Small rustout spots can be patched. This pipe is usually curved and often has been damaged by hitting curbs or stumps. Many times rocks thrown back by the front wheels will damage this pipe. Any broken or badly rusted pipe should be replaced.

The muffler should be sound and solid. The brackets holding it should be solid and firmly attached to the muffler and frame. Minor holes in the muffler can be repaired, but any damage to either end or serious rustout spots require muffler replacement.

The pipe that runs to the back of the car should be firmly clamped to the muffler. This is a slipover joint, with the muffler outlet sliding inside the pipe. Any small holes in this pipe can be patched. If a portion is badly rusted out or broken, yet another part is in good shape, the pipe can be spliced.

Along the exhaust system at various points, there are brackets holding the system to the frame. Some of these are flexible brackets to allow for motor vibration and twisting and flexing of the car's frame without cracking the pipes. Be sure all the brackets are firmly attached to the frame and to the pipes. Pay particular attention to those brackets which must carry the weight of the muffler, also to the attachment at the hump in the pipe that goes up and over the rear axle. Near the end of the tailpipe, there'll be a bracket that is often broken—caused when the car has backed into something that hit the pipe. Be sure the end of the pipe is open, so there's nothing restricting the flow of the exhaust.

MANIFOLD

Repair or Replacement

A cracked exhaust manifold must be welded or replaced. Removing the bolts that hold the manifold to the block requires sheer brute strength. Soak them good with a rust-removing solvent. If you feel you'll need help, this is the job on which to ask the help of a hefty friend. Because of exposure to intense heat over a period of years, you'll swear the bolts are welded in place. They'll come out, though, in time.

First disconnect the flanges holding the exhaust pipe to the manifold: this will give you an idea of what you're in for. Fit the right size socket to the bolt. Be certain there's no play in the socket and that it's a tight fit. Use the longest drive or handle the space will allow. If you have room, sometimes a piece of pipe slipped over the handle will give the added leverage you need. Before applying pressure, again soak the threads with a rust solvent.

Start at one end of the manifold, applying enough pressure to make a half turn on the bolt. Do the same on the other end. Follow this pattern as you release pressure evenly. After all the bolts have been broken loose, you can go ahead and remove them completely.

The manifold is a heavy casting and you may find it wise to support its weight by leaving in the two end bolts till you're ready to lift it out. You may want a block underneath the manifold to give it support during removal. *Do not drop it:* being a casting, it can break if it hits a concrete floor at the right angle.

Before replacing the manifold, give it a good scrubbing with a wire-bristled brush. Be sure to clean the parts of the block that connect to it. These are called ports and should match up with the replacement gaskets. You can use a little gasket cement around the ports and on the matching side of the manifold when installing new gaskets. You can cover each side of the gasket with the cement too, if you like. Any you get on your hands and tools makes the job more difficult, as you'll find everything sticking together.

The gaskets should fit over any studs or bolts without being forced. Equal pressure along the whole length of the gasket at the same time will usually accomplish this without warping the new gasket.

Tighten the bolts holding the manifold to the block in the same pattern you used in removing them. You should apply pressure equally to get a tight fit and not crack the manifold. You may want to call on your hefty friend again for the real tightening. After being run about a hundred miles, a final tightening is sometimes necessary. Reconnect the exhaust pipe to complete the job.

Reducing fittings are readily available to join different-sized components. Bendable tubing allows restorer to fit pipe over rear axle; flexible mountings protect exhaust system from engine vibration.

EXHAUST PIPES

Replacement of a segment of exhaust pipe requires removing bolts from any flanges, clamps or hangers involved. These are often hard to break loose because of the heat they've been subjected to, in addition to road grime and rust. If necessary, drill out the bolts in a flange, then use new bolts. A nut splitter will crack open a nut that won't come loose. You should scrub threads clean with a wire-bristled brush and apply a rust-removing solvent before working with your wrenches.

When you install a new segment of pipe, use new bolts if the heads or threads of the former ones were damaged. Make certain they are tight to do the job properly.

If you found only a few holes in a pipe, there are patches available to do a good repair job easily and quickly. Buy a water solvent putty that's made for exhaust systems. Press a wad of this into the hole and flatten the lump extending outside the hole. Let this dry according to instructions, then wrap the patch with a special tape made for this use. This works great for small holes.

The same type of patching will work for small holes or rusted spots on the muffler, too. With a screwdriver, break away the rust and flaky material. If the holes sre small, use the same patching putty as you did for the pipes. If it's a larger hole, cut a piece of galvanized sheet metal (metal used for ducts to your furnace), drill a hole in each corner, and use it as a sort of clamp over the hole. Metal screws will hold this in place. Make the patch enough larger than the hole to ensure that you'll be attaching it to solid metal. Before applying, either insert a piece of sheet asbestos on the patch or smear patching putty around the edge of the hole and the patch. When you draw this up tight, it will make a good seal.

You may want to wrap the patch afterward with the special tape mentioned previously. In some cases, it may be wise to make a circular band of lightweight strap iron to hold the patch in place. That strap iron with holes every half inch is especially handy when working on exhaust system repairs.

MUFFLER

If you have a badly deteriorated muffler, replacement is necessary. If you can't locate one specified for your car, measure the diameter of the pipe leading to the muffler, the diameter of the pipe at the rear of the muffler, and the length and the diameter of the muffler. With these measurements, you'll have no trouble locating a replacement. Get new clamps at the same time.

If you had to accept a replacement that is slightly different in length or diameter, but pipe diameters are the same, you may need to reposition some of the hangers and brackets. These won't make any difference in the operation of the car, as long as there's room in the chassis to fit the replacement muffler. Be sure all holding brackets, hangers and clamps are tight.

TAILPIPE

If the only problems you found in the exhaust system were behind the muffler, you can either replace the tailpipe, or patch it if there are only small holes or rustouts. Patch any holes as described for the exhaust pipe. If only a portion of the pipe is bad, you can cut out the bad portion and splice the pipe. Auto supply stores sell lengths of exhaust pipe and slipover joints for connecting pipes. Be sure to give the outside diameter measurement of your pipe. From front to rear, each piece of pipe should slip *inside* any pipe it joins: this helps prevent exhaust leaks around joints. Always tighten clamps and brackets as firmly as you can. Use spring washers to keep bolts and nuts tight.

Sometimes you'll find the piece of pipe that curves up over the rear axle is rotted out. In this case, saw the pipe at its last solid place. This will leave you with a solid system as far as it goes, short of reaching the end of the car. Measure the diameter of the outside of the existing pipe. Auto supply stores sell pipes that have a flexible section in them. You slip this over the end of the existing pipe and clamp it tightly in place. Curve it up over the axle and attach holding brackets to the frame. This gives you a rebuilt tailpipe that will clear the movement of the rear axle. It's inexpensive and easy to install. Of course, if you prefer, you can install a new pipe that is made to fit your car. Either way is satisfactory.

When you're done with all the repairs, it's a wise idea to buy an aerosol can of aluminum paint made expressly for painting exhaust systems. This is a high-heat resistant paint. The purpose is mainly to protect the system from rust. It serves a second purpose too, in that it makes inspection for future exhaust leaks easy. Do not spray it on the manifold. Start with the first flange joint and cover the entire system, new and old parts. It dries quickly and covers well.

Because of the danger of carbon monoxide asphixiation from exhaust fumes leaking into the car, it's not good judgment to make too many patches or repairs to an old system. If you can't be sure you've got a really tight exhaust system with the existing parts repaired, you should get replacement parts and play safe.

SECTION III

Body
Restoration

CHAPTER 15

Restoration
Choices

Before tackling any body restoration, it's a good idea to study the problems your particular car presents. You may want to call on knowledgeable friends who can give you advice. Owners of similar cars are a good source of information; material contained in factory releases is invaluable. Try to get all the information and advice you feel you need. Of course, you'll make the final decision yourself. Because you want the body beautiful, take time in studying the problems before you tear into this job: it will be time well spent.

You have a wide range of choices in body restoration. It depends upon your final objective with a specific car. Do you want to restore it to its original condition? Does authenticity mean enough to you to spend the hours and dollars necessary to hunt original parts and components? Is your car worth what restoration to original condition will cost? Do you just want to upgrade the car's present condition and let it go at that? Will you be content if certain parts end up painted instead of plated? Will you settle for a vinyl interior instead of leather, as in the original? You'll want to weigh the answers to these questions before starting to restore the body.

Original Condition

If you elect to restore it to original condition, congratulations! This is best, of course. Start by listing the things you must do. Make a list of the parts that will need replacement because they aren't repairable. List the parts that can be returned to good-as-new condition. Hunt sources for replacement parts; locate shops for repairing and rebuilding parts you don't feel you can handle. However, don't overlook the many jobs you can do, as this reduces your expenditure and gives added personal satisfaction.

Obtain pictures or snapshots of the original body style. These can come from sales catalogs or owners' manuals. Old magazines on file in your library may contain original ads with pictures. Articles in old car magazines are a good source. Photos of similar makes and models already restored can help. Get as complete a group of pictures or drawings as possible. These will all help give you something to work toward.

Conversion

Conversions are cars that have been changed or converted into a different

193

A restoration alternative: speedster bodies are fun to plan and easy to build for cars with bodies that may be beyond your ability or desire to repair them. Special bucket seats, gas tanks, windshields, horns, etc., are readily available.

body style. Many times they end up worth more than if they'd been restored to original condition. In some cases, it's easier to convert a car to a different body style than it is to restore it to original condition. This is especially true of certain coupes, coaches and sedans where the wooden-frame body may be in a bad state of decay. It's usually more fun to have a convertible or open car than a stodgy old sedan. By removing that portion of the body that extends above the window sill level, or certain molding lines, you can easily convert these to open cars. You may want to leave the windows and work toward a true convertible design. I once changed a Franklin Standard Coupe—in which the upper wood had rotted badly—into a convertible coupe that was almost indistinguishable from the factory version. In some cases you may want to remove the windows and cut the body down to the belt line: this provides an open car without windows. You can decide if you want to make side curtains to give added weather protection.

Before: Because of similarity in body stampings, it's easy to change coupes to smart convertibles. Cut out rotten wood; hinge quarter post at window level; make new windshield header and roof bows.

It was a common practice for manufacturers to use many of the same body stampings for their open and closed models. If you have any pictures or drawings of an open model of your make car, you can see the many similarities. Coupes can easily be made into convertible coupes or roadsters. Sedans easily become touring cars. Coaches can be made into highly desirable two-door phaetons. Sometimes, if the body isn't worth restoration effort and expense, it can be cut off behind the cowl or firewall and a speedster body built with bucket seats, exposed gas tank and tool box, similar to the old Stutz Bearcat or Mercer Raceabout. The fact that your particular make never produced or offered a speedster body isn't particularly important.

Pickup trucks are another easy conversion, though many need extensive

After: With doors rebuilt and nickel-plated frames fitted on windows, a convertible top was made to original specifications. Landau bars were added; car was reupholstered, repainted and replated. It took on new life as a convertible.

mechanical restoration. With the bed shortened, they become real fun vehicles. I've seen a pickup with the bed removed, a large trunk and dual rear-mounted spares added. A really smart-looking "touring coupe" was the result.

Don't overlook old hearses, flower cars or panel deliveries as a source for conversion vehicles. They can be made into the equivalent of today's station wagons or into large open-bodied touring cars. Most hearses and flower cars were well maintained mechanically and often had quite low mileage when retired.

The object to keep in mind in any conversion is that you want to have fun doing it and, later on, fun using it. If an open car has more appeal to you, by all means consider making a conversion from your present closed car.

Try to get pictures of the factory-produced model you want to copy. Sales catalogs or owners' manuals may be a source. Perhaps you can get snapshots of the model you want at a car club meet or from an owner. If you do locate a factory-produced model of the car you want to copy, get as many snapshots of details as possible. If it is to have a folding roof, try to photograph the roof bow arrangement, hold-down clamps on the windshield, size of the rear window frame, etc. Get a photo of the differences in window treatment, door and body moldings. These will be very valuable to you as you work along.

Make a drawing of your planned body restoration. Usually ⅛:1 or ¼:1 inch scale will be relatively easy to draw. This drawing will give you a practical gauge of what you'll have when you're finished. Make careful measurements to indicate just what will be removed and what will remain as it. You may find it wise to install some temporary braces to hold doors and door posts in their proper position before you remove the unwanted portions. Permanent braces may need to be installed later on. Get as complete a mental picture as possible of what you plan to do. Augment this mental picture with as many photographs, pictures, details and drawings as possible to aid you in your work.

You can customize your car if you've got a clear picture of what you want. Many medium-priced makes offered customized versions. Usually these were regular production models with goodies added, much like the many options offered on contemporary cars. A four-door, seven window sedan can easily be made into a five-window berlin by blanking out the rear quarter windows, making the rear window smaller and adding a vinyl top

Customized Model

Custom conversions can be far out and cost a great deal, or they can be ultrasimple. A second rear-mounted spare was added to this '41 Continental Coupe (too much of a good thing).

Now a smart two-door phaeton, originally a two-door sedan. Great care taken in making changes shows in finished product.

and landau bars. Or an original four-door sedan can be made into a landaulet by removing the rear quarter roof and windows and making a folding roof for this portion. In auto body language, the rear window is always added to the count. A seven-window sedan has three windows on each side, plus the back. A five-window coupe has two windows on each side, plus a back window. A three-window coupe has one window on each side, plus the back one. The windshield is not included in the window count.

New roof bows change original conformation and a new canvas top replaces the original to give this victoria coupe the look of a custom convertible.

On certain makes, the body design is such that you can remove the fixed portion over the front seat and make your humble auto into a town car. There are many ways you can customize an ordinary car. A word of caution, however: if you get too far out, you may end up with a car that you like, but one that has little value other than as an attention getter. So have a care on customizing.

Customizing may pertain only to additional refinements on the inside of the car. Using plywood, you may want to make a new back for the front seat of your sedan—it could include a small folding bar. The space in the doors below window level can be made to hold flasks or thermos bottles. You may want to add a trunk to your car. These can be done very easily and authentic trunk hardware is readily available.

There's a wide-open field in customizing your car. Depending upon what you do, customizing can easily increase the value of the car. On the other hand, to the purist you may have lowered the car's value, as it won't be really authentic. The choice is yours. Determine what you want and what you can do with your particular car; plan your work toward that end.

Unless you know for certain that a factory-built version of what you want to achieve has been produced, you'll have to work largely from pictures of other makes with the body style you want. This isn't difficult, as you can easily figure out necessary changes due to a longer hood, lower belt line, different moldings, etc. You'll need to make near-scale drawings of your plans which will require accurate measurements. Don't get overly anxious at this point and start customizing before you're really sure of what you want to do. If your customizing will require removal of any structural part, be sure you've installed a temporary brace to hold parts in their correct position. Later, you may find you'll need to install permanent braces or other structural members to keep the car solid. Try to locate matching hardware or other fittings you may need so your completed project will be up to, or exceed, original standards.

Once you know exactly what you want to do and have made the necessary plans, you can start to disassenble the parts involved. As you go along, you may want to mark certain parts so you'll know just where they go in reassembly. Freezer tape, masking tape or string tags are great for tagging parts: use a ballpoint or felt tipped marker for the job. Simple drawings showing the relationship of nuts, pins, washers and other parts are very helpful in getting window mechanisms and other assemblies back together correctly. Jot down measurements of parts that have to be replaced or rebuilt. Don't rely solely on your memory for relationship of parts. Label as many parts as you can.

In dissassembling body parts, save pieces for use as patterns for making replacements. Save hardware and metal braces, etc. There's no use in throwing out a usable brace or hinge and later having to buy a replacement. However, unless nuts, bolts and screws you remove are rustfree and in good condition, don't attempt to reuse them: you may need to save some as guides in determining sizes. If, when disassembling, you have to remove windshield or window glass, check to see if it's safety glass. If not, use the old glass as a pattern for a glass shop to cut you new pieces of safety glass. The use of safety glass may well be a law in your state, but you'll want it anyway.

Store parts that you won't be using for awhile in an out-of-the-way place

Beginning Work

where you won't trip over them and where they won't get damaged. You can mark sheetmetal parts with a felt tip marker. Remember to mark the top, front and right or left, so you can't possibly forget. Store small nuts, bolts, screws and parts in a can labled to show where they belong. Take care to keep the car, its parts and your work area as clean as possible during the disassembly process.

There are many variations in body construction and body types. Each manufacturer had his own method for building and assembling cars. The main ones will be covered in detail on following pages and apply to either wooden or steel body construction.

Basically, the two main types of body construction were wooden frame body and all-steel body. The restoration process is generally the same on either type. Structural members, whether wood or steel, that have rotted or rusted away must be replaced with new wood or metal. Weakened pieces must be strengthened or reinforced. It's often necessary to install extra bracing.

Don't get uptight about making repairs to the structural parts of the body. Just be sure that any bracing additions you make don't put stress or strain on a part that isn't strong enough to handle the additional burden. Also, be sure any additional braces you install don't change the alignment of parts that must fit together.

CHAPTER 16

Body Repairs
and Construction

As you work on your car's body, you'll find that its beauty is more than skin deep. It was common practice in body building to construct a wooden frame: most panels or stampings were then attached to cover the wooden framework. This gave a strong structure. However, it was time-consuming and expensive to build. As these wooden-frame bodies aged, they were apt to suffer from wood rot. This was especially true of open models and cars that stood outdoors a lot of the time. Weather was their biggest enemy.

With mass production, huge stamping presses and spot welding were developed. The wooden-frame body gave way to all-steel body construction. However, many smaller manufacturers stayed with the wooden-frame body until the Depression did them in. Custom-built bodies on the most expensive cars were wooden-framed until World War II. Some foreign cars through the Sixties continued with the wooden-frame construction.

Structural Replacement

Rotten wood loses its strength and won't hold the panels in their proper position or alignment. The bolts or screws usually rusted and lost their strength as the wood rotted. Rotten wood will have to be replaced with new pieces that will give the required strength. This is very common on doors, posts, rear-quarter and roof supports.

Because the replacement wood will probably have two curving sides, you may think making replacement is too hairy for you to attempt. It's not, if you cut one curve at a time and take care in making the pattern.

PATTERNS

You have several choices in making patterns for wood or steel. The easiest way is to trace the pattern from a similar make and model which is sound. Try to locate such a car for a pattern. If you can't find one, use your own car for the pattern. Replacement wood or steel for the left front door will have the same contours as the wood or steel in the right front door. However, it will have to be reversed when put in position before a second curve is cut.

In a cross-section view, most bodies were wider at the middle of the door along the belt line than at the bottom of the door. The vertical, or upright, wood or steel in the door must follow this contour. Also, most bodies were wider at the center post than they were at the cowl. Horizontal wood or steel in the doors must follow this contour. Cowl framing must have the same vertical contour as the front framing of the front door. The back edge of the front door will have the same contour as the center post between doors, as well as the leading edge of the rear door. The rear edge of the rear door will have the same contour as the front edge of the rear quarter panel.

Remember that the left side of the car will have the same contours as the right side of the car. This means you've probably got your piece to trace as a pattern. However, these must be flipped or reversed before tracing a second contour or cutting in notches for braces.

Trace a pattern for structural members on new wood. Make a preliminary cut to allow easier handling, then make final cut to pattern line.

The easiest way to make a pattern is to trace the desired contour onto a piece of fairly stiff cardboard. Suit or dress boxes from department stores are excellent; corrugated cardboard boxes aren't good at all for this purpose. You can buy pieces of cardboard from an office supply or stationery store. You can also make your tracing on plywood if you want: this is particularly good for pieces that extend across the car—like roof bows—as the extra stiffness of the plywood gives more accuracy on large patterns.

Cut the cardboard or plywood slightly larger than the piece you're using as a pattern. Lay or clamp the piece flat against the original. Using a sharp pencil or ballpoint pen, trace the outline *accurately*. Mark screw holes and other placements on the pattern. Be sure the cardboard or plywood doesn't move at all as you trace. After tracing, mark top, bottom, front, back, left, right, as needed so you'll know how to position the piece. If the piece you're tracing is incomplete, estimate the missing portion and allow a little extra on your pattern. This can be easily trimmed off when you start replacing the wood or steel. It's a good idea to take exact measurements, either from the other side of the car or from the metal stampings. This is a precaution you may appreciate later.

STRUCTURAL SUPPORTS

The average four-door sedan had ten pieces of vertical wood or steel used as supports per side. This count includes the two pieces on the cutout or

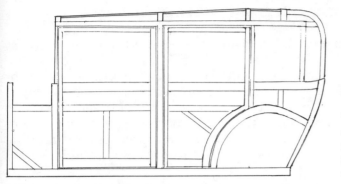

Typical wood framing for four-door sedan. Body stampings fitted over framework to add moldings, belt line and shape of windows.

curved portion of the rear door. There was a curved piece of wood or stamped steel over the wheel cutout window. Across the back there were usually two uprights, plus the framing for the rear spaces. Normally the windshield posts were steel, but on some older cars these were wood covered with a steel stamping. The header over the windshield was wood or steel. The bows supporting the roof materials were usually wood, even on cars with all-steel bodies, before the steel roof panel came into common use in the mid-Thirties.

The length of the car usually determined the number of cross bows supporting the roof material. There was one over the center post and another over the back post of the rear door. Other cross members were placed as needed to keep the material from sagging. Two-door sedans and coupes required fewer structural upright pieces of wood or steel.

Three horizontal pieces per door was common construction, with a diagonal brace on each door from the middle piece to the bottom. Some cars had a wooden or steel sill or frame on which the body was constructed. This was bolted in from four to six places onto the chassis frame, with insulating pads placed to prevent squeaks. Other cars bolted or welded the upright braces to an angle-iron bottom sill. Two-door sedans and coupes required fewer separate horizontal structural wood or steel pieces.

You only have to replace wood or steel that is rotten or rusted through. If some of the old framing is solid, there's no need to replace it. However, you may want to use a slightly longer or wider screw or bolt in the old holes. If you use your hacksaw properly, in many instances you may only have to replace a portion of the wooden or steel structural support. You can splice the support sometimes. However, if you do splice any support, use extra bracing to be sure you have a solid piece overall. New steel can be bolted to old steel, or welded in, for added safety and strength. It's better not to splice structural pieces if you can avoid it. Many times it's a satisfactory replacement method. If there's room, you may find it wise to install an extra piece or two of wood or steel here and there to give added support. Corners and joints on many wooden frames were notched so the pieces had more strength. If this type construction was used in your car, you'll probably want to use the same method in replacing wooden pieces, though it's not absolutely necessary. Steel corner braces were often added for extra strength.

BRACES, BRACKETS AND ANGLE IRON PIECES

If braces, brackets and angle-iron parts are in good condition, reuse them. Be sure they're free of rust or scale. I suggest a primer coat before reusing them. Plan on using new screws or bolts, sometimes slightly longer or thicker than the original for a tight fit. This may require reaming the holes in the braces to accommodate the larger size. Unless your hardware store sells heavyweight steel braces, angle irons, etc., plan on making your own. Lightweight corner braces and angle irons that come prepackaged are fine for shelving and household carpentry. They're not strong enough for car bodies.

Get the flat, heavyweight hardened steel bars from a hardware store to cut and make your own braces. These aren't hard to make with a sharp hacksaw and bit. They'll hold much better and can be made larger than the original if needed. You may find turnbuckles were used on doors. Running diagonally, these helped keep the door in shape. If these are still in good condition, you can reuse them. Scratch a mark near the center portion indicating how far it was threaded in. This way you won't overtighten it and draw the door out of shape.

You must use hardwood—ash, oak, etc.—when replacing structural wood. This is slightly more difficult to work with than a softer wood, but it's far stronger and will hold screws and bolts more tightly. A soft wood such as fir or pine can be used for convertible roof bows or in places where upholstery is to be fastened. However, use a soft wood only for places where real strength isn't required.

Closed Bodies

Four-door sedans, coaches, coupes, victoria coupes, etc., became popular in the Twenties and outsold open cars because of their added comfort and safety. They counted on the added strength of the fixed roof.

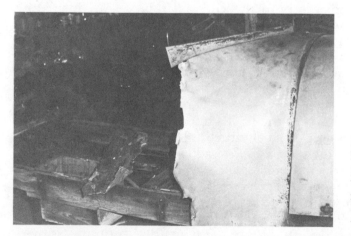

Aluminum body skin on '23 Franklin was torn when supporting wood rotted and door weight tore the cowl. Aluminum can be welded, but in this case piece was reused after new wood and patching job.

The cowl started at the firewall. This was a steel stamping on most cars or a casting on some expensive ones. The cowl was the first body section: it supported the back of the hood and the windshield posts. Most cars had a wooden or steel upright attached to the firewall and another upright at the end of the cowl at the door post. Depending upon how the door was hinged, this piece either held the door hinges or contained the catch. Doors hinged at the front were more common, as the cowl gave added support for wider doors. A cross brace in the cowl at belt line was common and a slanting brace to hold toe boards was installed. A curved cross member connected two uprights behind the dashboard. Some body builders added diagonal braces running from the lower end of the firewall up to the dashboard for rigidity.

As the necessity for better vision increased, windshield posts which were formerly steel-covered wood became steel stampings or castings. These were attached to the top of the wooden or steel cowl upright supports. A wooden or steel cross member at the top of the windshield posts was also attached to the side top rails running lengthwise on the car. A strong brace attached the end of the rear cowl upright supports to the body sill or chassis frame. The cowl uprights took tremendous stress. It's imperative in any restoration that these pieces be completely solid. The rear cowl upright supports have the same contour as the leading edge of the front door and aren't hard to make or replace.

DOORS AND PILLARS

The front door was hinged at either the front or back, depending upon the style the manufacturer accepted. The front door had two uprights, one at each end. At the bottom (windowsill level) and at the top, there were horizontal pieces of wood or steel completing the door framing. An extra horizontal piece was placed a short distance below the windowsill level to hold the bottom of the window winding mechanism. Framing was also provided to hold the door opening mechanism. A diagonal cross brace was often used and in some cases a turnbuckle was mounted diagonally. Steel angle irons and corner braces were screwed or bolted to the structural pieces. The door framework was lightweight and sturdy. Any restoration work should keep that goal foremost.

A center pillar was placed between the front and rear doors. This took tremendous strain. Again, depanding upon how the doors opened, this contained either hinges or door latch fittings. Occasionally, the center post was a steel stamping, even on wooden-frame cars. Usually it was wood

Wooden framing for door must be strong and solid. Scrub metal on inside with wire-bristled brush to remove surface rust, then spray with primer. Plastic filler should only be used when no support is required.

with a steel skin attached to it. The center post was braced three ways at the bottom and three ways at the top. Angle-iron braces were used to attach the center post to the floor and the top rail over the doors. If this post is rotten at top or bottom, it should be replaced. However, some restorers have successfully avoided replacement by making a set of angle-iron braces that extend up from the bottom, or down from the top, a greater distance till they reach solid wood. Your objective is to make the center post extremely solid: use the bracing method only as a last resort. On some four-door sedans, a cross brace between the center posts became the support for the back of the front seat cushion. This was particularly true in seven-passenger sedans or sedans with a glass partition between the front and rear. Smaller cars normally didn't have room for this cross brace.

The rear doors had a wooden or steel upright at each end, plus the bottom, middle and top horizontal pieces. Depending upon how much of the rear wheel arch intruded into the door space, there was a curved piece at the lower rear edge of the door. This corresponded in contour to the leading edge of the rear quarter upright. A fourth horizontal piece held the bottom of the window-opening mechanism. Extra framing was necessary to hold the door opening mechanism. Angle-iron braces were used at the four corners of the framework. Additional iron brackets were used at the joint of the windowsill horizontal brace. Often, wood or steel diagonal braces were used below the window level. Some used a turnbuckle. As with the front door, a solid lightweight framework for the door was the manufacturer's aim. These are the goals the restorer must keep in mind in reworking the framework of a door.

REAR QUARTER PANEL

This panel starts behind the rear door and continues around the back of the car to the back of the rear door on the other side. In early cars this consisted of three pieces of metal skin. Later on, it became a single piece of stamped steel: the framework started with the body upright behind the rear door. This either contained the rear door hinges or the door catch, depending upon how the door was hinged. The panel had a curved section to clear the wheel arch and the framing was made up of two structural pieces; the curved piece and the upright attached to it. This was attached to a cross-member roof support at the top and to the body sill at the bottom. A curved support followed the wheel arch cutout. This was connected to the rear body cross sill. A brace ran horizontally at window sill level. Possibly there was a second piece below it to hold the window opening mechanism for the rear quarter window. There may have been cross pieces of wood or steel to hold the bottom rear seat cushion, though these were usually a steel stamping. A curved brace ran laterally at the belt line level around the back of the car. This may have been arched upward in the middle or level as it crossed the rear of the body. Vertical braces ran between the lower sill to the aforementioned crosspiece. Uprights from the crosspiece held the framing for the rear window and continued upward to the rear roof brace. Horizontal pieces formed the upper and lower rear window framework.

Wooden crossbows support slats for fabric-covered center roof section on most Twenties and early Thirties cars. The restorer can replace rotten wood and recover the top with little difficulty.

ROOF STRUCTURE

Structure of the roof varied according to body builder, as well as length of the car. Generally these were horizontal wooden or steel rails on each side that extended from the top of the windshield posts to the rear upright support. These matched the lengthwise contours that were formed by the door tops. Arched pieces ran up and across from these rails to that portion of the roof that was covered with fabric. On some cars there was a horizontal support running between the top of the door rail and the roof aperture. Separate cross braces made up the roof structure, which was usually covered with chicken wire, a light padding and a rubberized, waterproof fabric. This type of roof was called "French construction," and was supposed to cut down on interior noise and drumming. These were used on even all-steel bodies until the steel stamped roof panel replaced it, starting about 1936. The roof cross braces were on the inside, of course, and it was to these braces that the head lining material was attached.

Coaches and Coupes. These had essentially the same body construction as four-door sedans. However, in some coupes and coach models, the front doors were larger and heavier, since there was but one door per side. To accommodate this extra weight, the vertical supports were sometimes heavier. An extra door hinge was added and the door framing generally beefed up. The number of vertical wooden or steel structural supports was less because of two fewer doors. Roof construction was along the same principle as sedans, but with shorter side rails and fewer cross members used.

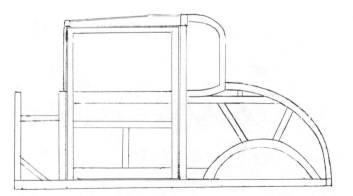

Typical wood framing for coupe. Slight changes in the deck bracing between rumble seat and luggage compartment were the only differences.

Coupes and Victoria Coupes. The average coupe was a two-passenger car in a three- or five-window version. The five-window coupe usually had a narrower front door and often utilized the same front door as the four-door sedan. The three-window coupe usually had a wider door, like the coach. Rumble seats were optional. The "business coupe" normally didn't have a rumble seat. The rear deck opened for storage space. The rumble seat version was often called a "sport coupe." On these, there was often a small door just in front of the right rear fender for storage. Also, the rear window usually could be lowered so front and rumble seat passengers could converse.

The victoria coupe was a four-passenger car. It had two front seats much like the coach. On some, the driver's seat was larger and the right seat considerably smaller. It was meant for auxiliary seating only and would fold quite compactly under the dashboard. These were known as "town coupes" or "opera coupes." The rear seat was close to the front seat. Sometimes there was a storage hamper built in behind the driver's seat. This made the rear seat much narrower. The rear deck opened for storage.

Structural framing for coupes followed the same pattern as sedans from the firewall to the front door. Some cars strengthened the cowl supports and added an extra hinge to support a wider door. Usually there's an added brace within the door framing. If not, sometimes heavier or larger framing was used. Depending upon the size of the car, the number of wooden or steel upright supports varied. The average coupe had six major vertical uprights. Added framing was necessary with the golf compartment.

The lateral structural framing on coupes differed considerably from sedans because of the rear deck. There was a cross member where the top joined the deck. Curved uprights joined this to make the rear roof framing and provide for the rear window. A crosspiece was needed at the front of the deck opening and another at the bottom of the deck opening. The deck itself usually had two or three vertical pieces and two or three cross members. Framing was provided for hinging. Rumble seats often had extra support on top and bottom to handle the weight of the passengers.

Rear deck crosspieces were cut to match the lateral contour of the deck. Hinges for the luggage deck lid were either exposed like door hinges or were concealed underneath the deck. In either case, they hinged against the cross brace ahead of the opening. There was usually a sliding arm to hold the lid open, if it wasn't counterbalanced by a spring. Often you'll find the

Wood framing for luggage lid outlines perimeter of the lid with extra wood around latch, hinges and support strut. Rumble lid may have additional center support and different bracing for hinges.

cross brace supporting the deck hinges has broken. Rust or rot makes a tight closing of the deck lid impossible. Because of poor sealing or clogged drainage openings, there was often leakage around the lid, causing the wooden framing to rot or the steel framing to rust through. Replacements aren't hard to make; with proper sealing to prevent water seeping in, a tight lid closing can be assured.

It's often necessary for the restorer to put an extra brace under fender-mounted rumble seats to give added strength. Stops or bumpers must be placed so lid doesn't rub against deck when opened.

Rumble seat lids were not hinged to the back support of the deck lid: they were attached to iron brackets on each side. The bracket pivoted below and ahead of the rear deck cross member. This allowed the lid to slide below the level of the deck at the back and seek support from stops attached to the compartment floor. On some cars, the pin on which the rumble seat lid pivoted was attached to a wooden upright. On other cars, this upright was a steel plate. Like the luggage compartment lid, because of poor sealing and clogged drainage openings, rumble seat lids often leaked. Leakage often caused the wooden deck framing to rot and steel framing to rust through. Often, this leakage caused rusting of the compartment floor and seat support and in some cases also caused rust-through on the bottom of body panels, as well as the structural supports for these panels.

Deck framing, whether for luggage compartment or rumble seat, is quite easy to repair. Extra bracing can be put in to stiffen the body if needed. One of the easiest methods is to cut a piece of half-inch plywood to fit behind the back of the front seat cushion. This will stiffen the body at midsection. Additional diagonal braces to the rear can be attached to this; additional upright supports at the deck opening can help.

Coaches. These two-door sedans became popular with the advent of the closed car. With two front seats and a back seat, they held four or five people. Coaches were usually lighter than sedans, so often gave better performance. In many cases the body was shorter than a four-door car, often ending just behind the midpoint of the rear wheel arch. A trunk was frequently added to provide luggage space and give a sporty appearance. The front doors were often wider to provide easier access to the rear seat.

Body framing was much the same as on the four-door sedan. The front door, being wider and heavier, was often fitted with an extra hinge and more interior bracing. Most coaches hinged the door at the front to make entry to the back seat easier. However, some hinged the door at midpost.

The average coach required seven structural wooden or steel vertical sup-

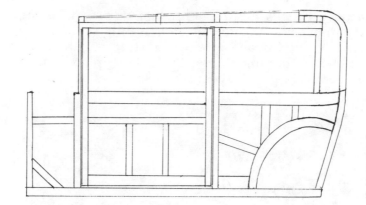

Typical wood framing for close-coupled two-door sedan. Quarter panels were often fabric covered and required more nonstructural framing.

ports. Since there was one less door per side, there was one less roof support. However, the wider door placed the midpost farther back and this compensated in part for the missing upright roof support.

In restoring structural wood or steel supports on coaches, you may find that you'll want to install some additional bracing behind the door post at midpoint to stiffen the body. This is particularly true on some wooden-frame cars. A diagonal brace from the joint of the body sill and the wheel arch to the midpost can stiffen the entire body. An extra, short brace from the wheel arch to the windowsill support can also help. A piece of half-inch plywood cut to fit at the rear of the upper back seat cushion and attached to the existing seat braces makes a solid yet lightweight brace. Usually no additional roof bracing need be installed.

Open Cars   Wood or steel framing is considerably different on open cars. Vertical framing had to be stronger, since there were no cross supports at the top as in closed bodies. The body must get its strength and rigidity from short upright supports. That's why open cars normally have narrower doors; you'll notice a considerable space between the front and rear doors. Some cars have a cross brace between the doors, but this was only on bodies that were long enough to allow this.

Touring Cars. These normally had ten upright supports. The first brace was at the firewall, as on all models. The cowl brace ends at the bottom of the windshield. The windshield posts on open cars were separate castings bolted through the cowl to the upright supports. The front door was normally hinged to the cowl upright supports. Since the doors were lower, as well as narrower on open cars, the door bracing didn't have to be as heavy. Normally the two vertical supports and two crosspieces were all that were required. A diagonal brace or turnbuckle was usually provided on each door. Since there was no window mechanism, framing for this was omitted.

The panel between the front and rear doors was an important structural

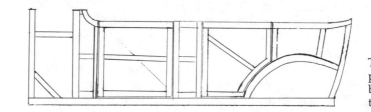

Typical wood framing for five-passenger touring car. Heavy brackets gave solid attachment to the chassis.

part of the body. This had two upright supports, plus a cross member at the top and bracing at the sill. Usually diagonal braces were added.

The rear door was normally hinged at the front and got its support from the section between the doors. Longer wheelbase cars with longer bodies had room for a brace to cross the body at the top of this section. Some cars had two braces and covered this area with metal, forming a second cowl or tonneau. If it was a seven-passenger vehicle, the jump seats were in this center section, which wasn't made into a folding tonneau. Five-passenger models often had a compartment in this section for storage of side curtains, top boot, etc. If your touring body doesn't have an upper cross brace and there is room, you can get extra bracing by installing an upper cross brace. It should be cut to the same contour as the cowl or rear of the front seat and should be covered with sheet metal.

On some sporty jobs, a hinged tonneau section was added. This had to be raised when passengers entered the rear seats. It was hinged at the front to the cross-section brace and latched part way back on the rear doors, or rear quarter when in position. Some of these cars had a folding windshield and wind wings attached to this section. These dual cowl phaetons are among today's most sought-after models.

Depending upon the space inside your touring body, you can add extra support if needed. As mentioned, a brace between the center panels will help. Also, a piece of half-inch plywood fitted at the back of the front seat adds stiffness. The same attached behind the rear seat cushion will also add stiffening and support to the body.

The leading vertical support on the rear panel contained the door latch if the door was hinged at the front, as most were. This may have a partial cut-out for the rear wheel arch, depending upon the length of the body. The placement of the rear door also affected this cutout. This vertical support can be strengthened by a diagonal brace from midpoint on the wheel arch: you can make strap iron braces yourself.

The folding roof on touring cars is attached by hinged roof bows. These get their main support from a rear roof support that runs diagonally upward from just behind the rear door to the back top of the roof. The main roof bow crosses the car at the back and runs diagonally forward and down to meet the body just behind the rear door on the other side. This called for strong bracing where this main roof bow is pivoted. A second roof bow usually ran from a point just above midway on the diagonal part of the rear roof bow. This crossed the body, usually a little ahead of the rear door. Attached near the top of the diagonal part of the second (counting from the rear) roof bow, a third roof bow was attached. This, again at a diagonal to the vertical, crossed the body around the back of the front seat. Attached to

Typical folding-top mechanism on touring car. Often bows were wood, but sometimes tubular metal was used. Seven-passenger and longer wheelbase cars often have an extra crossbow for added support.

this bow on each side were folding braces that supported the front roof bow. The front roof bow attached to the top of the windshield posts with clamps or latches to hold it tight. This completed the folding top mechanism. There may be variances on certain cars, but this was the normal pattern.

Webbing running lengthwise on the car attached to each roof bow. There were usually three or four lengths of webbing equally spaced to support the fabric top. Padding ran lengthwise at each side of the folding mechanism to protect the roofing material and make a smoother fit. There were sometimes adjustable straps inside the back portion of the top, between the rear roof bow and the top of the rear body panel. These could be tightened to make the rear roof bow pull the fabric roof tight. Directions for making repairs to roof bows and folding mechanisms are covered later.

Roadsters. These bodies had much the same wooden or steel framework as coupes. However, because of the lack of cross bracing from a solid top, their upright structural members also had to be stronger. Like touring bodies, they had windshield posts that were separate castings and bolted to the cowl supports. Also like touring cars, they had lower and shorter doors. These required a simple, yet strong framing. The rear post to which the door closed or hinged, depending upon the car, had to be very strong. Also the cross supports behind the seat at the leading edge of the rear deck opening had to be strong. Many bodies developed cracks in the metal, known as "metal fatigue," because of inadequate framing or rot and rust-through as the car aged. Cracks appeared in the corners of the rear deck openings. Sometimes cracks appeared in the metal behind the door. Metal cracks can be welded, of course. But to correct the cause, extra bracing or new supports must be made for these areas.

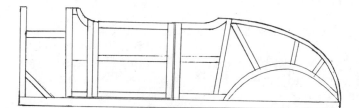

Typical wood framing for roadster body. Windshield posts were usually separate castings. Braces were screwed or bolted to add strength to joints and turnbuckles used on doors.

Roadster tops had supporting bows like the touring cars. A rear roof bow runs diagonally upward from just behind the door to the back top of the roof. It crosses the body to the rear of the seat back, then runs diagonally forward to meet the body just behind the door on the other side. A second bow attaches to a point just above midway on the diagonal upright of the rear roof bow. This crosses the body just ahead of the rear of the door. A front or header bow was attached to the second roof bow by a folding mechanism. The front bow attached to the windshield posts. Clamps or catches held these in place. Webbing and padding were used for the same reasons and in the same positions as on touring tops.

From the firewall to the back of the cowl, the framing was the same as on coupes or touring cars. The door had a front to back upper and lower support, as well as a front and back vertical support. Usually a diagonal brace or a turnbuckle was fitted in the door to prevent sagging. The pillar at the

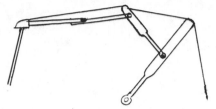

Typical folding-top mechanism for roadster. It must fold compactly, yet give rigidity when in position.

leading edge of the rear body section, to which the door hinged or closed, also helped furnish support to the main rear roof bow pivot. An upright support was usually installed in back of the passenger compartment where it joined the rear deck. Another vertical support was usually used between the wheel arch and the deck opening framing. On longer bodies, there were more upright supports required.

One thing to bear in mind with any open car body is that they often had to contend with water on the inside of the car. Provisions for draining water that gets inside of the body should be cleaned out so they can do the job. In some cases, extra drain holes may be needed.

One of the easiest ways to brace a roadster body is to fit a piece of half-inch plywood behind the back of the upper cushion. From this, angle-iron or wooden braces can extend back into the deck area, as well as toward the door opening support. You want to make the sides rigid so they'll support the top mechanism and absorb road shocks and vibrations.

CHAPTER 17

Body Rebuilding

If you find you have the job of rebuilding the body, or a portion of the body, don't let the thought throw you. There is nothing that you can't do except possibly some welding, and that is easily obtainable. You need to study the rebuilding very carefully and plan your work so you'll know what you're doing to make each operation count. One of the biggest mistakes a beginner–restorer can make is trying to rebuild more of the body than is necessary. Remember that the structural members, whether wooden or steel, must be sound. Any replacements must have the same contours as the original piece. When you've stripped the body or area on which you're going to work, you can easily determine what needs replacement and what can be strengthened or repaired instead. Body rebuilding boils down to one simple fact: when the old won't do, you'll have to make new.

If auto body is too badly deteriorated to repair, sound bodies like this '31 Ford sedan are available at wrecking yards or from other restorers.

Removing the body from the chassis frame usually isn't necessary. It may be too much of a job for the beginner. Wooden framed bodies were built on subframes called body rails. These ran parallel to the chassis of the car. The subframes were attached to the chassis in four or more places with steel

212

brackets. After removing the bolts in these brackets and disconnecting the wiring harness, the body can be lifted off the chassis if necessary. Only in extreme cases of deterioration need this be done. Steel framed bodies were built in much the same way. Many were on a separate subframe and can be lifted off once the holding bolts are removed and wiring harness disconnected.

The frame rails may be rotten if they're wooden, or badly rusted if they're steel. Since these are the main supports for the body, they must be sound. If you must replace one or both, plan on doing one at a time. Many wooden frame rails were set inside an angle-iron form, so you have a pattern there. If one rail is rotten, yet the other one is solid, use the good one for a pattern, remembering you'll have to flip it when making any secondary cuts or installing it. Of course, if the frame rail is straight, not tapered or curved, this isn't necessary.

Most wooden frame bodies were built on steel frame rails with brackets to attach to chassis. Clean out rust, primer and paint before tracing outline on new hardwood lumber. Paint or varnish lumber before installing it inside frame rails.

Body frame rails, whether wooden or steel, were set inside the outer measurements of the body, but outside and parallel to the chassis. They start at the firewall and run the length of the body. There were cross members, usually located where the door posts met the frame. You can easily check the frame rails from underneath the car. They can also be readily examined from the inside once the floorboards and seat cushions are removed.

FRAME RAIL REPAIR

Depending upon the condition of the rails—if deterioration is slight and confined to a small area—repair is usually possible. A steel bar or plate cut slightly larger than the area to be covered can be held in place by bolts or screws. Angle iron can be cut to fit for additional strengthening. A common practice is to "fish plate" the frame. This simply means to cut a piece of flat steel plate to the desired dimensions and bolt it to the existing frame rail to strengthen it. Any work on frame rails should be done one at a time. This

New ash chassis rails for '28 Franklin were cut and glued by a lumber yard. Preserve them with a solution of equal parts linseed oil and turpentine or a commercially prepared preservative. Give rails two to three coats.

Refinished front frame ends for '28 Franklin bolt to wooden chassis rail ends. Graphite-saturated inserts fit between metal and wood to prevent squeaks.

allows whatever support is given by the other side to help maintain alignment. The wood or steel must be strong and solid at the point where the door posts or other vertical structural members join the frame rails. If your car has rotted or rusted through, with weak spots under more than one structural vertical support, it's better to replace the frame rail.

To replace the rail, remove the brackets attaching it to the upright and cross members. You don't need to remove the screws or bolts holding the brace to the vertical or cross member, unless you want to. With the braces loosened, the rail should be free and can be taken out. You may find it necessary to remove the weight of the body from the side you're working on by placing a car jack against a 2 × 4 that will span a couple of the cross braces. By applying a little lift to the jack, it'll remove the weight from the frame rail.

Just as you should stain or paint the new frame rail for protection against

The wooden chassis rotted through on this '23 Franklin and had to be replaced. Replacement rails were located for this particular car.

deterioration, spray the exposed ends of the structural members that are attached to it. You may want to sand and spray the brackets and braces. Only use the original screws and bolts if they're strong and rust-free. In buying replacement screws or bolts, be sure to secure the hardened steel kind. Ordinary over-the-counter screws and bolts aren't strong enough for this work.

CENTER POST

The center post is very important to the strength of the car: in closed cars, it helps support the roof. The doors are either hinged on it or close to it. If it's not perfectly solid, you'll have to find out why and correct the situation.

First remove the upholstery that covers it. In most cases the cloth was stretched over a piece of cardboard and glued on the back side. This is either attached to the center post by screws or clips like the door panels. You may have to loosen the headliner at this particular spot, but avoid that if possible. Once the upholstery is removed, you can see the post from top to bottom. If there's rot or rust at the top, it indicates there's been a leak in the roof or around the gutter over the doors. Depending upon how serious the deterioration, consider installing new angle-iron braces to make it solid. Find the leak and repair it to prevent future deterioration.

If you find the top solid, but the bottom rotten or rusted through, it's probably because the frame rail or body sill has rotted or rusted, too. If they are now sound, you can consider splicing in a new piece of wood or steel to replace that part of the post that's affected. If you do this, use solid hard wood and brace the joint with vertical steel strips. You can cut and drill these yourself. Also consider using longer angle-iron braces at the bottom of the post. You can drill completely through the post, countersink the hole at the outside of the post, and insert new slot-headed bolts directly through the outside body metal, the post and any new braces or brackets. Body putty will cover the bolt head on the outside and when feathered, sanded and painted, it won't show.

If the post is in really bad shape, you'd better replace it. You can remove it, metal skin and all. Usually screws held the hinges or door catches, as well as rubber bumpers and door stoppers. Make a pattern for the wooden or steel replacement. You can use a wooden post as a replacement in an all-steel body if you like, as the body metal will cover the post anyway. For a pattern, use the post on the other side or the contours of the doors that fit against the post. You may have to spread the U-shaped skin over the post to get the old wood or metal out: you can tap it back into shape easily. It's easier to put the skin back on before you attempt to replace the repaired post on the body. Be sure to align the hinges and latches exactly as they were before. As with any replacement wood or metal, treat it with a preservative or paint before installing it.

REBUILDING A DOOR

If it's necessary to rebuild a door, disassemble as much of it while it's in place on the car as possible. But only take off the necessary minimum, since each piece contributes to overall rigidity of the door. Remove the inside

Wood framework on rear door of convertible. Note rotten wood and rusted metal at bottom of the door. Window winding mechanism and door latch are contained in steel framework attached to wooden frame with screws.

window moldings: these are usually in four pieces and held in place by screws. There may be a trim piece, either wood or metal extending below the window. With the frame removed, you can see the screws or clips holding this in place. Store any small screws or clips in a properly marked can for future use.

The window crank and inside door handle are usually held in place by a pin. Press the escutcheon plate toward the outside of the door, exposing the pin. Using either a blunt nail or a small punch, tap gently to start the pin. Sometimes a little oil is required. If the pin is tapered, as some were, drive it from the small side. With the pin out, remove the handle, spring and escutcheon plate and store for future use. Some cars attached the cranks and handles by a set screw on the shaft or a slot-headed bolt visible at the end of the handle. In either case, removal is simple. On some cars the door handle extended up through the window frame and operated from the top. In these cases, the ornamental top handle usually unscrews or is pinned to the shaft. If there's a separate door lock button or a pull strap, these need to be removed, too. Sometimes a strap-type door stop was used. If so, remove the screws holding the loop bracket to the door.

Framework on front door of '39 Buick convertible sedan, with window control and door latch mechanism removed. Note insulation on inside of door; turnbuckle helps hold shape.

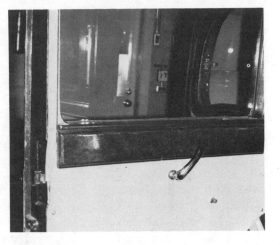

First step in removing upholstery panels is to remove door hardware, then window frames. Window cranks and door handles are normally held in place with tapered pins.

To remove the upholstery panels, proceed slowly so you don't tear the cardboard backing. Remove any exposed screws and washers. Using a thin screwdriver or putty knife, insert it between the upholstery panel and the door. You'll find there are spring clips holding the panel to the door: pry these out, taking care not to bend them. If the upholstery is good enough to reuse, take care not to damage it. If not, you don't have to be so careful unless you want to use the cardboard panel another time. With these parts removed, you've exposed the framework of the door.

If you have to remove window glass, crank the glass all the way up. Since the window moldings have been removed, the glass should rise higher than previously and can be lifted out.

Window raising mechanisms are simple. A crank turns a little toothed wheel. This meshes with two larger wheels. An arm is attached to the large wheels. A coiled spring or springs hold the tension on the wheels so the window will stay where cranked. As you turn the window crank, the arm attached to each large wheel moves along slots on the bottom of the frame holding the glass. As they push out along these slots, the window lowers. As they pull back toward the middle of the frame, the window raises. These may require some cleaning and oiling to get them working smoothly. When the two arms are all the way up, they almost come together. At this point, they'll move outside the channel in which they normally operate and the glass with its frame can be lifted up and out. If the channel at the bottom of the glass is rusted through, this is easily replaced, as many cars used the same size. They usually can be repaired, though, making replacement unnecessary.

The window operating mechanism is attached to the door frame by a series of screws. Remove these and the mechanism will come off the door. Before reinstalling it, it's a good idea to clean it thoroughly with a wire-bristled brush. After cleaning, oil it lightly. To avoid rust, a spray coat of rust-resistant primer helps.

On some cars the door stop is a rod attached to the door post, extending through a hole in the door frame. A rubber faced washer is held in place at the threaded end of the rod. Remove the holding nut or cotter pin if you want to remove the door. Remove the door opening mechanism, if this is in the area you'll need to rebuild. This is located at the edge of the door near the belt line and opposite the hinges. The outside door handle is usually held in place by two screws. With these removed, the door handle will pull out of its slot. The latch mechanism is contained in a plate about four inches square that extends around to the face of the door. Either bolts or screws hold this in place. The movable latch is attached to a quadrant at the inside handle location. One or more springs assist it in operation. On cars where the inside door handle may be some distance from the latch mechanism, there will be an attaching rod that can be disconnected at either end. Like the window operating mechanism, you should inspect the latch carefully and clean it thoroughly. Any bent parts should be straightened, springs lubricated and the ends securely in place. When you've cleaned and lubricated the mechanism, give it a light coat of rust-resistant primer.

You now have the skeleton door frame in clear view. Take any necessary measurements before you remove the door. Note which pieces of wood or steel must be replaced, as well as any that could use some reinforcing.

"Skin" can be removed from wooden doors to replace rotten wood. Install extra bracing if necessary and apply a coat of preservative.

To remove the door from the car, drive the pin out of the hinges, or you can remove the screws or bolts holding the hinges to either the door or the door post. Choose whichever is easier for you. You'll find it easier to rebuild the door if you lay it flat, either on your workbench or the floor.

Because of the importance of having a strong door, be sure to replace or reinforce any rotten wood or rusted-through metal. Use hardwood for replacements. If you don't want to saw the pieces yourself, trace your pattern and have a lumber yard that offers millwork services do it for you. Their cost will be small. If you can't notch or mortise the replacement wood, be sure to use corner or angle braces to hold the joints solid. When mortising or notching wood, use glue as well as screws to hold pieces solid. You can shape pieces of sheet metal in your vise to make replacement pieces for rusted-through steel.

When repairing doors, it's not absolutely necessary to use the same method the manufacturer used. If you feel you can shape a piece of wood easier than sheet steel, do so. Many restorers have rebuilt the basically all-steel body with shaped wooden pieces replacing rusted-out steel supports. On the other hand, you can replace rotten wood pieces with properly shaped steel pieces. Do whichever is easier for you to handle.

Take care in fitting replacement pieces, as you must have the door prop-

After installing new wood frame for door, you'll get extra strength by replacing cardboard upholstery panel with plywood. Paint both sides of wood to protect against deterioration from moisture.

Warped bottom edge of '29 Ford roadster won't allow door to close properly. Metal on bottom and around hinges has weakened.

A good welder can join metals so perfectly they can be plated and will not show a joint. Various types of metal can be welded to each other with proper skill, care and equipment.

erly aligned when finished. Remember that the contour of the front door edge will be the same as the back of the cowl. Also, the contour of the rear edge of the door will be the same as the upright against which it fits. With this in mind, you'll have no trouble in making a pattern that will have the correct contours. To maintain the front-to-back contour of the door, use the bottom door jamb or sill as a pattern. If you find it easier to work with two one-inch pieces of wood rather than one two-inch piece, do so and screw the pieces together when shaped.

When you've cut and shaped the replacement pieces, fit them carefully and screw or bolt them in place securely. Put the door in place to see how it fits before reassembling the latch and window mechanisms. If you have a difference in door contours, make note of how much correction you have to make. Door moldings or striping on the outside of the door should match adjoining sections. Occasionally a washer behind a door hinge will act as a shim and help line up the door. However, it's better to work at it till you get the contour and fit as good as you can make them, only using shims as a last resort.

METAL SKIN

Unfortunately, as the wooden or steel framework on a door deteriorates, the outside metal skin often rusts away with it. When you have the door off and the wooden or steel framework replaced, that's the time to work on the metal skin. In most cases, the rustout will be along the bottom. The sheet metal is not structural; it is easily replaced or repaired. The best way is to have new metal welded in to replace the old. When finished, it won't be noticeable and you have a stronger repair because of it. If you don't want to do this, you can repair it yourself with a piece of galvanized sheet steel.

Rust is beginning to eat through the bottom of rear door on '36 Olds. Spot can be leaded in or new metal welded in place. Alternative method is to apply a metal patch on inside, with fibreglass or plastic filler on outside.

It's easy to patch small rustouts and they're better placed on the inside of the panel, cut to overlap the existing metal. Cut away the worst metal. Make your patch larger than the area so you'll have some solid metal to attach it to. Drill or punch the necessary holes from the outside in. After drilling them, ream the outside slightly to hold a countersunk screw or bolt head.

Bugatti door on right had rusted through. Old metal was cut out and new steel skin welded in for a first class repair.

Use plenty of metal screws or slot-headed bolts. If the rustout extends over the door framework, you can use bolts or screws long enough to secure the patch firmly. There are plenty of body fillers or epoxy materials available to cover the screw heads and patched areas. Or you can lead it in if you want: once the lead or epoxy is in place, it can be feathered at the edges so the patch will be completely invisible when properly painted.

Galvanized sheet steel was cut to fit the rocker panel at back of rear door. When attached by metal screws over old section and properly filled and finished, this makes satisfactory repair.

If you need to have the replacement metal go under the door as well as up the side, either ask a sheet-metal shop to crimp it for you in their metal break or do it yourself. To bend sheet metal to a 90-degree angle, scratch a mark along the line to be bent. Use a sharp nail or punch to make a visible mark. Cut two pieces of wood slightly longer than the metal piece. Place them in a vise with the metal in between. Be sure the mark is even with the top of the wood. Using a third block of wood and a hammer, start bending the metal from the middle in each direction. Bend it only a little at a time until it's all bent in the right direction along the line. Keep bending it until it's flat against the wood: this gives you a 90-degree angle. You can then trim the contour you need. It may be necessary from time to time to make a cut from the outside just to the bend line, to follow curving contours. Fasten the part extending up the door first. Once that is secure, start in the middle of the bottom and secure this point. Work both ways. Either allow the metal to cross over itself where you made your cuts or cut a shallow V to make them meet. Occasionally leave a little tab of metal that can be bent up to secure the new piece to the inside bottom door framework. Use the same procedure to crimp metal for upright portions on the leading or trailing edge of the door. If you worked on the bottom of the door, be sure to make drainage holes to let water out and avoid more rot or rust. When the framework and metal patches are completed, spray the inside with a flat rust-resistant primer. If you want, you can attach insulating material to the metal as long as it won't get in the way of the window operating mechanism. More than once I've coated the inside of a repaired door with a heavy asphalt roofing paint that preserves and insulates at the same time.

When reassembling the door, be sure the latching mechanism is operating properly and lines up with the latch on the post. After the door latch is on and properly operating, install the window operating mechanism. Connect the arms to the bottom window frame by turning them all the way up so they slide into the channels on the frame. Use oil or graphite on the little rollers at the end of the rods to keep them operating smoothly.

If the rubberized or fabric channel in which the glass slides up and down the door is frayed or worn, now is the time to replace it. It's inexpensive

Clips on back of body molding hold it in place. When replacing moldings, be sure they line up properly as on this '37 Buick.

and readily available at most auto supply stores. It's held in place by countersunk screws or glue.

On many old cars, the rubber bumpers that cushion the door closing and keep the doors from rattling have either worn out or deteriorated because of age. Pick the best one you have when looking for replacements. There are places that carry all the rubber replacements a car needs. If for some reason you can't match yours exactly, get the next larger size and trim it down with a razor blade. Companies that supplied these parts originally did so for many manufacturers, so there's great interchangeability among them. If the rubber is still soft and pliable, but only worn down, you can still use it by cutting a couple of cardboard shims to fit behind it and push it out far enough to make replacement unnecessary. Usually at an auto wrecking yard, you'll be able to pick up all sorts of rubber door bumpers for less than a dollar. So don't feel you have to spend a lot of money to locate an exact duplicate.

REAR QUARTER PANEL

You should consider the rear quarter panel in two parts: the section *below* the belt line that extends from the back of one rear door to the back of the other rear door; the other section, *above* the belt line for the same panel.
Lower Rear Quarter. Often the metal at the bottom of the rear quarter panel rusted out where it joined the fenders or along the bottom of the body. This was usually caused by water that leaked in around the windows and didn't drain out properly or by moisture that didn't dry out along fender weltings.

If metal in rear quarter section has rusted through, cut out old metal. Bolt in new metal to hold it in correct position for welding. Make your own strap iron braces using contour guide for correct fit.

The best repair, of course, is to cut out the rusted metal and have new metal welded in. This isn't expensive and makes the best and most permanent type of body repair. However, if your car has a molding along the bottom of the body section, around the fender line, etc., the job is slightly more difficult.

In either case, you must first check the framework supporting these sections. There are usually four upright supports in the rear section between the sill and the belt line. These can be either spliced or replaced if they seem to need it. However, pay particular attention to the bottom sill; if the upright supports are rotten, there will probably be rot where they join the body sill.

In most cases it isn't necessary to replace the bottom sill that runs across the back of the body. Usually you can cut a one-inch piece of hardwood to fit over the existing sill, then screw or bolt the new piece to it. This will provide a solid base for new or repaired upright pieces. Use old vertical pieces as patterns. You can add extra upright supports if you feel the car needs it. A piece of half-inch plywood cut to fit across the back of the body behind the rear back cushion will add stiffness. This can be screwed to the upright supports. Cut out any rusted-through metal before installing new wood, as it makes metal replacement easier once the new wood is in. When you have the framework solid and secure, you're ready to patch the metal. If you cut out the rusted metal, as suggested, cut the patch larger than the area it's to cover. Either punch or dill holes; use metal screws that can be set flush with the outside metal. Bolts are usually more satisfactory if you hold the nut as you tighten the threads. Sometimes metal screws will work loose.

If the metal rustout is in the wheel arch, you may want to make a cardboard pattern before you start with the galvanized sheet steel. You can scribe the pattern onto the metal using a sharp nail or punch. Make the curve fit the outside part of the wheel arch. Mark a similar line about one inch out from the line on which you intend to bend the metal. Cut Vs in that portion that extends beyond the original line. When bent to a 90-degree angle, these can be attached to the body by screws or bolts. Screws or bolts should be used to secure the metal to the wheel arch. When a filler is added to hide the heads and an undercoat properly sanded, you'll never know where the screw heads are. The fender welting between the body and fender will help hide minor imperfections in your work.

In any patching operation, no matter where, always put the new metal on the inside and secure it firmly to the existing metal and any adjacent supports. Epoxy or fibreglass fillers will cover the patched area; when properly sanded and primed, they'll finish off excellently. It's a good idea to spray the inside of each panel with a rust-resistant primer or any other paint you have on hand to prevent further rusting.

Upper Rear Quarter. Rot or rust is not as easily repaired as on the bottom section, but you can do it. There was considerable variety in construction of top rear quarter sections. Some cars had steel above the belt line molding. These seldom had metal rustout, but could easily have rust or rot in the supporting framework if the roof leaked. Once you're sure the wood or steel supporting pieces are solid, either punch or drill holes to hold a patch behind the existing metal. On cars with fabric or leather above the belt line, you'll usually have to rip out the old material to view the supporting framework.

Placing spare tire inside, as on this '39 Chrysler, cut costs and allowed easier entry to luggage compartment. Torn corner on upholstery should be repaired before more damage occurs.

If the headliner shows water stains or mildew, these indicate the roof has leaked. The same is true for upholstery around the quarter or rear window. Where there has been water leakage over a period of time, there's bound to be rust or rot. You may have to remove at least the rear portion of the headliner and the upholstery panels around the rear quarter. This will probably require removing the window moldings. With the upholstery removed, you can easily spot any serious rot or rust.

UPPER FRAMEWORK

With the headliner and upholstery removed, look for rusted metal or rotten wood. These pieces will be curved to match the metal skin. They join the lateral support that runs across the back of the body near the belt line. If this lateral support is solid, you can install T braces if the decay is only slight on the vertical pieces. However, if these won't correct the situation, plan to cut and install new pieces. You may want to leave the old ones in and install new ones at different spots. You can usually use the old ones as a pattern, making allowances for the parts rotted away. You can also cut a piece of cardboard that fits the metal contour on the outside of the body and use it as a pattern.

The framing for the windows is important and is usually held in place by supports down to the belt line, with curved supports up above to the rear roof rail. Check the bottom supporting framework, as water leaks will cause deterioration here first.

Indication of leakage around the rear window requires removal of the glass: then clean out the channel and reseal the glass. A new rubber molding around the glass will probably be easier to install than trying to patch the old one, especially if it's been badly deteriorated by weather. Use a sealing compound between the molding and frame, as well as between the frame and glass. The sealing compound shouldn't be visible from the inside or outside once the window and frame are reinstalled.

On some cars, the metal stamping for the upper rear quarter section was joined *inside* the metal stamping for the lower rear quarter section. Why, no one knows, as this invites leaks inside the body. If your car is constructed this way, remove the molding that covers the joint and put in new caulking. The kind sold at hardware stores for use around home storm windows is excellent for this purpose. It goes in easily and is quite permanent. Once the molding is back in place, the caulking won't show and the seam will be watertight.

Remember that most leakage into the rear quarter will come from the point where the roof panel joins the metal part of the body. There's little use in repairing leak damage if you don't correct the initial source of leaks.

Fabric-covered quarter sections are found on the more deluxe or sporty coupes and sedans. These top sections required more wood or steel framing than the regular metal sections. They often had an oval or round window at the side—or no window at all—and a smaller than ordinary rear window. Some were fitted with nonfolding landau bars as decoration.

Because the fabric-covered rear quarter sections usually precluded any sort of outside metal window frames, there was often seepage that caused rot around these sections. This type of construction utilized metal or thin pieces of wood or plywood to fill in spaces where windows were omitted. Usually there was a light padding over the wood or metal to protect the fabric covering and give a smoother appearance. Unfortunately, this padding held moisture if leaks started and this type of top often needed repair after a few years.

Some cars had a "blind" quarter panel: no window in the fabric-covered area other than the rear window. In these cases the window area was blanked out with metal or wood and formed a base for the padded fabric covering.

Normally patching or repainting fabric will correct nothing other than very minor defects: usually you have to replace it. To do this, make a pattern and get measurements before you start removing the fabric. It's wise to trace the pattern on unbleached muslin or some other inexpensive fabric before you cut the more expensive top material. If your car is equipped with nonfolding landau bars, a nut at top and bottom makes removal easy. Take the molding off by prying carefully—a little at a time—to loosen it. If it is a fabric molding that crimps over to hide the nails, this can seldom be reused, so get it off the easiest way. It's only the metal molding that's reusable and should be saved. With the molding off, start on the fabric at one corner and loosen it. As you remove the fabric, the padding will be exposed. If this appears to be reusable, save it; otherwise, measure it accurately before giving it the pitch. The new polyethylene foam paddings now available are much better than the old-time cotton padding.

At this point, the framework should be visible. Note any pieces that need to be replaced, as well as any that can serve their purpose with splicing or repair. Remove the rotten wood and make a pattern to cut replacement pieces. You may want to install an extra upright support or two. Often it's easier to cut new lateral framework and install it than fuss with the old pieces. Use long bolts with a washer next to the wood on each end. Give the new wood or metal plates and any parts you leave in place a good coat of rust-resistant primer before reassembly. When installing either new or old padding, be sure to get it as smooth as possible. Use plenty of tacks so it won't pull loose or bunch up. Use plenty of good sealant at joints around the landau bar supports so water won't seep in later.

FLOORBOARDS

On many cars, the original floorboards were over a half-inch thick. These were bolted or screwed in place and gave added rigidity to the body. They

If floorboards are in good condition, clean and give them a coat of preservative. If new boards are needed, draw a pattern using a center line to take widening body measurements into consideration.

should be solid and free from rot or splinters. Old ones can usually be used as a pattern in making new ones. If not, you can measure the space to be covered and make your own. So the floor padding and mats will fit properly, use the same thickness of replacement wood, if possible. If not, a washer under each holding screw will hold the top of the floorboard to the desired level. When making a pattern for a replacement floorboard, get precise measurements. You may notice that the floorboard is wider at the back than at the front. To be sure you cut properly, draw a center line on your pattern and make your measurements equidistant from it.

It's easier to cut floorboards out of a good grade of plywood than solid lumber. Plywood is stronger and lighter, too. Mark where the holes are to be drilled for screws and bolts. Many cars had a piece of felt or other fabric where the floorboards met the frame to cut down on squeaks. It's wise to have this on replacement boards. You may also notice metal clips on one board that slip into matching slots on the adjoining board: be sure to include these if they were used. Spray the replacement boards with a primer paint or treat them with a wood preservative before installing them.

Often floors in rear compartments were lowered below the frame to give added foot room, with a metal tunnel along the middle to make room for the drive shaft. These lowered spaces were called "foot wells." In earlier cars the bodies were higher and the rear floors flat, as in front. On later cars, stamped steel panels were used as floorboards. They often rusted through and have to be patched with heavy galvanized steel sheets. Cut out the rusted area, treat the old panel with plenty of primer, then screw or bolt the new piece over it. I've used house roof cement between the two pieces of metal to get a good seal.

In the front compartment there may be a metal hump over the transmission, with the floorboards slightly lower on each side. The transmission cover and rear compartment tunnel came into use as stylists designed lower cars. Be sure the plate over the transmission, as well as the one over the rear tunnel, is well painted before being covered with carpet.

Since floorboards, as well as metal floor pans, are exposed to weather conditions underneath and moisture brought inside by wet shoes, etc., it's a good idea to either paint new boards and panels or treat them with a creosote preservative before installation.

SEAT SUPPORTS

Normally, seat supports are not structural; however, on some wooden framed bodies, every piece of wood was made to give added strength to the

Many cars had metal framework bolted to a cross member to hold the bottom seat cushion. Battery was frequently placed on one side and tool storage compartment on the other.

body. Depending upon body style and construction, seat cushion supports varied. It was common practice to have a space under the front seat to contain the battery and some tools.

In body construction the front seat, or at least the driver's side, was made adjustable. Early models simply added a hinged part to the front seat support. In one position, the seat was average height. With the hinged portion in place, the front of the cushion would be elevated by the depth of the hinged piece. Some cars had a solid back to the front seat, but there were split cushions to allow the driver to sit at a different position than the passenger. A common front-to-back adjustment was a threaded rod with a decent-sized knob on the front. By twisting the knob, the driver was able to move the whole seat arrangement on short tracks. Later cars had a notched bracket device supporting the cushion. By releasing the lever that latched into the notches and moving his body, the driver could move the seat.

Back seats were seldom adjustable, though some cars had provisions for a block to be added to raise the front edge of the cushion. Because of the space required for the up-and-down movement of the rear axle, the rear seat was usually higher from the ground than the front seat. The front brace that held the rear seat cushion in place was frequently a carpeted cross piece. The seat cushion pushed in behind it or there were pegs on the frame of the cushion that fitted into corresponding holes in the floor. Most cars had a metal pan between the rear seat cushion and the frame. A few had wooden boards over this. In some cases there was a metal inspection plate over the top of the differential.

The framework that supports the seats should be firmly attached to the body frame. The back seat usually depended upon the pegs on the seat cushion or cross member to keep it in place. Frames for front seats, either movable or solid, relied upon being bolted to a solid cross member or solid floorboard. It's important in restoration that the seat framework (called squabs) be solid. Any adjusting mechanisms should be firmly anchored, cleaned and given a light coat of graphite or oil to work properly.

Since you'll probably want to install seat belts, this is the time to look for the best location for the anchor bolts.

Because of fumes given off by the battery, the cover to the battery box should fit tightly. Also, to avoid engine or exhaust fumes from entering the passenger compartment, all floorboards and floor pans should be solid and firmly attached in place.

WINDSHIELD

In most cars, both open and closed, the windshield could be opened. This provided additional ventilation in the days before air conditioning. By now, the rubber gaskets are probably wornout and many cars will have developed leaks around the windshield. Since there were several types of opening mechanisms, the most popular ones will be covered.

Open Cars and Convertibles. Many of these had "fold flat" windshields. By loosening a winged or round nut at each post, the windshield could be folded flat against the cowl. On this type of windshield, some frames were held to the posts at both top and bottom. Others were hinged at the top of the post and could be pushed out from the bottom, leaving the posts in their upright position. To replace the rubber gasket or glass, remove the frame from the posts. You'll find the frame has flush slot-headed bolts holding the sections together. After a little soaking in oil or rust remover, the bolts can be unscrewed, disassembling the frame. The glass can then be taken out. You'll have no trouble buying new rubber gaskets; some restorers have successfully made replacements from old inner tubes. Use a sealant when replacing the glass in the frame.

Other open cars had the windshield set in posts that did not fold: the frame was hinged at the top and opened outward. On this type, there may be an opening mechanism on each windshield post. These are easily disassembled to allow the windshield to open out far enough to get at the screws holding the hinges at the top. Either the frame will come apart in two halves, or the top piece of the frame may be removed. You'll find the rubber or fabric in the channels that hold the glass, along with a rubber gasket to prevent leakage around the frame. This usually has to be replaced in the same manner as previously described. On cars with a center knob that operated the windshield, turn the mechanism out far enough to expose the screws holding the frame, then remove them. Remove the frame by removing the hinges at the top.

Closed Cars. These had windshields that either cranked up into the header board or were hinged at the top and swung out when clamping arms were properly positioned. On the wind-up type, there may be a separate framework. Some arrangements depended upon the channel at the top holding the glass, as it moved up and down in U-shaped channels just like window glass. In some cases the header panel must be removed, along with the framework or molding. You can easily replace the channels in which the glass moves and the gasket along the bottom of the windshield. Work on the winding mechanism is similar to that on the windows; attack it by removing the header board.

On the crank-out type windshield, you can disconnect the cranking mechanism, remove the inside moldings and expose the hinges at the top. Remember, on a swing-out windshield you must have a good tight seal around all four sides of the frame.

Some cars built through the mid-Twenties had two-piece windshields. The bottom section extended upward three or more inches, and a top section overlapped it by about a half inch when closed. Some of these had a thin piece of rubber fitted to the top of the bottom panel, but as this made a visible line across the windshield, most relied on the overlap to keep out water.

Usually, only the upper glass was movable and it was hinged at the top. Winged nuts through brackets held the windshield in place, open or closed. Windshields of this era preceded the use of safety glass; unless it was installed later in your car, plan on installing it now, as you replace the rubber gasket.

Broken Windows. You don't have to remove the upholstery to replace broken window glass on most cars. Usually it's only necessary to remove the window moldings and crank the window all the way up. With the moldings removed, the bottom window holding frame will be exposed. You'll notice an open section near the middle of the metal tracks in which the operating arms ride. Move these to the center till they're out of the holding tracks. The glass and frame can then be lifted free of the door.

With the glass on a flat area, use a rubber hammer or tap with a piece of wood to free the glass from the bottom holding frame. Usually there'll be a rubber or fabric strip between the glass and the frame; you may also find that a sealing compound was used. Clean the metal channel and give it a coat of a rust-resistant primer. Use new fabric or rubber if the old isn't in good condition. Tap the new glass into the frame lightly. Once in the frame, place the glass in the door. Slide the operating arms into the tracks on the bottom of the metal holding frame. Give them a drop or two of oil. You can then crank the glass down. Run it up and down a couple of times to be sure it's operating properly before reinstalling the window moldings.

CHAPTER 18

Body Trim

The appearance of your car's interior is a significant asset to its overall value, as well as your enjoyment of the car. Although body trim items have little to do with the car's general operation, they do add convenience and comfort. By and large, trim items are easy to refurbish and inexpensive if replacement is necessary. The number and variety of trim items varied by make and model of car. The more expensive the car, the more trim items it had. Window shades, robe rails, vanity cases, ashtrays, lighters, clocks, mirrors, assist cords, foot rests, dome and courtesy lights, are all classified as body trim items. So you see, it's the little things that mean so much.

Trim items usually require very little attention. For the restorer, it's a matter of cleaning, polishing and occasionally refinishing. Clocks may need professional repair and mirrors resilvered. Some of the electric items may need repair. In most cases, however, the restorer can properly refurbish trim items to a highly acceptable degree.

As a restorer you should consider the functional trim items first, then work on the convenience group.

DASHBOARD

A good looking, functional dashboard considerably enhances interior appearance and enjoyment of the car. It can make driving easier and it's worth the time to restore it properly. The instruments must be made to work: cleaning is all that's often necessary to make the oil pressure gauge work and it's seldom that anything goes wrong with the ammeter gauge. Occasionally a fluid-type gas gauge will need additional fluid. If the speedometer doesn't work, the problem is usually in the flexible cable that drives it. Since instruments were always covered with glass, the dials and pointers should not require attention unless the glass has been broken. Occasionally you'll find that the instrument will require replacement or repair by a machine shop, but these are exceptions. There are shops that specialize in

Reworked dashboard on '41 Lincoln Continental with chrome knobs replacing deteriorated plastic knobs. Instruments were masked off and the dash sprayed. Four light coats, sanded between coats, produced glass-like finish.

rebuilding dash instruments and advertise regularly in old car magazines. During restoration of well over fifty cars, I've had to call on professional help only a couple of times; these were for speedometer parts I couldn't locate.

Make sure that the lights behind the instrument panel are working properly. The explanation of the electrical circuitry has been covered. If a new fuse or bulb won't correct inoperative dash lights, run a new wire, as it's important to see the gauges when driving at night.

Dashboards have changed over the years. Taking the name from buggies, early cars grouped their few instruments and controls on the dashboard. In early cars this was sometimes the firewall. Later it became a different panel, separated from the firewall by the length of the cowl. As the number of instruments and controls grew, the panel became known as the instrument board. As the influence of the stylist became greater, instruments were made more decorative and grouped. Glove or map compartments were added, as were ashtrays and places for radio controls and speakers. The instrument board became the focal point of the interior styling.

On some cars the dashboard was made of wood. Instruments were viewed through holes in the wood and were attached to the back of the board. Lower priced cars used steel stamping, either painted or finished to resemble wood.

In some instances, the dash was made of two separate pieces. One fitted against the bottom inside of the windshield frame and extended down a few inches, following the curve of the top of the cowl. A second piece extended from one side of the cowl to the other and contained the instruments. On most cars these were combined into one piece. Often instruments were clustered and either individually glassed, or the cluster was covered by one piece of glass. Control knobs were mounted below the dash or through holes in it.

If the dashboard was painted black or a solid color and is not rusty, you won't need to remove it. Mask off the instruments and knobs and sand the finish until it's smooth. It may take two or three coats of primer, with sanding in between coats, to get the smooth base you want. Once you have it, spray a coat or two of glossy paint. Lightly sand between coats. In spraying the dash, as in other spray painting, it's better to use several light coats than one heavy coat to avoid runs. After the final coat has hardened, a good waxing should preserve the finish.

If your car has a wooden dash or a metal one that is in bad shape, you

Remove instruments and glove compartment doors when refinishing dashboard. Sand lightly between coats. Use enough coats to get depth of finish you want.

Wooden dashboard should be removed from car and refinished like fine furniture. Avoid liquid paint remover, as it can lift veneers if cracked. Sand between coats and rub with fine pumice stone to get desired finish.

should remove it for the refinishing process. Disconnect the instruments: tag the wires so you'll know how to reconnect them. Most instruments are held to the dash by screws or brackets and will come out easily. The coupling on the speedometer cable housing will unscrew easily. The oil gauge may have a small pipe running to it: when disconnected, wrap a bandaid or bit of tape over the end to preclude dirt entering the tube.

You may find that the steering column is attached to the dashboard. If so, remove the bolts holding it. You'll find screws or bolts holding the dashboard to the cowl on each side, as well as across the top. With these removed, the panel should pull back and out. Some of these screws or bolts may be difficult to reach and you'll wonder how the hell they ever got there in the first place—remember that these may have been assembled in the body-building process before other stampings or panels were added.

Metal. Once the panel is out, lay it flat and clean it good with a strong detergent solution. Remove any rust with a thorough sanding before giving a primer coat. Apply as many primer coats as necessary to build up a good base for the glossy paint. Sand lightly between coats to remove any blemishes or rough spots. Once you have the base coats to your satisfaction, spray the glossy coats, sanding lightly between applications to give the proper finish. A final rubdown with pumice stone or extra-soft steel wool will produce a glasslike finish. Use a clear varnish or lacquer final coat if you like.

Wooden. If the dashboard is made of wood, you'd refinish it like any piece of furniture. Remove the old finish by scraping or sanding, or with a liquid paint remover. Wash all traces of liquid paint remover off before filling any cracks or blemishes with wood filler. Sand the board till smooth and apply either a color stain or shellac. Sand lightly and repeat this step if necessary. Apply either a semigloss or high-gloss varnish. Sand lightly and apply a second coat. Build up as many coats of varnish as you feel necessary. Finally, rub it down with pumice stone or soft steel wool. A final coat of wax will keep the finish you've produced.

Remove instrument clusters, ash trays and glove compartment doors to get proper finish. This '36 Auburn and some other autos had chrome-plated fascia above dash. If chrome doesn't clean up to please you, replating is necessary.

GIVING METAL A WOOD-LIKE FINISH

On some cars the dashboard and window frames were metal, but finished to look like wood. You have a choice of methods if you want to restore these. If you don't feel you can do it satisfactorily, there are places advertised in old car magazines that will do the job for you. You can take the dashboard and window reveals to a paint store and there's a good chance they'll suggest a painter who can handle the work for you.

It's better to restore, or have restored, any parts that originally were wood finished. It's always wise to restore a car to as nearly original as possible, only accepting substitutes in materials and methods when you have to. If you don't want to, or can't afford to restore these parts to the original, you can apply wood-grained adhesive-backed shelf paper. This is about what's done on today's station wagons. If you do this, be sure you allow the material to extend under or around any flanges, so it won't start to peel with use. Once it's applied properly, a spray coat of clear lacquer or plastic finish helps preserve it.

If you decide to apply paint and want to give a wood-like finish, decide on the base coat color. Usually a medium flat brown enamel is best. A couple of coats, sanded in between, should be sufficient. Pick two or three graining colors that you want. It helps if you have a piece of wood with the finish you plan to copy. Give a light application of one graining color: this must go on streaked, as you're not trying for a solid color. After it dries, apply a coat of the second graining color, etc. It's not necessary to sand between graining coats unless you want to. You can use a toothbrush, stiff brush or coarse steel wool for these applications. When all graining coats are applied and dried, sand lightly and varnish. Several coats of varnish may be necessary to give the depth of finish you want. A rubdown with pumice stone or soft steel and waxing should complete the job.

WINDOW FRAMES

Window frames should have essentially the same treatment as the dashboard. If they're wood, refinish them as you did the dash panel. If they're painted, they're often a color that harmonizes with upholstery, a neutral color or match the car. You're never wrong with black. If they're wood-grain finish, refinish them using the same methods as outlined for the dashboard.

Occasionally you'll come across a car that has highly polished or plated

Window frames from a convertible like this '32 Marmon can be removed when controlling arms are out of channel and windowsill removed from door. Broken bottom channel must have new metal welded in or replacement installed to hold frame solid. Replace rubber or fabric channel if worn.

Beautiful wood veneers and cabinetry surround swiveling jump seats on Brunn-bodied Pierce Arrow. Because of excellent workmanship and materials, unless upholstery is torn, it'll usually clean up satisfactorily. Replace glasses and flasks in bar.

dashboard and window trims. If this is the case, usually a thorough cleaning with a strong detergent and power polishing are all that are necessary. If the plating is worn through in places, you can either have the pieces replated or paint the whole ensemble.

INSTRUMENT CLUSTERS

Cleaning is all that's required for many instrument panels. Occasionally, glass will have been broken and require a new piece. Sometimes the rims on instruments need replating. Clusters can usually be removed without having to disconnect each separate instrument. This will allow you to trace a pattern and have a glass shop cut you a new piece. When replacing the cluster, be sure any gasket is in place, so you don't crack the new glass as you tighten the cluster.

Some cars had a steel insert with small semicircular designs around the instruments. This was machine turned and the process was called *damascening*. These can usually be restored by polishing, then coating with clear finish. There's also available a chrome tape with an adhesive backing. This comes in several widths, has a true engine-turned appearance, and is easy to apply. It can be used to recover these cluster panels. Since they're usually flat, there's no problem in cutting and trimming the material to give a tight fit. Once on, a spray coat of clear finish will give added protection.

GLOVE COMPARTMENT

Some cars had one or two compartments in the dashboard. These were used for storage of small articles. In most cases, the doors were finished like the rest of the panel, but in some models were a contrasting color. They should be given the original finish.

The inside of these compartments were either wood, steel or fibreboard. You can easily make a replacement if necessary. From time to time, leakage around the windshield caused the compartments to deteriorate; other times they were loaded too heavily and simply wore out.

Making replacements isn't difficult. Make a pattern so you know the dimensions you have to work with. Either use plywood or fibreboard to make the new box. The inside can be covered with pieces of felt cut to size and glued in place, or any other vinyl or fabric. There is a wrinkle-finish paint available in spray cans which is excellent for the inside of these compartments. Check the hinges and latches, being sure they're properly secured. If the latch is worn down, you may find a shim underneath it will make it hold when closed. Ordinarily, these boxes were attached to the dash panel at the front and had a simple brace in the back. You may want to add some bracing if you make a replacement box. While you have the box out, be sure to seal any leaks that may have caused deterioration in the first place.

INTERIOR LIGHTS

The electrical portion of repairing interior lights has been covered in Chapter 12. Once you're sure the current gets to the light, refurbishing the light is the next step.

Dash Lights. Lights that are mounted externally on the instrument panel to give light to the instruments, as well as the surrounding areas, were usually chrome or nickel plated. Often these had a removable shade portion that allowed for changing the bulb and directing the beam of light. Soaking in a strong detergent solution will remove any grime or light rust film. They can be scrubbed with a detergent pad and sprayed with a clear finish to keep them shiny. If they won't clean up sufficiently, consider painting them the color of the dashboard or having them replated.

Map Lights. On some cars, these were on a cord attached to a reel and could be drawn out and held over maps. These usually had a plated cover over the socket and bulb, as well as a plated receptacle on the dash. Most interior plating will clean up with a scouring pad and detergent solution. If not, they can be painted like the dash or replated.

Some map lights were recessed in the header bar over the instrument panel; only a small frame, lens and switch show. Again, if the framework won't clean up, it can be painted or replated. This type of light may have a silvered reflector inside. If the reflector won't clean up sufficiently it can be sprayed with aluminum paint to give the necessary reflection.

Trouble Light. An accessory on some cars, standard on others, a trouble light stored in the glove compartment or on a clip under the cowl. The lamp fixture usually had a small handle and a reflector to help intensify the light. Normally, there was no switch on this type lamp, as it had to be plugged into a small receptable to get current. If the lamp was plated, try to clean it up with a scouring pad and detergent solution. If this won't clean it to your satisfaction, consider painting it if you don't feel it warrants the cost of replating. If the reflector doesn't clean up properly, it can be sprayed with aluminum paint or resilvered. Check the bracket and plug while you're at it to be sure everything's tight.

Dome and Courtesy Lights. Most cars had one, two or more lights in the ceiling of the car. Others had lights in the rear quarters. These were controlled by a switch on the dash, on the door pillar, or a combination of switches. In some cases the light switch was activated when the doors were opened. These lights sometimes had quite fancy lenses and ornate frames matching the pattern of other interior hardware. Usually the frames will clean up satisfactorily with washing in a strong detergent solution. Sometimes a little extra rubbing with a fine scouring pad will help. When cleaned they should be sprayed with a clear finish or given a light coat of wax. The reflectors inside the lamps will usually clean up; occasionally, you'll have to spray them with aluminum paint.

If the lens is broken, try to locate a replacement through the ads in old car magazines or car flea markets. You may have to settle temporarily for a plain glass lens. The type of covering made for bathroom windows can be cut and applied to a plain glass insert, if there is only one dome light in the car. It is much better than using a plastic lens.

Courtesy lights appeared in different positions inside or outside the car. The most common was mounted on the apron above the running board, usually centered. It turned on when the door was opened and gave light on the running board. These usually had a simple plated frame around a frosted lens. If the rim won't clean up, consider having it plated. You can always paint it as a last resort. Some courtesy lights were mounted on a panel below the rear door floor sill. They were out of sight when the door was closed and operated by a switch when the door opened. Most of these had a plated rim and a flat frosted lens. If they won't clean up properly and you don't feel you want the expense of plating them, they can be painted easily. Since courtesy lights were low output lights, aluminum paint on rusty reflectors gives a satisfactory job.

There are several things to keep in mind when reworking interior lights. If your car has more than one interior light that shows, try to match the rims and lenses. Many manufacturers bought their interior hardware from the same company, so you may be able to find suitable replacements in another make. Don't overlook flea markets or car-part sales held by car clubs, as a source. Many car magazines carry ads on parts for sale. A good tip is to look under the parts wanted ads: you may find someone with a car similar to yours advertising for parts. A letter containing a stamped, self-addressed envelope asking about parts you need may bring results.

It may take some extra time to locate the lenses or rims you want; if so, it's worthwhile. A piece of clear plastic or glass cut to fit will protect the inside of the light while you're looking for a replacement.

OTHER TRIM ITEMS

Each trim item should have adequate attention to be sure it's doing its job properly. None are difficult to repair, and once done, you'll appreciate having them in place and working.

Door Check Straps. These are very important: they keep the door from opening beyond the proper distance and putting extra strain on the door framework and supporting pillar. New ones are readily available at automotive supply stores. You can make your own if you wish. I've often bought web belts from Army Surplus stores and covered them with vinyl. They work fine. Or leather belting will do the job. Be sure the securing screws through the end plates are holding firmly when replaced, as there's a lot of strain on these straps.

Robe Rails and Assist Cords. If these are frayed or torn, you can recover them in a fabric matching the upholstery. It's unlikely you'll find ready-made replacements unless you have a popular make car. Cut the material slightly longer than the cord to be covered and turn back the raw edges. Either sew the material together inside-out on a machine or wrap it around the cord and hand stitch along the back where it won't show. Be sure to clean the attaching hardware before reinstalling.

Foot Rests. These were normally hinged so they could be moved out of the way when not in use. The hardware on the ends was usually plated, but can be painted if it won't clean up satisfactorily. The rail itself was either wood or steel, normally covered with carpet. If the carpet is worn, it can be replaced. Remove the assembly from the car; the rail will either come out of the end brackets by itself or there may be a screw in each end. Once the old carpet is removed, clean the rail and measure for the replacement material. In some cases the material was glued on and forced into a slit that ran lengthwise along the back. On others, it was tacked to the wooden bar. You may want to glue the replacement cover in place and attach it to the back with metal screws or tacks. You may feel that hand sewing the carpet edges together along the back will give you a better job. Do as you choose, as it's easy any way you do it.

Window Shades. Often these will be water stained or mildewed because of roof leaks. Some mildew may come out if the shade is exposed to strong sunlight. However, even dry cleaning doesn't often help and the shades will have to be replaced. If the rollers are not broken, you can make new shades to attach to them. Rollers are spring loaded and the little ratchet on the end may need cleaning and lubricating before installing the new cover. Match the original fabric as closely as possible. New shades can be stitched on a home sewing machine. Hardware stores will carry the thin dowel for the bottom if you need new ones, as well as the little screw-eyes that the guide cords run through. The new cloth should either be stapled or tacked to the roller. Clean the brackets before installing the shade. New guide cords are easily attached if necessary.

Inside Visors. When the visors disappeared from the outside of the car, they reappeared on the inside. Outside visors were victims of efforts to streamline cars. The inside visors were usually cloth or leather covered and hinged to the header board above the windshield. Standard cars normally had one visor for the driver. A second visor on the passenger's side was included in deluxe jobs. Some of these were mounted on one arm, with a swivel attachment for adjusting the angle. Others had two mountings, one of which unplugged so the visor could be moved to protect from glare coming in a side window.

If the hardware holding the visor is OK, the visor itself can be recovered if necessary. If the visor is badly broken, you can cut a new one: use either light plywood or fibreboard as a base and recover with cloth or vinyl.

Mounting hardware is not difficult to locate if some is missing, as many cars used identical mountings. If making a replacement visor, sew the cloth or vinyl together inside-out on three sides. Turn it right side out and whip-stitch the top edge. You may want to use a light padding between the board and cloth or vinyl.

Mirrors. Usually a rear-view mirror for the driver was mounted at the center of the windshield header, aimed at the rear window. This should be put into perfect condition or replaced, as it has to do with the safety of the car's occupants. Other mirrors were often placed for the use of passengers, e.g., mounted on the inside of the right visor. Some were in corners of the rear quarter section. All the restorer can do is check and adjust the mountings. These were either plated or painted. If the mirrors need attention, they can be resilvered or new mirrors cut to fit. Mirrors are inexpensive and should be in excellent condition.

Clocks. On older cars these were hand-wound; later models were electrically operated. They were standard equipment on many of the more expensive cars, and an accessory on lower priced cars. Usually they were mounted on the dashboard and in some cases a second clock was mounted on the top railing at the rear of the front seat or in vanity cases. The hand wound ones can be repaired at a clock and watch repair shop. Electric ones can be repaired, of course, but check the fuse and wiring before having the clock works repaired. A common accessory was a clock in a mirror to be mounted on the windshield header board. You probably can't do any clock repairs yourself, but they are inexpensive, and an accurate clock adds to enjoyment of the car.

Ashtrays. A source of rattles on many cars! Be sure the holding brackets are tight; install a thin shim if necessary. Check the tension on the spring that holds the lid closed. Most receptacles had a tray on the inside. The tray may be rusted out and if so can be easily replaced. If the receptable is plated, it will usually respond to soaking in a strong detergent solution. You can paint it, if replating sounds too expensive.

Lighters. Some cars had a unit that was pushed in to make contact and had to be held in to heat the element. Others had a pop-out type that needed only to be pushed in. Still other lighters were on a long cord attached to a reel. When this type was heated, it could be passed around and the cord would wind itself back on the reel after use. Many times the element or tiny coiled wire inside the lighter would become brittle and eventually break. You can usually find replacement elements, as most companies bought from several manufacturers.

Lighters were usually on a separate electric circuit. Most did not require that the ignition be turned on to complete the circuit. If your lighter is not working and the element seems to be in good shape, check the fuse, then the wires. If there are but a few cracks in the insulation, you can tape them. However, it's usually better to replace the entire wire and be sure the circuit is grounded. Check to see if there's a rubber or bakelite gasket insulating the lighter receptacle from the dashboard or mounting surface. On the reel type, check the tension on the pulley wheel and the little ratchet device. Usually a drop of oil will let it work freely.

Vanity Cases. One, sometimes two, cases were found in the rear compartment. These varied greatly with the cost of the car. Some were stamped steel, leatherette covered and contained only an ashtray. Others were finely polished wood with several compartments. Removable ashtrays, mirrors, perfume flasks, etc., were included. Others had note pads, pencils and smoking equipment. Most can be easily removed from the car and refinished like a piece of cabinetry. Check the wiring to be sure there are no breaks in the insulation.

It's often possible to find replacement fittings that will be suitable at stationery stores and gift shops. Decide what refinishing needs to be done and give it a try. These have nothing to do with the operation of the car, so the cost of refitting or professionally refinishing depends upon what you want to spend.

Leather or vinyl trays can be recovered by tracing outline on new material. Allow enough extra on edges to glue, tack or staple. Replace clips and hinges after formica or wood is in place.

Bars, Compartments, Folding Trays. The more deluxe expensive cars had these goodies in varying degree and size. They were usually mounted on the back of the front seat facing the rear seat passengers. Usually of wood, they need to be refinished as furniture with careful sanding and filling, staining, varnishing, rubbing, etc. These all take time, but make a terrific difference in the finished appearance of the car. They also give added pleasure when using the car, so give them whatever attention you feel they

Replace chipped or split veneer on folding tray tables by tracing shape on new material. Remove all hardware, clamp new material in place until glue has dried, then trim edges.

need. Flasks, glasses, etc., can also be located to fit these bars. You can even have them monogrammed for a personal touch.

Door Handles and Window Cranks. These accessories should be cleaned and should match. If you have any that don't match, use what you have until you can locate what you need. Many of these were interchangeable among cars, so you should be able to find just what you need in time. To clean them properly, you should remove them from the car and give them a good soaking in a strong detergent solution, plus a light scrubbing with a soft scouring pad. In most cases, they'll clean up very easily and the overall interior appearance will be greatly improved.

CHAPTER 19

Convertible Tops

Nothing enhances the appearance, pleasure and value of an open car more than a good looking, properly working top. A new folding top can be easily made by the beginner–restorer if a replacement isn't available. Access to a sewing machine, room enough to cut the material, and a little patience are the main prerequisites. You can let the sunshine in, but only when you want it!

Before making the new top, it's necessary to be sure the top bows and folding arms are in good working condition. You'll need to assure yourself that the clamping, or hold-down mechanism that attaches and holds the front roof bow to the windshield posts is tight and strong.

Special automotive and upholstery shops carry an assortment of replacement materials for convertible tops. If there isn't one one near you, you can order from ads appearing in the national old car magazines. Be sure to get samples and prices. Choose a material as close to the original as possible to maintain the value of your car. Also select a color that is near original, or a color offered as an option. When choosing the bindings, weltings, and top hardware, choose items as near the original as possible. You'll maintain the value of your car better if you stick to original specification replacements.

ROOF BOWS

On touring cars, there were usually three roof bows, plus the front or header bow. These were attached to each other in such a manner that they would hold the top in a rigid position, yet fold in a reasonably easy and compact manner. Ease of operation was so important that advertising campaigns stressed a "one man top."

The rear roof bow was usually attached to arms that ran diagonally down from the back roof line to the belt line of the car just behind the rear door. These were pivoted at the bottom. Part way up this diagonal arm, a second roof bow was attached at an angle that placed the cross member about even

Make replacement bows of hardwood for strength. Sand and varnish for looks, long life and protection. Attach bracing, landau bars and webbing. Make sure folding arms work properly before installing padding and top covering.

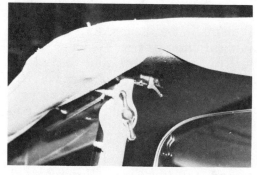

Make sure roof bow attachment is secure and that second bow and folding mechanism are strong and in good condition before installing top.

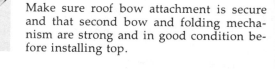

Fittings to attach header bow to top of windshield vary from car to car. Thumb screw on Model A is simple and strong. Make sure fittings are firmly attached.

with, or slightly ahead of, the rear door opening. Near the top of this diagonal brace and usually hidden by the top covering itself, another brace was attached—running forward to a third cross member about even with the rear of the front seat. To this brace, an arm was attached which connected with the front bow and placed it directly over, or slightly ahead of, the windshield posts. It was attached to the windshield posts by clamps. Seven-passenger cars, because of their added length, often required an extra cross roof bow. Roadsters required fewer.

There may be some differences among makes because of individual design and manufacturing techniques. The bow and holding arrangement was always such that when the top was folded, it was behind the seat and out of the passengers' way.

Most roof bows were highly varnished wood. Originally, most were steam bent to give the curved shape desired. Later on, bows were cut to

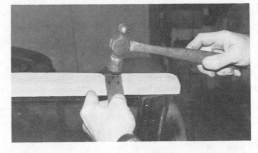

Make slight indentations in bows so the webbing will lie flat and not make a ridge. Use several tacks at each point where webbing crosses a bow. Stretch it tight between bows so it will give good support to top material.

shape and many were encased in steel as an economy measure. Some models used steel bows in place of wooden ones. Most were wrapped with top material to prevent chafing.

The restorer can make replacement bows out of solid wood or even plywood. There are sources that manufacture steam-bent bows; if yours is among the makes for which these are offered, it's best to get them to maintain originality. Old car magazines carry ads for these firms, as do some of the car club publications.

If you decide to make your own bows, first make a pattern on plywood or cardboard. Trace the pattern onto the wood you plan to use. Cut with a coping saw if you're using plywood or a regular saw if you're using solid wood. Sanding or filing to avoid rough edges and splinters is necessary once the piece is cut to shape: expend the effort to shape them properly. Replacement bows should be shellaced and varnished to prevent moisture seeping in and causing rot. Use either a hard or soft wood, but hardwood is preferred. Occasionally a roof bow will be shaped in such a way that it will require three pieces of wood to form it: two short pieces to form the side members (which usually included a curve) and a third piece along the top. These can be mortised, notched, or held together by steel joining strips. When cutting a roof bow, be sure to make each side even so you won't have a lopsided top.

Take special care to ensure that the pins in the joints aren't worn, as these are the pivots on which the mechanism operates. New pins can be easily made from the proper diameter bolts with the threads filed down, if replacement pins aren't available.

Paint or plate the supporting arms and lubricate the joints lightly so they'll fold easily. Be sure the "stops"—either crimped metal or set screws—are in proper position so the top bows seat correctly.

If your car has the metal roof bows common in the late Thirties—

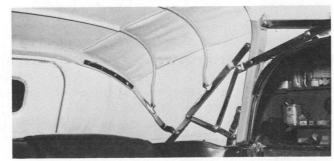

Roof padding is tacked to rear bow and main bows, then attached to secondary bows to give smooth curve to roof line and avoid starved cow look, as on this '39 Buick.

especially on convertible sedans and club coupes—you can still make any replacement bows necessary. These were either steel tubing bent to shape or, more often, steel rods. Measure the dimensions and cut a piece of plywood to the correct pattern. The steel tubing or rod can then be bent over this plywood form to get the exact shape. You may have to thread the ends to fit the attachments, or have them welded, depending upon how the original sockets were attached. They should be sanded, primed and painted.

OTHER COMPONENTS

Between the roof bows, running lengthwise along the car, are web straps that act as reinforcements and keep the strain off the top material. Lengthwise strips of cotton padding inside a fabric sleeve give the tops a smooth appearance. These fit along the curved portion of the roof near each edge and keep the material from being pinched between the bows and folding mechanism. Some cars had tie-down straps that held the top in its folded position. On most cars, a boot to slip over the folded top gave a neater appearance and better protection. These, plus the clamps that hold the front bow to the windshield posts or header, comprise the top mechanism.

Roof padding should be attached to bows to cover curved portion of roof and hide folding mechanism. Loops made of top material cover metal bows to protect the roof.

CONVERTIBLE TOPS

The folding tops on convertible coupes and sedans were much the same as on touring cars and roadsters. Since the convertibles featured a fabric quarter panel that fitted to the door or window frame, there had to be both extra framing and extra material. Usually there was a hinged section that fitted against the door or window frame and the top material was stretched and tacked to this. Often at the bottom corner, one or two snaps would be fitted so the material wouldn't tear when folded. Often an outside brace called a landau bar was employed as the folding mechanism that held the top rigid when closed. On more expensive cars, the inside of the folding top was often upholstered. This hid the top bows, arms, padding, etc. Another difference between the touring car and convertible sedan was, of course, windows in place of side curtains. Windows required a folding or removable post at the center: this attached to the roof when in position.

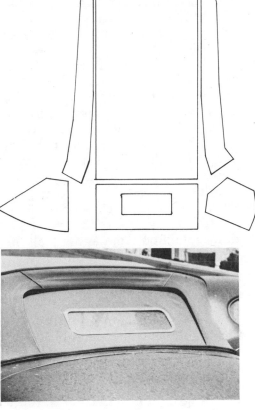

Pieces similar to these, when sewn together, make a convertible top. Left side shows typical "gypsy" style, with all of main rear roof bow covered by rear quarter section of top. Right side is "sport" style top, with more open area around rear roof bow. Roadster top was shorter, but similar.

Rear curtain on '40 Ford folds to give added ventilation: it is attached at bottom and with side zippers to give weather-tight closure. Use original as pattern or make a pattern on light cloth or paper. Reuse window frame.

MAKING REPLACEMENT TOP

You can easily make a new top. It helps if you have the old top as a pattern, but it isn't impossible without it. If a model similar to yours is available, study it and take measurements. Any pictures, diagrams or other information on the original top will be helpful to you. When making the new pattern, it's best to use inexpensive cotton cloth. I've bought remnants on

Use old top for pattern if possible, as on this '51 Plymouth. Remove old material carefully to preserve it for use as pattern. Take measurements with bows in place.

sale at fabric stores for this, as they are inexpensive and will save you from making a mistake on the expensive top material.

Folding tops usually consisted of seven separate pieces sewn together. The main piece ran lengthwise along the car from the front header to the rear bow. This piece covered the flat portion of the top, was centered, and usually extended between eight to ten inches from each edge of the top. On each side of the center section, a piece was sewn that ran down to the edge of the top: this covered the folding arms that position the roof. The fourth piece was the rear panel, extending from the rear roof bow to the top of the car body: on some cars, because of a center portion that could be raised, this section was made in three pieces. A side piece that fits between the body and diagonal rear roof bow support completes the roof's side profile. Inner flaps on each side protected against leakage around side curtains and windows. A flap, permanently attached to the front bow, snapped to the top of the windshield to complete the top.

After being sure the roof bows and folding mechanism are in good condition, you should cut and install the webbing. Put the roof framework in the "up" position and tighten all clamps. Start from the front header and work toward the back. Usually there are three web straps, each about three inches wide. Wider cars may have four web straps. Attach the webbing to the front bow in such a manner that the material will fold back over itself, hiding the tack heads. Use aluminum or blued tacks and drive them in firmly so the head is flat. Fold the webbing back over the tacks and stretch it to the next bow. Uually there is a slight indentation in the top of the bows to allow for the webbing. The webbing is to protect the top material from sagging under the weight of snow or rain, as well as keep the top bows in position. The webbing is never attached to the top material itself, only to the bows.

Work from front to rear, doing all webs from bow to bow. Don't work one web all the way back then start on the other ones, or you'll be apt to make the top crooked. Stretch the webbing tightly from bow to bow till you've reached the final anchorage at the rear bow. On some cars the webbing stops at the rear bow. On others, it will extend from the rear bow to the top of the body. It may be attached to the body, looped through a holder that's on the body. If so, this requires hand sewing with strong thread. Work for evenness between bows and make a solid attachment at each bow.

ROOF PADS

These easy-to-make pads are important to proper fit of the top. The width may vary from car to car, but they're usually from six to eight inches wide and you'll need one for each side of the roof. These fit lengthwise along the car from the windshield header to the rear bow. On some cars they also extended from the rear bow down to the body line. They were placed near the outer edges of the top, on the curved portion of the roof bows, to protect the top material from being cut by the folding arms, as well as to give the top a smoother fit.

In making new pads, use the same width as the originals: the top bows were usually indented to allow for the pads. Use a good grade of cotton duck or canvas, or one of the new vinyl fabrics. Use a strong mercerized or nylon thread. Instead of cotton padding as in the original, the newer foam rubber or polyethylene materials will do a better job. They won't absorb water or bunch up, as cotton pads sometimes do.

Sew the pads lengthwise. The material should be sewn on each side, with a second seam about one-half inch from the outside. This gives you a place to tack through without ripping the material. Sew across the padding from time to time, as this will keep the filling from shifting as the top is folded.

As you tack the padding in place, start at the front and place the material so it folds back over itself to hide the tacks. If this appears to make the material bunch up, you may find that you need to sew a tab onto the front of the pad for tacking through if the front bow didn't allow for this added thickness. The padding must be securely tacked to each bow. This makes it stay in place and gives a smoother fit on the top, as well as protecting the material when the top is folded.

With the webbing and padding in place, be sure the top folds properly and that nothing binds or gets pinched in the operation. The next step is to make the pattern. Using inexpensive cloth, measure and cut the center portion. This should extend from the header to about one inch beyond the rear bow. On some cars this center portion may extend down to the top of the car body. This piece should cover only the flat portion of the roof bows and cannot extend down over the curved side portion of the bows. Allow about one-half inch on each side for seaming. This piece should extend over the front bow so it can be tacked onto the bottom of the bow; in some cases, it wraps around the part of the bow that faces the driver. After measuring and cutting this piece, tack it lightly in place.

Before making a pattern for the side pieces, tack a piece of stout string from the side of the front header back to each bow to give the outline edge of the cloth roof. You have some leeway here to give the top the appearance you want. Measure each side to be sure you make them both the same.

Each side piece extends from the center piece down over the curved portion of the roof bows. At the front, they'll either be even with the bottom of the bow or may extend a slight distance below. As you cut and fit the pattern cloth, allow one-half inch extra on each edge for seaming. Cut each piece about one inch longer than necessary and trim off excess later.

You'll need to make an inside flap, two to three inches wide and the length of these side pieces. One piece is attached to each side and provides protection against rain coming in over the side curtains or windows. Pin this flap on the inside of the side piece.

After each side is cut and fitted, tack each one lightly into place, allowing a half-inch overlap with the center panel. At this point, view the outline of the top to see if it's what you want. This will be your last chance to make changes in top configuration.

Depending upon the style of the rear portion of the top, it may be in one piece. It will consist of three pieces if there's a center portion that raises. On some cars this rear portion extends around each side to attach to the main diagonal rear bow support. On other cars, the rear side pieces cover only the rear side curve of the body, leaving the main diagonal roof bow support visible.

When planning the rear upright section, make it simple, using as few pieces as possible. However, you must use enough separate pieces so you get a smooth fit.

When cutting the pattern cloth for the rear piece(s) allow one-half inch on

Material was cut a little too short here and has stretched between fasteners to body on '29 Ford. Some tops have a strip of metal inserted in a "sleeve" through which fasteners are attached to body to prevent stretching.

each side for seaming and about one inch on the top to bottom measurements. If you're planning on a center portion that raises, you'll need to make an inside flap of about one inch on each side piece so that the center portion will fasten between these flaps when closed.

Since the actual top covering material is expensive and you want the best fit possible, you may want to stitch the pattern pieces together and see how they fit before tracing them on the material you'll use. If you don't feel this is necessary, at least pin the seams together to check on your fit.

Most top material is 54 inches wide. Be sure it's laid out straight and flat with the inside facing up. Trace your pattern with a soft lead pencil on the wrong side. You can later erase any marks that show. Note any weave or graining in the material and cut the pieces so the weave will be the same on each. Cut the main center panel, using one edge of the material as the outer edge of the seam. Use a wooden yard stick for all measuring and as a straightedge when marking lines.

Before marking or cutting, place the pattern pieces on the cloth so you can make the best use of the material. Allow a little extra cloth between each piece. Trace or mark each piece before you cut any of them. Remember you're working from the inside of the cloth. Cut each piece along pattern lines. If you need to mark "left" or "right" to avoid confusion, do so.

Before sewing any of the pieces, pin them together from the inside along

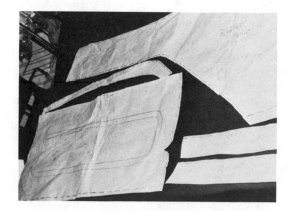

Position all pattern pieces on material before marking it to avoid wasting material. If there is a weave or pattern, place pieces so when cut they will have correct graining.

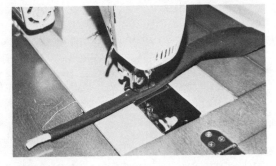

To make cording or welting, cut material on bias. Use cording foot on home sewing machine. Make cording strips for roofing, upholstery, tire covers, roof boots—wherever materials are joined that require cording.

the seam marks, and see how the ensemble fits over the top framework. At this point, everything should be larger than necessary. If anything appears too tight, alter it at this stage.

You may want to make some cording to go along the seams. Get the cording from curtain or drapery shops; cut your roofing material into one inch strips on the bias. Use the cording foot on a sewing machine to enclose the cording in the material.

If you want, you can fold the roofing material directly over the cording to produce a corded edge on the material itself. This is a matter of personal preference and works exceptionally well on the center panel, as you have two less layers of material to sew through when attaching side and center panels.

Top materials can be easily sewn together. You'll need a fairly heavy needle in the sewing machine. Since you don't want the top to pull apart, use a strong mercerized or nylon thread in matching color.

Replacement top on '48 Hillman was stitched on household sewing machine. Single center panel stretches from front bow to rear body line. Welting hides tacks at front bow and clear plastic rear window was stitched into place.

It's easier, and you'll have less bulk to handle, if you sew the inside flaps on the side pieces. Also, sew any flaps on the back piece. Sew these so you won't have any unfinished edges showing. Either use a binding on the outer edge of the flap and side piece or fold the material back and sew a seam about one-eighth inch from the edge. If you're applying a cording, fold the material back so the cording can be sewn without exposing a raw outside edge. It's always a good idea to sew a second seam line close to the first one for added strength.

Matching up the actual seam lines on the top panel, pin the material together, folding the half inch you allowed for seaming. Place the material so the center panel will be on the top of the side piece when sewn. This gives a better appearance and helps make the top watertight.

Before joining the top panel to the side sections, put the side sections into position on the roof bows for a final check. You may have to tack them lightly in place. Place the top center panel in place, tacking lightly at front and rear. Make a final check on how these pieces will fit together. You may want to pin them together, as most machines will sew over pins that can be removed later.

Sew seams slowly, getting them straight along the lines you've marked. Once you've sewn the main seam line, make a second seam about one-eighth inch inside it. Keep seam lines straight. When the material is right side out, the seams will look OK and won't be bulky. You can trim off excess material, but be sure not to trim so close to your seams that the material will pull loose.

After you've completed this work, you have the top center panel and the two side sections, with flaps, sewn into one piece. Put this aside for now, and start on the back upright section.

If the back is to be a three-part section, as it was on most roadsters to allow conversation with rumble seat passengers, sew the vertical flaps inside each rear side portion so you'll have less bulk to handle. The inside flaps should be about one inch inside the outer edge so there'll be protection against water blowing in. These inside vertical flaps should be about one inch short of the top, so there'll be room for the curtain to fold into the car. As with other pieces, turn the material under so there'll be no exposed edges.

After sewing each of the rear side sections, start on the center panel. It's wise to make the center panel double thickness because it must support the weight of the rear window and frame. This section will look better if it's bound on three sides. If you don't want to bind it, sew the two thicknesses of material together inside out on the bottom and both sides. Turn it right side out after sewing. The top edge that tacks to the rear roof bow doesn't have to be sewn together unless you want it to be.

REAR WINDOW

If you have the old top as a guide, you'll know where to place the rear window. If not, be sure to use your rear view mirror in deciding where to locate it. Measure the curtain to indicate the center line of the car. Normally the window will be centered and slightly above the middle line of the distance between the rear roof bow and the top of the body.

Window frames are in two sections, held together by slot-headed bolts.

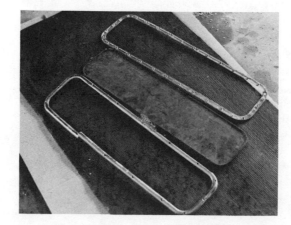

Rear window is in three pieces: the two frames with glass sandwiched between. There may be a rubber gasket around the glass.

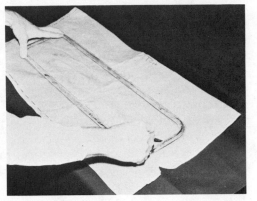

Position rear window on pattern material and trace it. Cut out your pattern and put it into place for a final check before cutting your final replacement.

Using a flat surface, dismantle the frame and place it on the curtain in the position you want it. Trace the inside outline of the frame and cut out this material. Mark the spots where the bolts go through and punch small holes at these marks.

Place the inside portion of the frame on the inside of the curtain and the outside portion on the outside of the curtain. There may be rubber gaskets on each side of the glass. If so, use them. If there is no gasket, a clear liquid sealer will do the job. Tighten the bolts to make a tight seal between the material, glass and frame. If any material should show on the glass area, it can be trimmed off with a razor blade. A little clear sealer around the glass and outside frame will keep it from leaking.

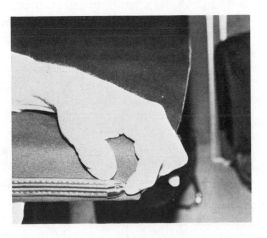

Welting hides tacks between material folds. Bright metal tip hides raw end, held in place with screw or plated tack.

ASSEMBLY

The top itself is held in place with tacks hidden behind a welting that gives the finished appearance you want. Bright metal ends are held over the ends of the welting by a screw. The top material will first be tacked to the wooden railing around the top of the body. There may also be some clips to install on the top and rear curtain. Basically, there are two types of fasteners: the *dot* type pushes over a pointed pin screwed into the body; another variety is the *twist*, which is attached to the body and slips through a slot in the material, twisting to a right angle to stay in place. Use the type that was originally on your car or your own preference. They're readily available and inexpensive.

The curtain containing the rear window must be fitted so it can be held in place when closed. You may want to sew in zippers on the curtain and flap to make a tight closure; if so, leave the closed portion of the zipper at the top. If you use fasteners, the male portion should be attached to the top and the female portion to the curtain.

Unless there is a molding that hides the tacks along the top joining to the body, you'll need fasteners. The number will depend upon the distance, but six on each side should be plenty. Put the male portion on the car body and the female portion on the top material.

Once the rear curtain is installed, you'll need about four male portions of the fasteners attached either to the next roof bow or to straps attached between the roof bows. The female portions on the rear curtain should line up with these to hold the curtain up.

If you're installing a roadster top with the three-panel rear section, install the three pieces as a unit. Mark the middle of the roof material and the middle of the front and rear roof bows. Line them up properly. With the bottom of the rear section in place, stretch the material to the front of the top of the rear bow and tack it securely. Start at the middle and work toward each side. Normally a tack every inch will hold. Use tacks at least one-half inch in length. After tacking this section firmly in place, trim off any excess material; be sure you leave enough material beyond the tack line so it won't pull loose.

Now you're ready to install the previously joined center and side panels. Starting at the center of the windshield header bow, tack the front section securely, being sure to center the cloth. With the front tacked, stretch the section back over the bows to the rear roof bow, making it tight and wrinkle free. Tack it only to the front bow. Tack the center of this section to the center mark on the rear roof bow. The material should overlap that of the rear panel already tacked to the bow. Work from the middle toward each end, stretching the material to make it wrinkle free as you tack it.

With the two sections tacked in place, trim off any excess material. At this point you have an option. You can either use a welting to cover the edge of the roofing material, or you can sew a flap that attaches to the top of the rear bow and extends down about two inches over the back section. Both methods were used. If you use the flap, either bind the lower edge or make it out of two thicknesses of material. You'll still need the welting where it attaches to the rear roof bow. Apply welting along the edge of the front bow and possibly one inch back onto the side of the front bow. Use a bright metal end piece to cover the raw end. Apply welting along the seam where the top material joins the body, with bright metal ends screwed in place.

Don't get uptight over a few wrinkles. You can soak the top and let it stand in the hot sun to stretch out any small wrinkles. Aside from some minor adjustments here and there, the top is finished.

TOP BOOT

A top boot is worthwhile and not difficult to make. Fold the top and secure any tie-down straps to make it compact. Make a pattern for the top profile first. This can be one piece or three pieces. It should cover the folded material and extend forward to the seat back, as well as along the sides to cover the folded arms and bow sections. Make a pattern for the upright portion, again one or three pieces. Join the top pieces together and then the side pieces. Some cars will require a bottom piece too, but it will usually be of different conformation than the top piece so will require a pattern. Either sew the top, side and bottom portions together from the inside of the material or turn the material back and attach a welting to the seam. This should slip over the folded top. You may need to install some extra male fasteners to the body, with the female portions to the boot material.

SIDE CURTAINS

Make side curtains after you have the top in place. These should extend below the windowsill level of the door and above the bottom of the inner part of the flap sewn to the top side panels. The flaps on the top side panels act to keep the rain from running off the top and down the inside of the curtains.

Side curtains are held upright by metal inserts that fit into sockets on the doors or body panels. They attach to the windshield post on cars with doors hinged at the front. The curtains are also attached along the bottom of the doors. On cars with the front doors hinged at the rear, there is a separate curtain that fastens to the windshield post and expands back a few inches to cover the space between the windshield and door curtain.

Side curtains often had bright metal inserts as stiffeners. Some metal curtain supports were painted and fitted into slots in door or body panels. Rubber weatherstripping is a good addition.

A roadster will normally have one curtain for each door, as well as a curtain to cover the area behind each door. The shape of the latter curtain depends upon the conformation of the roof at that point. On some cars there was an extra piece that fastened to the side roof flaps and extended down over the curtain about one inch. Rear doors usually had two curtain rods and, depending upon the length of the space between the front and rear doors, there may be an additional separate curtain.

With curtain rods firmly in place, make a pattern on cloth or paper for each curtain. Leave about one-half inch of extra material on each piece. Side curtains should be double thickness, plus an added thickness to fit over the sleeve into which the curtain rod fits.

With the outside measurements traced on your cloth, sew the two pieces together inside out. You may want cording along the outer edges of the curtain to give additional stiffness. Some cars had a light piece of metal or wood secured in slots along the outside edges of curtains for rigidity.

At this point, the curtains are solid material with no window places cut in. These you add after sewing on the sleeves that hold the curtain rods in place. Measure where the sleeve should be and cut one or two thicknesses of material, enough wider than the rod to allow it to slide easily and provide enough material for a double seam on each side. Sew one side of the sleeve to the curtain and slip the curtain into place. With a pencil you can mark how close you need to sew the other side of the sleeve to the curtain to get a tight fit. If you do this for each rod, you'll get the tight fit necessary to keep water out.

On the driver's side, you may need to cut an opening and sew a flap over the front and top edges to allow you to stick your arm out for signaling turns.

Some roadsters and touring cars didn't have outside door handles. If your car is like this, you'll have to cut a slot and make a flap to go over the top and leading edges so you can reach through and open the door from outside. Normally, even on touring cars, this was on the front curtains only, the driver or passenger reaching back to open the rear doors.

After the fasteners are in place and the curtains fit properly, you're ready to measure and cut the windows. There are excellent grades of clear plastic material available today for making windows far superior to the original equipment. Some cars had glass inserts and if you want these, you should get safety glass. The installation for glass inserts is the same as for the rear window glass.

With the window openings traced on the material, sew one or two seams all around the openings about a half inch from the line. The plastic should be about one-half inch larger in each dimension than the opening in the material. Insert the plastic between the two thicknesses of material and turn the material back just far enough so there are no raw edges. You'll be able to sew through the material and plastic and should have two seams holding the plastic in place.

You may want a narrow cording around the opening for the plastic, instead of turning the material back under itself. If you do, be sure the stitches go through the two layers of material, the plastic and the cording to get a secure insert. You may find it necessary to use a clear cement around the plastic windows as a sealer.

Some cars had a large envelope made of top material, in which side curtains could be stored when not in use. Others suggested that the windows be rolled for storage. Whatever you decide to do, make some provision for storing the curtains where the transparent portions won't get scratched or torn. The flat envelope probably makes the best storage.

TIRE COVERS

Tire covers to match the top material (or in another material) can be made up in several ways. There were several styles, too, and you should pick the style that was originally made for your car or the one that most appeals to you.

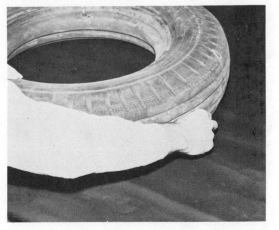

The first step in making a tire cover is to trace outer edge onto a pattern, then measure tread width and circumference of tread, including a seam allowance as you cut your pattern.

Drum Style. This is the tire cover that also obscures the outside of the wheel. Some had cutouts for the hub cab, while others covered the hub. Make a circle one inch larger in diameter than the tire. This gives you a seam allowance. Cut a strip the circumference of the tire, plus one inch for seaming. This piece should be the width of the tire tread or the width of the tire at its widest part. To go on the inside, cut a circular piece that is one inch more than the diameter of the tire.

The tread cover doesn't have to be in one piece, although it was on the most expensive cars. This can be made up of three or four shorter pieces sewn together. Also, the part that fits on the inside of the tire doesn't need to be one piece, as smaller pieces can be sewn together to make one piece.

Sew pieces of cording the length of the piece that covers the tread and seam these to the outside piece. Naturally, you sew the material either turned back or to the inside so there'll be no raw edges. With the cording attached to the outside piece, sew it to the piece that covers the tread. Do not join the ends of the piece that covers the tread. Double back about one-half inch at the end of this piece, so snap fasteners can later be installed.

Sew the cording on the inside of the piece that covers the tire tread, leaving each end of the cording attached only to the ends of the tread cover. So that you can slip the cover over the tire, you should attach the inside piece only halfway around the tread cover. Turn the portion not attached back over itself and sew a seam to hide the raw edge and provide a double thickness for the fasteners.

You should have two snap fasteners on the tread cover and from four to six snaps fastening the inside tire cover to the tread cover. The cover will slip over the wheel and the snap fasteners will draw it tight and keep it on.

Open Wheel Covers. Use the same procedure for measuring, cutting and sewing the tread cover. Draw your pattern for the tire circumference, allowing one inch over so there'll be material for seaming. This type of cover should hide only the tire, leaving the wheel exposed.

You can use one, two or more pieces for the two side covers, but the fewer the better. Attach these pieces to each other; for the section that goes on the outside of the wheel, sew them completely together. On the portion that'll be on the inside, leave about half unsewn for installation of snap fasteners.

Sew the cording to the tread cover first, then to the outside portion of the

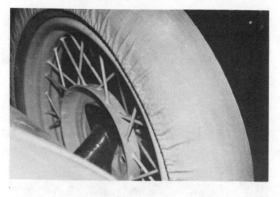

To get a tight fit with fabric tire covers, either sew elastic inside seam at back or put snaps on elastic tabs. Position snaps to provide snug fit.

wheel cover. Two seams should give adequate strength. Sew slowly, being sure to get even lines of stitches. Sew the inside portion of the tire cover next, leaving the unsewn part to match up with the unjoined parts of the tread cover. Turn the material right side out and place it over the tire. Mark where you need to install the two tread fasteners, as well as the inside fasteners.

If you have, or can buy, your car's insignia, it should be sewn to the tire cover for an elegant finishing touch.

Dual Rear Spares. Choose either a drum or rim style covering: most dual mounted spares used one wide cover for both tires. You make this the same as a single cover, increasing the width of the tread piece enough to cover both treads, plus the space between. Remember to leave the lower half of the inside portion of the cover free of the tread cover, so you can attach the snap fasteners needed to hold it snug.

Sidemounted Spares. Normally there's no differemce in the construction of the tire cover, whether it's carried on the front fender wall or at the back. That is, unless there isn't adequate width in the fender well to accomodate the tire cover material. In this case, make the cover the same way, but don't install the snap fasteners. Measure the amount that must be trimmed off to allow a snug fit in the fender well and sew additional cording along this part, then cut off the extra material. You may want to sew an elastic strip connecting the tread covers, as well as two elastic strips with a fastener on the end of each to fasten two snaps on the inside wheel portion of the cover.

With every tire cover, you want to be sure you have a tight enough fit so it looks good. In some cases, you may want to sew elastic into the inside wheel portion. This will keep the cover tight on the wheel, but doesn't replace the snap fasteners at the ends of the tread cover or that portion of the tire cover that snaps to the tread cover.

TRUNK COVER

Many cars had a dust cover for the trunk that matched either the car's top or the spare tire covers. This is easily made by measuring the outside of the trunk. Make a pattern for each end, allowing a half-inch extra for seaming. Cut the large piece to cover the wide part of the trunk, again allowing a half-inch extra for seaming. This piece should be long enough to cover the three sides of the trunk.

Your trunk will look better if you have cording along the edges. Make up

Make necessary wood replacement for trunks with plywood. Sand and finish smoothly. There are any number of decorative coverings that can be applied to inside of trunk.

enough cording to cover the bottoms of the end pieces, as well as the edges where the end pieces join the sides and top, and both edges of the side and top cover.

Matching the edges of the cording and material (inside out), sew the cording and large piece together. Then sew the cording and the end pieces together. When finished, this gives a cover that will slip over your trunk.

Make new cover for trunk or refinish old cover, using paint that won't crack. Remove bright metal parts if recovering trunk, then glue and staple on new material. If repainting, mask off bright metal parts. Give several light spray coats to avoid runs.

You may want to make cutouts for trunk handles. You may also want to make the trunk cover so it snaps together at each end rather than being a slipover style. This is easily done by sewing together only the portions you want attached to each other and attaching snap fasteners to the other edges. Double any material that will hold snap fasteners and sew it back to itself so you have both a finished and strong edge.

CHAPTER 20

Upholstery

A wide variety of styles and materials were used for upholstering cars over the years. This gives you a choice in the restoration process. Since upholstery isn't necessary for the operation of the car, consider it the last inside job. It can be done before or after the car is painted, but it's wiser to do it before painting to prevent marks on the new paint.

When reupholstering a car, the first thing to consider is what you're aiming for in your restoration. It's best, of course, to restore everything to original or near-original specifications. On some cars this will be very expensive, but should be considered preferable if you have the desire, money and time. If you don't, then consider the alternatives: reupholster in vinyl instead of leather, a less expensive material in place of wool broadcloth, etc. You may even want to consider seat covers as an inexpensive way to dress up the seats if the panels on the doors and sides are OK.

The beginner–restorer will probably settle for an interior that is comfortable, attractive and serviceable. Also fairly high on the list of priorities should be an interior that's fairly easy to accomplish. It's toward these ends that this chapter is written: your old bus never had it so good!

Original cloth upholstery on this '41 Lincoln Continental was replaced by black naugahide with white inserts. Push-button door openers and pull handles were replated.

If it's leather you're needing, there are several sources, some of which may be near your home. Try any leather store first. If they don't have what you want, you may be able to get the name of a good source from a fellow club member. The national auto magazines catering to the old-car market usually carry ads for leather goods. Get samples and prices.

You can locate upholstery fabrics in about the same way. Again, get samples and prices. You can also contact local fabric and upholstery shops that cater to furniture reupholstery and may very well locate a close replacement for your material. If you're trying to match original fabric, get a sample from a portion that shows the least wear and is as clean as possible.

Headliner. Try to match the original covering material as closely as possible. You can try local fabric shops first, then the automotive top and upholstery shops. Again, the national old-car magazines carry ads by upholstery suppliers who will carry headliner material. Write for samples and prices.

MATERIAL SELECTION

There are upholstery materials on the market that weren't even thought of twenty, thirty or forty years ago. Consequently, this allows you to add color, texture and serviceability not available when the car was manufactured. Choose the nearest to original that is available to you for the best restoration job. However, if you don't have the money for this and feel you want to substitute another material, that should definitely be your second choice. The new vinyls are much less expensive and far easier to work with than leather or the old-fashioned leatherette. Many of today's upholstery materials are treated to repel stains, making them more serviceable. New stronger fabrics will give added wear. All in all, with proper care given to selection and workmanship, you'll end up with a car that is better upholstered than it was originally.

The material used for doors and side panels doesn't have to be the same as that used for the seats. In many cases the factory produced them this way and the contrast was effective.

Seat Cushions. These take more wear than the side panels and the covering

To repair leather seats, first trace a pattern for replacement sections before cutting or removing any upholstery from cushions. Use saddle soap or leather softener to condition material.

When stitching has torn out, it's best to remove the cover and cut a pattern for new material. Stitch the cover together before attaching it to the cushion frame.

usually wore out first. It's a wise choice to redo the seat cushions in a serviceable material. A figured pattern will show stains less than a plain solid color. Remember not to choose a fabric too heavy to stitch on your sewing machine. If yours is an open car, there are a wide variety of expanded vinyls from which to choose: these are easy to cut, fit and sew. In closed cars if you don't want vinyl, there are weaves and prints that are treated to resist soil. Consider using a contrasting color for seat cording or for inserts on the cushions to add a touch of color.

Side Panels. These are sometimes slightly padded and often have a stitched design. They're usually cloth or artificial leather, except on the more expensive open cars or in the chauffer's compartment on town cars, etc., where leather was used. Both materials were usually glued around the tucked-over edges to a fibreboard backing. Clips and screws hold the panels in place along three sides and the window molding usually holds the top. Often the backing was torn or became badly warped or rotten from moisture. It's wise to consider cutting new panels if this has happened to your car. Don't get uptight over pockets or pouches in the door, as they're not hard to make.

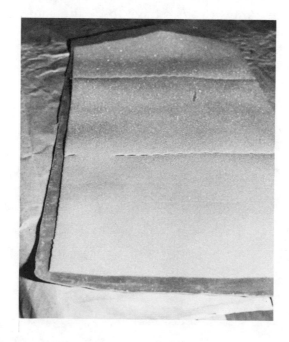

When installing light padding under upholstery, cut to exact measurements and glue to panel or inside material to prevent bunching.

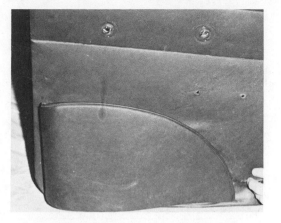

Map pocket or storage compartment for doors can be made by covering plywood or fibreboard framework and attaching, adding convenience and enjoyment of car.

Arm rests attached to the door or side panels are easily removed for recovering. Side panels can be made of a lighter material than that used on the cushions. A contrasting color on side panels may be a wise choice. On many cars, there was bound carpet along the bottom of doors and side panels to add protection. As a restorer you have a wide variety of colors and materials from which to choose.

Kick Panels. These are the panels beneath the dashboard on each side of the cowl. Sometimes they contained a pocket or compartment. These usually got a lot of wear, as they were subjected to dirt and moisture from the feet of the front seat occupants. On some cars they were leather covered, others used carpeting. Some used fibreboard with a printed finish to simulate leather. All were held in place by clips or screws. You'll probably need to cut new backing pieces before recovering kick panels. You may want to add a pocket or compartment when making your replacements. These are easy to make and a handy addition to the car.

You can stretch material over metal panels and glue it into place. Light foam padding should be placed between panel and material.

Headliners. Usually found in closed cars only, but occasionally in more expensive convertibles, the headliner is the cloth that covers the inside of the top. It may start with the top of the door or window openings or there may be separate panels over the tops of the doors and windows. If there are panels, they'll be cloth glued over cardboard, held in place by clips or screws. Headliners usually had cloth strips sewn to the back of them. These strips were attached to the windshield header and the roof supports from front to rear. Quarter panels covered the area from the top of the rear cush-

Although it appears difficult, making a new headliner isn't beyond beginner's ability. Work from center front and attach headliner at center of each support. Once center is tight from front to back, work toward the sides on each seam.

ion to the headliner and were usually covered with the same material. Any badly stained, mildewed or deteriorated material should be replaced. There are spray finishes that can be applied over the old cloth if staining is the only damage. Be sure that whatever leaks caused the mildew or rotting have been corrected before you repair or replace these parts. Headliners may look tricky to replace, but they're not if you take the time to do them right.

RECOVERING SEATS

Seats have probably taken a beating and will need recovering or reupholstering. The degree of wear and the condition of the padding, springs, etc., will be the determining factors. Special spray coverings are available to dress up solid cushions, but do not repair damage.

If the cushions are basically sound, they can be recovered easily. The covers should be tacked, stapled or tied into place. If you do this, consider fitting a one-inch pad of foam latex or polyethylene over the old cushions before installing new covers.

In older cars, the seats were made up differently than in later models. Seats were manufactured like pieces of furniture and required considerable hand work and detailing. Many cars had a framework of wood or steel for each seat. The exposed parts, seat back, sides, arm rests, etc., were all upholstered. Later on, as labor and material costs increased, seats were made with less care and attention to detail. Cushions were of lighter construction and upholstered with less care. Much of the hand work disappeared. Seats and cushions were installed as a unit.

Torn front seat cushion on '39 Lincoln can be easily repaired. Sew torn material back together and sew patch over area. It's a good idea to insert a thin layer of padding over patched cushion before installing a new cover.

Remove the bottom cushion from the seat squab or frame. Choose a heavier material than you would for reupholstering, as the covers will be attached in fewer places. The cushion should be in good condition first: sew a patch over any torn spot; tie down any piece of spring that may be exposed. Cover the cushion with a pad of polyethylene or latex foam. Secure the padding along the edges to prevent bunching under the seat cover. Measure the cushion and make a simple pattern or mark the measurements directly on the underside of the material. Make the bottom cushion of two or more pieces: one will be the top of the cushion, the other(s) the sides and front panel. Either join these together by seaming about one-half inch from the edges on the underside or make a cording to sew onto the top piece before joining.

You'll need to attach short tabs from time to time, for stapling or tacking to the framework. In some cases, these will need to be long enough to tie around the seat frame or springs.

If you can remove the seat back cushion, do so: it'll make the cover fit more nicely. Measure and either make a pattern or draw the outline on the material. Leave a seam allowance and sew double seams. The cushion will probably require three pieces of material, possibly four, if you want to consider the piece along the top as separate. Sew them together from the underside of the material, using cording if you like. Make attaching tabs to get a tight fit.

When making and fitting seat covers, be sure the area to be covered doesn't have any sharp pieces of metal sticking through and that all torn spots are patched. Just make the cushions as serviceable as possible before recovering.

There's no problem in reupholstering the seats if recovering won't give you what you want. Remove the cushions and as much of the seat squab or framework as possible. Make a little sketch showing how the seat was originally covered. Note the tufting and seaming so you can make the cushion nearly original in appearance. Check the framework to make sure it's sound and solid so you'll have something to work from.

Remove the old upholstery material, exposing the padding and springs. A wide variety of cushion construction was used. There'll be a basic frame, coil springs and connectors between the springs. Webbing was used across

Rip off old material to get down to basic framework of badly deteriorated seats. Clean out any rust and spray with primer coat before reupholstering.

the top, running in both directions to hold the cushion in shape. Coiled hair padding was often used to give shape and an overall cotton padding used as a top layer directly under the upholstery material. With more expensive construction, a canvas or duck cover was installed under the upholstery material to take the strain, leaving the exposed upholstery material for decorative purposes only. Either burlap or a scrim material covered the bottom part of the cushion.

You should get down to the springs, so you'll need to remove padding and webbing. Save these for reuse if they're in good condition. Check the attachment of the springs to the basic cushion framework. Secure any loose spring by wrapping wire between the spring and frame. Check the wires connecting the springs at top and bottom, sometimes in the middle. Examine the connectors and you'll see how easy replacements can be made from wire coat hangers. Often stout cord was used to tie springs, too. Be sure each spring is secured in place.

Sew or clip webbing over cushion frame; use over and under pattern with webbing. Sew or clip webbing strips where they cross each other. Rubberized hair or foam padding goes over webbing.

Attach the webbing to the framework at one end. Stretch it in an over–under pattern, with the webbing running in the other direction. You may need to install extra webbing if the springs appear weak or if passengers will be extra heavy. Be sure the webbing is attached to the spring. Upholstery shops use "hog rings" and a plier-like tool to do this. You can use the same, or wire and pliers.

With webbing in place over the firmly secured springs, next install the padding. Use plenty of padding and consider adding the one-inch latex or polyethylene foam padding over the top of the cotton padding. This won't alter the configuration of the cushion and makes a much more serviceable and comfortable seat.

If you want to do a really good job, make a cover for the cushion of canvas or heavy muslin. This is easy to make and allows the upholstery to fit better. This "inner skin" should be tight enough to give the shape you want, yet not compress the springs. With this cover installed, you'll know how the seat will look and feel. If you're satisfied on all counts, start on the upholstery material.

Make your pattern and draw it on the inside of the material. Allow about a half inch extra for seaming. You'll probably want cording around the top edge of the cushion. If so, cut strips of material on the bias. Use the cording foot on the sewing machine and run off lengths of cording. You'll probably

Torn seat upholstery can be easily repaired. Make measurements and pattern before removing material from framework. A patch cemented or sewn over a tear like this should only be a last resort.

Measure and cut strips to be sewn together for cushion cover. Heavy needle in home machine is satisfactory for this job. Since material is expensive, make your measurements and pattern carefully.

find it easier to sew the cording onto one piece of material first, rather than trying to join both pieces plus the cording in the same operation.

If your original cushion was ribbed, you can easily duplicate it. Draw and cut the strips, leaving material for seaming. Sew them edge to edge on the inside of the material: when turned right side out, you'll have the ribbed effect you want. You can easily add padding to these ribs.

For ribbing on cushions or panels, either cut materials into strips and sew together or sew narrow seams at measured intervals to give appearance of ribbing.

With the pieces sewn together, you have the new upholstery ready to cover the cushion. Mark the center of the material and the center of the cushion so they'll line up properly. Place the upper part of the cushion edge in place. Stretch the material over the frame and tack this in place. Work from the middle toward the outside edges, being sure you're getting it on straight and wrinkle free. A little extra care in locating the first tack position is wise. With the front in place, tack the back edge next, starting in the middle and working toward each end. With this finished, tack each end. Occasionally, you'll need to do a little hand stitching at the back corners of the cushion to assure a snug fit. If so, use curved needles and strong thread. This should only be necessary for an inch or two and won't show when the cushion is in place. Tack down the burlap or scrim cloth covering the bottom of the framework to complete the job.

Folding center arm rests can be removed from seat and recovered. Sew material from inside, then turn right side out and slip over form. If padding is required, use foam or cotton.

When working on the upright cushions, be sure to check the anchoring of the springs. These tended to sag after years of use. Be sure the webbing is tight and consider extra webbing if necessary. Any springs that may have broken can be stretched and recrimped, or you can get replacement springs from old cushions at wrecking yards. They can be "wound in" with the existing springs for added strength. Secure all padding along the upright cushion in several places so it won't sag in use.

If your upright seat cushion has a folding arm rest, you should remove it when working on the cushion. It'll be easier to reupholster out of the unit and can be reinstalled easily when the cushion is completed. In some cars, the rear seat arm rests were separate panels. These are easily removed when the seat cushions are out and can be upholstered to match the seats. Measure and cut the material. If the present arm rests appear to be in good condition, don't bother to remove the present material. Just fit your new upholstery over them and secure it from the back side. However, if the original

It is best to remove center arm rest before removing leather covering for replacement or repair. You may want to sew on extra tabs so upholstery cover can be reattached securely.

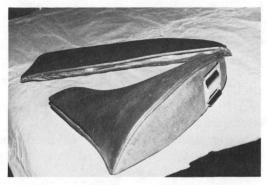

Remove arm rest framework and recover, using cording to join pieces. Cut a slot where ashtray fits and tack edges to framework.

material is torn and the padding pulled out, it's best to remove the old and install new padding before reupholstering.

I've found it wise to have some extra padding on hand to put here and there after you've started to attach the upholstery material. This will help give a better fit. When everything is back in place in the car, you'll have a job you can be proud of.

Seat cushion appears ribbed, but is made of one piece. Narrow seams were sewn at correct distance to provide ribs. Padding strips can be cut to correct measurements and inserted in ribs.

SIDE PANELS

When making new side panels, first remove the old ones. This requires removal of the window frame and door and window hardware. With the frame and moldings removed, you may see a line of tacks holding the material at the top. Usually panels were held on by screws and clips. Pry gently

Stretch completed door upholstery over fibre panels and glue or staple on back. Cut holes to match the holes in panel backing for door and window controls.

with a thin screwdriver or putty knife around the edges to locate the clips. When located, pry on each side of the clip at the same time to lift it out of the hole.

With the panel off, you can take measurements for a new panel, if necessary. Use either a strong fibreboard or light plywood. If you use plywood, shellac it after cutting it to size. Cut openings for door or window cranks and mark the location of any brackets to hold arm rests, ashtrays, door straps or pulls.

Some side panels had a stitched pattern on the upholstery. If you want this, use a light cotton or foam padding on the back of the material and sew the stitch pattern you want.

Usually there was a light padding under the side panels and this was often held to the fibre panel with a light coat of glue, even though it may be sewn to the outer material.

When you have the backing completed, you're ready to trace the pattern onto the inside of the material. Allow up to two inches on each side of the material for attaching it to the panel. Mark the center of the holes for the window crank and door handle. From this mark, draw lines to the rim of the opening. Cut along these lines to make small pie-shaped wedges to be brought through the panel and glued to the back side. Install the holding clips to the panel, being sure they're securely in place and lined up with the holes into which they must fit.

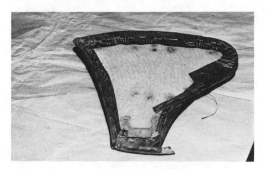

Upholstery material can be glued and stapled to fibreboard backing material as on this arm rest. Clips and screws hold it to door panels.

Place the covering material face down and lay any separate padding over it. On top of these, place the panel, spreading a thin layer of glue to the edges of the panel if necessary. Turn back the extra material around the edges until you have the panel tightly covered. You'll need to make little slits where the material fits over the clips. If the panel is thick enough, you may use small staples to help hold the upholstery material tight. In some cases, you may want to use a needle and coarse thread to loop through the material from one edge to the other. These long pieces of thread will help hold the material in place while the glue dries. Later you can remove these threads if you like (I once disassembled a Jaguar door to find that the factory had used this method and left the threads in place). Place weights to hold the material tight till the glue dries. An easy method is to use a couple of clamps with a board on each side of the upholstery and panel. The clamps will hold the boards tight against the surfaces till they dry sufficiently.

If your car had a scuff pad on the bottom of the panel, this should be made up separately and attached after the upholstery has been applied.

Usually it's better to bind carpet pieces, although they're often outlined by a strip of cording that hides any raw edges. They're attached to the panel by bright metal screws and washers or round-headed gimp tacks that won't show through the pile of the material. Usually they're also glued to the panel.

With the reupholstered panel completed, line up the clips with the holes and push them into place. Secure corners or other necessary places with bright metal screws and washers. Always use washers so the material doesn't twist as you turn the screw. Attach any brackets for arm rests, ashtrays and door straps. Install the escutcheon plate over its spring and attach the window crank and door handle. Replace the window frame and molding and the finished panel should have the appearance you want.

DOOR WELTING

Welting around the doors is easy to replace. You can buy the ready-made kind very inexpensively if the color you want is available. Called "windlace welting," it's a round rubber tube or strip covered with vinyl, leather or upholstery. The newer sponge rubber is easier to work with than rubber tubing and usually less expensive. Sometimes a lightweight spring is inserted between the rubber and cloth to help hide tacks. In most cases, the strip that's tacked is behind the upholstery panels so the tacks don't show. The purpose of the welting is to make a tight seal around the doors and other openings. Often welting is scuffed and torn and should be replaced.

Proper folding at ends will allow finished appearance on the welting to be used around doors and side panels. Some cars had metal tips on ends of welting.

You make welting just like cording. Cut the material you want to use in strips along the bias; use the cording foot on the sewing machine to cover the tubing, keeping the seam as close to the tubing as possible. Fold back the material at each end of the strip or leave enough to be folded over and tacked, so there won't be a raw edge. You can buy bright metal ends for the welting at auto upholstery shops to hide raw ends and give a more finished look. Usually you'll have to remove upholstery panels to install the welting.

Use same thickness of cording as originally used on car: usually narrow on door panels, medium width on cushions, and wide around doors. Cording is available at fabric shops.

HEADLINER

To make a new headliner, remove the present one. This may require that you remove the visors, if they're inside, and also the dome light. Note how many sections were sewn together to make the original liner. Use the present one for a pattern if possible. If not, make a pattern for cutting a new headliner. Measure the width at the front end and at each roof bow or support where the original liner was attached. In these measurements, allow about one inch extra for attaching to the sides of the body. Measure along the length of the headliner, from windshield to rear. Because the headliner follows the contours of the car body, make a center line on the pattern and mark all measurements from the center line. This will keep the new headliner from being lopsided. You'll probably find there are four or five pieces or sections to the headliner on a sedan and two or three in a coupe.

With measurements complete, mark them on your pattern or material, working from the center. Allow a little extra material for sewing sections together. Sew from the inside. The material beyond the seam will be used for attaching the headliner to the cross supports. Mark where the dome light will be located and cut the cross marks when you get to that place when installing the liner.

Installation isn't tricky, but since there's a lot of material to work with, there are some suggestions to keep you from feeling swamped. Start installation at the center of the front: secure this point with a tack or two. To make the material easier to handle place a holding tack, driven only part way in, at each side of the front edge of the liner. Secure the center of each sewn seam section from front to back to the center mark on each cross support. Stretch the material from support to support, working from front to back. Place a holding tack on each side of each section after securing the center point. This makes less material to wrestle with as you go along. Once the center sections are secured from front to rear, drive a tack about two inches from each side of the center tack, stretching the material toward each side as you go. Again work from front to rear, stretching the material to each side of each cross support. This will guarantee a tight fit. Repeat this process, placing tacks about two inches apart until you reach the outer edges of the liner.

On some cars, there will be a small panel above each door and window opening. If so, the headliner installs behind these panels. Others had a "cove" style headliner which omitted the upper side panels and attached behind the welting above doors, or behind window frames in nondoor panels.

Naturally, you don't want tack heads showing in your upholstery. To achieve a finished look, you can do several things. A popular method is to glue the ends of the upholstery that fold over the panels. If you do, be sure to use glue in places where it won't saturate the material. Drive the tacks holding these panels down to within a close distance of the cloth. Use a needle to stretch the material out and over the tack head: then give the head one last tap and it'll disappear under the material.

Upholstery to cover panels between doors can be glued and stapled in place. Make cuts toward foldover line for a smooth fitting curve.

Always try to place tacks behind frames or moldings that will hide the heads. There is a handy, inexpensive little upholstery tool that forces material behind moldings, where it will usually stay in place without tacking.

Occasionally, you'll find there is just no way to hide a tack head: use either a bright metal screw and washer or an ornamental head tack. If you have to resort to these, use only enough to hold the panel and place them in the same relative position on each side.

MATS AND CARPETS

If the front mat is worn only where the driver's feet go, you can put a small rubber or vinyl mat over it. Usually, though, you'll find mats and carpets worn and rotten, so replacement is necessary. Use the old one as a pattern if possible; otherwise, make a new one by tracing the measurements on the back of the material.

Mark all measurements from a center line so your new mat or carpet will fit the body contours. Make outside measurements about one inch oversize till you're sure everything fits, then trim it down. Mark in openings for shift levers, pedals, etc. Remember, you're working on the wrong side of the material, so mark these on the righthand, instead of lefthand, side. Mark all openings slightly smaller than actual, then cut them larger as you fit the mat. Once you're satisfied with the fit, sew the binding around the edges and openings. Cut rubber matting to exact fit. Many times carpets and mats extended under door plates or other moldings: be sure these are in place tightly enough to hold the edges.

If you're replacing a front rubber mat with a carpet, plan to install a piece of rubber or vinyl as heel pads on one or both sides to protect the carpet. This is easier to sew on, but can be glued in place if you like.

Rear carpets may be badly worn; if installing inserts won't render them acceptable, you can make replacements. Depending upon the car, you'll have to figure out if you need a carpet under or along the sides of the front seat, if the seat isn't attached to the middle pillar. Make measurements every six inches or so along a center line, unless you know there are no changes in outer edges.

Unless you have the old carpet from which to make a tracing, cut a pattern from heavy paper to get correct fit. Sew binding on edges to prevent unravelling and give finished appearance.

If your car has recessed foot wells, this is more difficult, as you'll have to make more measurements and cut more pieces. It's worth taking your time to make careful measurements on these irregularly shaped pieces. They must be sewn to cloth tape on the back to hold them together or you can make them as separately bound sections if you prefer.

Cut the material, leaving about an inch extra on outside measurements. This can be trimmed once you have the fit you want. If the edges of the carpet aren't held in place by moldings, you'll need to sew on regular rug binding or narrow vinyl strips to give a finished edge. Sometimes there are bright metal screws or other fittings that hold carpets in place. Be sure these are secured firmly to keep the carpet from moving around.

Carpet and floor matting materials are readily available from any number of sources. You can get various weights and choose about what you want. Usually you can get bindings that will match carpet colors.

It's a good idea to cut padding to fit under front and rear carpets, as these help cut down on noise and give better wear. The pad should be only a fraction of an inch smaller than the finished mat or carpet so it doesn't show. In fact, if you're cutting new mats and carpets from patterns you've made, cut the pad first to be sure your pattern is correct.

CHAPTER 21

Painting
the Car

There is a wide choice of color schemes for a car. You can repaint it as it was originally or use some other color offered by the manufacturer for the same year and model. Several paint manufacturers carry color chips that are cataloged by make, model and year of car. This service will assure an authentic color if that's what you want. You may want to choose an entirely different scheme—perhaps colors you particularly like or colors you think would look good on your car. Part of the fun of car restoration is choosing a color scheme that pleases you. So let your car express the real you.

Usually the restorer has decided what color the car will be long before it's ready to be painted, even before the upholstery was chosen. No matter what color or colors you select, remember that preparation for the paint job is all-important. Allow yourself ample time for surface preparation to assure the kind of paint job you want. Shiny new paint will only magnify any surface imperfections, so work them out before painting.

Old cars often used two or three different colors or shades of the same color on a single car. Moldings were usually the dividing line: these were

Color
Schemes

Unusual body molding on '36 Windover-bodied Rolls lends itself to contrasting colors for emphasis. Cars with interesting moldings on body or fenders give restorer a wide choice in treatment.

273

Two tones of blue lacquer make attractive color scheme on '53 Rolls. Lighter shade on top makes car look lower.

often black or a contrasting color. Various panels were sometimes a different color or shade, as were window reveals, louvers, fenders and wheels. Fenders and splash aprons were usually black on standard models, but painted body color or a contrasting color on the deluxe versions. There are any number of combinations open to the restorer.

Two-tone paint jobs usually were separated or divided by a molding on the body. Everything above was one color, everything below another color. Generally the lighter color was on the bottom, but this becomes the restorer's choice. When deciding upon a two-tone paint job, remember that the lighter color on top will make the car look lower; the darker color on top will emphasize the height of the car.

Dark colors make a car look more sedate and dignified, if this is the impression you're after. A dark color also makes a car look smaller than it really is. If your car is a big sedan, limousine or touring car, you may decide a dark color is preferable.

Light colors usually make a car look larger: they also give it a sporty look. This makes lighter shades a logical choice for roadsters, convertibles and other sports models.

Body molding colors varied, but were often black—as on this '35 Chevrolet. Dark moldings on light body accentuate car's lines. Mask off body panels and spray moldings after body coats have dried.

Body moldings running horizontally emphasize the length of the car. If these are painted black or a contrasting color, they'll make the car look lower. Vertical moldings in a different color emphasize height and will give the impression of added height to the car.

Black fenders and splash aprons are always right for old cars, but certainly

Black fenders and aprons were standard on many cars during the Twenties and Thirties, and require separate masking and painting. It's best to remove fenders when car is being refinished and paint inside housings.

not necessary. Most manufacturers offered their cars with fenders painted to match the body of the car for a few dollars extra. Wheels could be had in a variety of colors: varnished wood in artillery wheels, bright colors in wire wheels or colors with contrasting striping on disc wheels. On cars with demountable rims, these were usually black or aluminum color.

You have a choice of finishes available to you that were unheard of even a few years ago. The new finishes are far superior to the enamels and lacquers originally used on cars. The new finishes are tougher, longer lasting and more fade-resistant products. There's no longer the big difference between an enamel and lacquer paint job that once existed. The new acrylic finishes are great.

Choice of Paint

A properly applied lacquer finish gives beautiful depth and gloss on '41 Lincoln Continental. Fenders were removed during repainting and new fender welting applied.

Lacquer finishes were used on the most expensive cars and are still preferred by many car enthusiasts. A lacquer finish gives a depth and gloss that's highly desirable. It will require a rubdown with rubbing compound when completed for a lustrous finish. It may also oxidize slightly over the years, making additional use of rubbing compound necessary. Lacquer finishes may chip around edges and joints as they age, but can be easily touched up.

Enamels enjoyed the greatest popularity for use on cars because they were easily applied and gave a tough finish. Enamel doesn't chip easily, can be

Enamel gives a tough, durable finish and is easy to apply. Moldings, in a different shade or color, only require extra masking and add authenticity to restoration.

had as a high gloss or semigloss finish. Some of the most expensive cars, with lacquer on the bodies and fenders, used enamel on the wheels because if its toughness and durability.

Choose an acrylic enamel or lacquer; one is now as good as the other and each is easy to apply. If you want a metallic finish on your car, ask that the aluminum powder be added and the paint thoroughly mixed. You may have to shake metallic paints, as the metallic flakes will sink to the bottom.

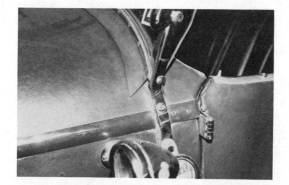

Chances are you won't come across a leather or fabric covered body like this '29 LaGonda Tourer. Hudson, Stutz and some other American cars offered this. The new expanded vinyls are easier to shape and far less costly than some of the original fabrics used.

Preparation of Surfaces

It is not necessary to remove the fenders or hood for painting, but you'll get a better job if you do. If the fenders are simply loosened and allowed to drop a half inch from the body, this will allow the paint to cover the inside edge of the fender, as well as the undersection of the wheel arches and front chassis fillets. This also allows you to install the fender welting after painting and thereby keep paint from chipping off fender welting. By removing the hood, you assure yourself that louvres and hood joints get a complete and even coat.

In either case—with fenders and hood in place or separate—the important thing to keep in mind is to have a clean, smooth surface for the paint. Remove door handles, bolts, plated parts.

Use a rubber sanding block to hold sandpaper or emery cloth. Sand and fill any blemished spots. Treat rusted spots with a rust inhibiting primer after sanding. There are excellent fillers now available to make rusted and rough spots smooth again. Smooth these on and allow to dry. Sand the edges till they're feathered and the joining is smooth. Spray with a primer and sand again. You'll find the blemishes have disappeared.

Liquid paint remover will peel off old finish to bare metal. A thorough washing and rinsing is necessary to get all traces out of crevices and joints. Sand-blasting is the easiest way to strip paint from wire wheels, but they should be primed soon afterward to prevent surface rust from forming.

After all rough spots are smoothed, you should sand the entire car. Use a good quality fine-grit sandpaper or emery cloth. You'll get faster and better results using sandpaper or emery cloth that is made for use with water. Keep the abrasive wet and rub in short strokes. Let each area dry, then wipe off accumulated grit. You may find you'll need to go over an area several times. With your eyes closed, rub your bare hand over the parts you consider ready for the primer coat. If you can't feel any imperfections, it's ready. If you do feel any imperfections with your bare hand, rework the area. When you're satisfied that the surface is smooth, wash the car down with clear water. After it dries, go over the crevices and joints with an air gun or the blowing attachment on your cleaner. Be sure to get all dust out of crevices and joints.

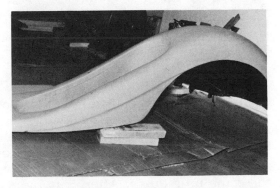

It may take several coats of primer, with sanding between coats, to get the smooth finish you want. This '33 Mercedes fender has been undercoated and will receive finish lacquer coats before being installed on car.

Mask the windows, using newspapers and masking tape: be sure the tape doesn't cover areas you're going to paint. Mask off the grill and any plated moldings or fittings you didn't remove. With everything that's not to be painted protected by masking tape, spray the car with a good quality primer. After this dries, sand it thoroughly but lightly. Dust off and spray a second coat of primer. Smooth the second coat with fine sandpaper or emery cloth. Use air blowing again to clean out any dust that may have collected in seams and joints.

WHEELS

To prepare wheels for painting, first remove them from the car. Take the tires or rims off the wheels: this makes for far easier handling. Scrape off what dirt and grease you can before getting the wheels wet. Wash the wheels with a strong detergent to cut grease and oil films. You may want to use a spoke brush or a scrub brush with the detergent solution. Scrub the wheels till all traces of dirt and grease are removed. Sand the wheels thoroughly to remove any rust. This is more difficult on wire wheels, but take the time necessary to sand the entire wheel. Pay particular attention to any chipped or rusted spots. Sand down to bare metal on these parts, feathering out the area around the spot. On disc or wire wheels, it's acceptable to use a liquid paint remover to get the old finish off. This can damage the wood on artillery wheels and is almost impossible to get out of the crevices where the spokes join and where they enter the steel rim. So don't use liquid paint remover on wooden wheels.

Unless you're going to varnish wooden wheels that have previously been painted, it's seldom necessary or even desirable to remove all the old paint. If you feel you really want all the old paint off the wheels, consider taking them to a place that does sandblasting. The sand under pressure will cut the old finish off in a hurry. Once cleaned this way, you've got to be sure to get all the sand out of crevices. You should spray a primer coat on them soon to prevent the bare metal from rusting.

Wire wheels, when properly painted as on this '36 Hispano Suiza, add a touch of class. Many restorers change to wire wheels, if originally offered on their car. A coat of clear lacquer helps preserve finish on wire wheels.

Once the surfaces are clean and smooth, give them a primer coat. Lay the wheel on paper with the inside facing up. From a position on one side of the wheel, spray two light coats of primer clockwise, then counterclockwise. Move to a position on the other side of the wheel and do the same thing. After the primer dries, turn the wheel with the outside facing up and repeat the same procedures. After priming, sand lightly. Remove any runs in the primer with sanding. If the wheels appear to need more priming to build up the surface, give them additional coats, sanding lightly between each coat.

A good paint job on the wheels increases the value of your car and improves its appearance greatly. Time spent preparing the wheels for painting is worthwhile.

Two-Tone Prep. Preparation isn't any different for a two-tone paint job as far as sanding, filling and priming are concerned. After the preparation is completed, with primer applied, mask off the areas that are to be a different color. If the fenders and aprons are to be a different color than the body, paint the body first. If the body is to be two colors, mask off the bottom and first paint the uppermost part.

When applying masking tape, be sure you leave about half of the tape's width to stick on the metal or glass you're covering. Remember that the inside edges and tops of doors must be painted, so don't do any masking that will prevent the doors from being opened to paint. If the inside of the car is upholstered at this stage, you must protect it by masking off door panels, windlace welting, carpets, etc.

Attach newspapers with masking tape to cover upholstery and other areas on which spray dust could settle. Use low pressure spray to avoid paint runs.

It's important to remember that on a two-tone job you mustn't remove the masking tape and papers until the parts are thoroughly dry. This means you'll have to leave areas covered until you spray a second coat, if required. If you've left the wheels on the car during the paint job, cover them with papers or cloth so they won't get spray dust on them from the painting of other parts.

You can paint in a garage, barn or any other closed area. It must be clean and warm and should have adequate ventilation. Never paint if the temperature is below 70 degrees—the warmer, the better. Clean the area before you start the primer coat, so you won't get dirt and dust on the primer, making the sanding job more difficult. Many restorers do the sanding and preparation work outside and wheel the car into the spraying area when it's ready for paint.

If you do the sanding and preparation work in the same area in which you plan to do the spraying, you'll have to clean the area thoroughly before the painting is started. A vacuum cleaner is good for this, as it doesn't stir up as much dust as sweeping. If you move the car out so you can clean the area, it's a good idea to hose the floor after sweeping, but only if there's some means of draining the water. A wet sheet hanging in an out-of-the-

**Applying
Paint**

Careful sanding, priming and painting will produce glass-like finish, as on this '35 Packard. Fenders, trunk lid and spare tire door were removed to get a first class job.

way place will collect and hold dust that might land on the car during painting.

You'll need ventilation while spray painting, but you can't have drafts. Open a window or door so there'll be some movement of air while you're spraying. I've often put a small electric fan on the floor, pointing out a window or door and running at low speeds to keep the air moving. Be sure to use a painting mask with a filter to keep from inhaling the spray paint. These masks have replaceable gauze filters. They're an inexpensive way to keep the spray paint out of your respiratory system. Check the gauze filter after spraying to see the amount of paint you kept out of your lungs: it'll amaze you.

PAINTING WHEELS

You may have learned from priming and preparing the wheels for painting that a circular motion with the spray gun is best. As recommended, the tire and rim should be removed from the wheel. Rims can either be brush painted or sprayed, on or off the tire. If you want to leave the tire or rim on the wheel during painting, you'll have to mask off the tire so you don't get paint on the sidewalls. This not only looks bad, but can cause the rubber to crack.

Wire wheels require careful preparation before priming and painting, as on these '34 Auburn wheels. Inner portion of wheel rim should be smoothed, primed and painted to prevent chafing the tube.

Some restorers prefer to leave the wheels on the car, then with the wheel jacked up, spin it while holding the gun steady. After spinning the wheel in one direction, it's then spun in the opposite direction. This will cover the outside of the wheel only; you'll have to get on the other side of the wheel to spray the area not covered from the outside. It also gets paint on the brake drums and inside the fenders. It's not recommended: you'll get a far better job by removing the wheels for painting.

Laying the wheels on papers, spray clockwise and counterclockwise, two coats from one position. Then go to the opposite side of the wheel and repeat the process, just as recommended for spraying the primer coat. When they're dry, turn the wheels over and follow the same procedure on the other side. Occasionally you'll need to add a coat to the rim area; if so, use a circular motion.

Don't attempt to mount tires until the paint is thoroughly dry. Then use a soapy solution on the rim and bead of the tire so you won't scar the rim. Brush paint the wooden or metal spoke wheels if you want. Be sure to paint out any brush marks and remove any bristles that may pull out of the brush. Paint the spokes first, then the hub area, leaving the rim till last.

SPECIAL TIPS FOR SPRAYING

If you follow some simple rules, you'll get a professional result. It's wise to practice with the spray gun if you've never used one before: test the paint and pressure on a piece of plywood or metal panel before starting on the car.

Be sure to buy the primer and paint that is prepared for use in a spray gun. These will be thinned to the right consistency and will have the drying qualities you want. Be sure to buy some paint thinner for cleanup purposes. It's a good idea to pick up a paint strainer if you're going to use a portion of a can and leave paint in the can for future use.

Try to borrow a compressor and spray outfit if you can. If you can't borrow one, it's suggested you rent one rather than buy an outfit. The little spray gun that comes as an accessory with some vacuum cleaners isn't satisfactory for painting your car, so don't bother with it. When renting a spray outfit, ask for at least a ¼- to ¾-horsepower compressor. A more powerful one is better if you can get it. The larger the compressor, the more pressure you'll have, along with a more even and steady force. You should specify a spray outfit that will deliver at least 30 pounds per square inch (psi). It should also deliver at least 4 standard cubic feet per minute (scfm). These factors are important, as they guarantee you adequate and sustained pressure during the spraying.

Check where the compressor will be placed in relation to where you'll be using the spray gun. It's better to rent an extra length of hose than to use an extension cord, since you want the compressor to have full power and avoid burning out the motor. Use extra hose from the compressor to the gun if necessary. Be sure the needle that fits into the nozzle of the spray gun is clean. Also, be sure that the orifice in the nozzle is clean. The gasket on top of the canister portion must give a tight seal so the paint won't spill out as you tip the gun in use.

When you spray, hold the gun about a foot away from the car. The trigger on the gun regulates the speed and amount of paint coming through the nozzle. A little experimentation will tell you at what position to hold the trigger. Keep the spray gun moving to avoid paint buildups and drips. Spray lightly with a back and forth motion, starting at the top of a panel and working down. You want the paint on evenly, so short movements of the gun are preferable to long sweeping motions.

If any paint runs, stop and wipe it off with a soft, lint-free cloth. Remember that it's better to give an area several light coats than one heavy coat. Spray one panel at a time, then move to the next panel. Go completely around the car, being sure the hose doesn't get pulled across the freshly painted surface. By the time you go completely around the car, the first areas are usually ready for a second light coat.

Remember not to remove the masking tape until the paint has time to dry. Don't do anything to stir up dust while painting or while the car is standing before the paint sets. After painting, be sure to clean the nozzle and needle in paint thinner. Also, when the canister is removed, run some air through the gun. Do this away from the car you've just painted. *Remember that paints and thinner are highly flammable*, so don't light up yet.

STRIPING

Striping can make a world of difference in the final appearance of a repainted car. Most cars produced in the Twenties had a lot of striping. This became somewhat less popular in the Thirties, as chrome moldings were used. Striping practically disappeared in the Forties and Fifties. It is being revived now.

Striping is something you can do yourself with a little practice. But before you apply any stripes, you want to know where they're going and the thickness and color of the stripes. You may have been able to tell this from your car before you painted it. Catalogs show colored renderings with the striping. Cars you'll see at shows and car meets can also give you some ideas.

There was frequently a stripe along the belt line, either above or below the molding. Some cars had double stripes, starting at the radiator. One continued around the belt line; the upper stripe separated along the cowl and either went around the body at the top of the molding or extended up over the doors and down to the molding behind the rear quarter window. It continued on the top of the molding around the back of the car to go up over the doors on the other side. On some cars, the hood panels were individually striped, with a vertical stripe just behind the point where the hood met the cowl. Some cars had a stripe at the back end of each louver on the hood. Striping along stampings on the fenders wasn't uncommon.

The thing to remember about striping is that it tends to break the car into segments and can be overdone. It's important that the size and number of stripes be studied. Some cars had two stripes running parallel to each other, approximately 1/16-inch apart: The bottom stripe was wider than the top stripe. Normally, the wheels and stripe would be the same color, if the wheels were other than black. White or cream was commonly used on dark colored bodies and black stripes on light bodies. Sometimes a gold-colored stripe was used. You can, of course, use whatever color striping you prefer.

The beginner–restorer might do well to use the ready made, adhesive-backed plastic striping that is on the market. This comes in a wide choice of sizes and colors. The adhesive backing makes it easy to apply and it gives a professional looking stripe. If you use this, apply the stripe only if the surface on which it's to go is clean and dry. The temperature of the metal should be above 70 degrees for good adhesion. Each piece of striping should be cut enough longer than the panel it's to cover so that there's "tuck back" material on each end. A light spray coat of clear plastic finish will keep it from peeling.

If you want to hand stripe your own car, you have two methods from which to choose. There are striping wheels available that work well. These little wheels come in a variety of widths, with spacers for putting between them if you want a double stripe. The paint is contained in a small bottle that is attached. A guide fixed to the apparatus helps you follow moldings, etc. Be sure to use paint for striping that is thicker than normal so it won't run. Practice with the wheel on other pieces of metal before you start on your car. A few practice stripes will show you the angle and pressure to use. Just in case something goes wrong while striping your car, keep a cloth soaked in paint thinner handy. If paint runs, wipe it off immediately, before it has a chance to dry and ruin your finish.

Cars were originally striped by hand, with the painter using a pointed brush. Usually these were camelhair brushes. They're not expensive and come in a variety of widths. To keep the width of the stripe even, you must increase the pressure on the brush as the paint runs out of it. Do some practicing first. The handicap with this method is picking up a smooth joining on long stripes where you can't hold enough paint in the brush for one solid movement. Again, protect yourself by keeping a pad soaked with paint thinner handy to wipe off any runs or wavery lines. With a brush, you have to move along faster than with a wheel to avoid any hand tremors giving a wavy line to the stripe.

PLATED PARTS

Plated parts should be inspected as they're removed from the car. In many cases they can be cleaned up satisfactorily. Soak them in a strong solution of detergent and water. After soaking, scrub them with a fine steelwool scouring pad that contains a cleansing agent. This will usually remove anything that's going to come off. Rinse parts in clear water and dry them after scouring. There are many good metal polishes on the market that should restore sufficient luster.

If the parts don't clean up satisfactorily and there are spots where plating has worn off, you'll have to have them replated. Plating is relatively inexpensive. There are some things you can do to reduce plating costs. Remove

Bright metal parts should be thoroughly cleaned before plating. Badly pitted metal should be filled with new metal and ground smooth to assure a good plating job.

brackets, screws and bolts that don't need to be plated. If you're working with headlights, remove the wiring, lens retaining clips and glass lenses. In other words, save the plater's time by taking to him only what needs replating.

Early cars had a lot of brass trim, but this gave way during the Teens to nickel plating. Nickel has a deep dull shine, is expensive, and gave way in the Twenties to chrome. You should use the same metal in replating that was originally used on your car. A car that has nickel-plated headlamps and radiator will look better and be worth more if the replating is nickel. Cars with chrome plating should have any parts that need replating done with chrome. Plating isn't prohibitively expensive and can be done a little at a time, if necessary. If you want to keep costs down, consider painting some parts that need replating. Headlights will function and look fine if they are painted, with only the lens rim plated. Radiator shells can be painted instead of plated. Headlight crossbars, tire carriers and other parts that were often plated can be painted and still give excellent service. In most instances, no one will notice the difference in the car's appearance.

Newly replated bumper and bumper guards on '37 Olds show how much plating can improve car's appearance. Bumper arms and braces should be sanded, primed and painted while parts are at the plating shop.

CHAPTER 22

After
Restoration

Once your car has been restored, you'll want to enjoy using it, yet keep it in handsome condition. There will be pleasant drives, calls on friends, old car meets, shows and parades. Don't overlook membership in one of the car clubs, as their planned activities are fun and give you a chance to meet people with the same interests.

A real jewel, this fully restored '32 Ford Model B five-window coupe shows what can be done to bring an old car to a new life.

It takes upkeep to keep values up, so to enjoy your old car without worrying about it, keep these tips in mind. Be sure it is properly licensed in your state, either as an antique or as a current operating model. A check with your license bureau will give you relevant information connected with licensing it as an antique. Some states require a safety inspection periodically. You want your car safe, of course. Some inspection stations are manned by people unfamiliar with old automobiles and this may give you some unnecessary trouble. If you have a choice among inspection stations,

285

try to locate one where the people running it are familiar with old cars and like them. Don't try to get by with anything that doesn't meet state requirements; on the other hand, there's no use in subjecting yourself to unnecessary headaches caused by people unfamiliar with old cars.

For your own peace of mind, you'll want to have the car insured. There are several first-rate companies that specialize in insuring old cars. You can find their ads in old-car magazines, as well as by asking other owners. Protect yourself with adequate liability. You should probably cover the car for fire and theft. Medical payments insurance may be available to you also. Because of the cost of repairing an old car that has been involved in an accident, collision insurance rates are necessarily high. You'll have to decide if that particular coverage is worth what it'll cost you.

Once you're done with your restoration, it's a good idea to clean out the area you used. Throw out any unusable or unrepairable parts that you may have put aside for making patterns. Keep any unused or extra parts you could use later on or sell to other restorers. Be sure to protect any parts you keep for future use against rust, rot or other deterioration. Coat metal parts with a light film of oil. Keep wooden parts dry. Clean and wrap any upholstery or rug pieces. Label these parts for future identification and store in a dry place that's out of the way.

Go through the tools you acquired during the restoration job. Clean them up for future use: gasoline, kerosene or another solvent will make this easy. Decide what tools you want to keep. You can sell the others. Keep absolutely necessary tools in your car, storing the others elsewhere. Be sure you get returned to you any deposit that may have been required when you rented tools. Also, be sure to return any tools you borrowed from someone else.

It's a good idea to keep a few emergency repair parts in your car: an extra fan belt, sparkplug, headlight and taillight bulbs, fuses, tube patching outfit, etc. Some cars are known to be hard on certain parts and break them from time to time: axle shafts, spring shackles, etc. If you've heard your car is one of these and you plan to travel very far or often from home base, it's wise to carry spare parts.

Storage   Most old cars are driven only occasionally and there are some suggestions for good care of these cars between uses. Keep your car clean. Wash it often and wipe it dry with a chamois. Don't leave water standing on it. Clean off the easy-to-reach portions of the engine occasionally. The garage space should be dry and have adequate ventilation. A simple muslin cover is a good idea. You can make this by sewing together enough yardage of unbleached muslin to cover your car: just a large rectangular piece will give adequate protection. If yours is an open car, it's a good idea to have a piece of muslin to throw over the seats.

It helps if the garage floor is near enough level so the car won't roll if the brake is off and its out of gear. You should leave the car in neutral, with the hand or parking brake *off*. Place a brick behind each rear wheel, if necessary. On some old cars, it's a wise idea to cut a piece of wood long enough to fit from the bottom of the dashboard to hold the clutch depressed. This will keep the clutch plate from sticking to the driving plate.

If yours is a closed car, leave a couple of windows lowered about a half inch. This will allow air to circulate, yet keep almost everything out of the car. It's a wise idea to lock the car between uses. Obviously, you'll make sure the ignition and the lights are off.

If the car will be driven occasionally, it's not necessary to put it on jacks or disconnect the battery. However, if you're in a climate where antifreeze is required, be sure the motor is protected with sufficient antifreeze. The new permanent type will give better cooling than plain water. They also contain a lubricant and rust inhibitor. Many old car owners keep it in year 'round.

To protect the car's finish, it's smart to see that it has an adequate coat of wax. Wax will help protect plated parts, too. To protect upholstery, give it a coat of Scotchgard.®¡ An occasional interior spraying with a bug repellant is wise. Interior woodwork should be waxed. The rubber beading and other small rubber parts should be treated every so often with glycerine or silicone spray.

Be sure to check the oil level, radiator coolant, battery water level and gas before you take it out on the road. Also check the tires to be sure they haven't lost pressure.

If your car will be stored for a couple of months or more, there are some precautions you should take to protect your investment. Take the weight off the tires by placing the car on blocks: the same blocks you used during restoration will do very well. Place them under either the axle or frame. A cement block with a wooden piece where the block meets the car is best. Remove the battery, have it charged, then store out of the car in a dry place. It's not recommended that you drain the radiator, just be sure there's adequate antifreeze. If you live in an area where antifreeze isn't necessary, you should keep a rust inhibitor in the coolant. Be sure the car is clean and dry. It should be waxed, including the plated parts. Upholstery and rugs should be brushed or vacuumed and the interior sprayed with an insect repellant. If yours is an open car, brush the top, curtains and roof boot. Many people like to keep side curtains in place during storage, Cover your car, as previously mentioned, and lock it if you can.

After the time and money you spent restoring your car, these few suggestions will help you keep value up and add to your enjoyment as you use it.

Index